1.45

THE FALL OF WISCONSIN

THE FALL OF WISCONSIN

THE CONSERVATIVE CONQUEST OF A PROGRESSIVE
BASTION AND THE FUTURE OF AMERICAN POLITICS

DAN KAUFMAN

W. W. NORTON & COMPANY

Independent Publishers Since 1923

New York | London

Portions of this work appeared, in different forms, in the *New York Times*
and on the website of *The New Yorker*.

For information about permission to reproduce selections from this book, write to
Permissions, W. W. Norton & Company, Inc., 500 Fifth Avenue, New York, NY 10110

For information about special discounts for bulk purchases, please contact
W. W. Norton Special Sales at specialsales@wwnorton.com or 800-233-4830

Manufacturing by LSC Communications Harrisonburg
Book design by Chris Welch Design
Production manager: Julia Druskin

ISBN 978-0-393-63520-1

W. W. Norton & Company, Inc., 500 Fifth Avenue, New York, N.Y. 10110
www.wwnorton.com

W. W. Norton & Company Ltd., 15 Carlisle Street, London W1D 3BS

1 2 3 4 5 6 7 8 9 0

For Juliette and Luca

And to the memory of my parents, Jerry and Judy

The question will arise and arise in your day, though perhaps not fully in mine, which shall rule—wealth or man; which shall lead—money or intellect; who shall fill public stations—educated and patriotic freemen, or the feudal serfs of corporate capital?

—EDWARD G. RYAN, CHIEF JUSTICE OF WISCONSIN, 1873

CONTENTS

THE FALL OF
WISCONSIN

PROLOGUE

Hillary Clinton was confident about winning Wisconsin. Throughout the lead-up to the 2016 election, she had never trailed Donald Trump in a single poll, and Wisconsin had not gone for a Republican presidential candidate since 1984, when Ronald Reagan swept every state except Minnesota. Her confidence was reflected by not going there—even once—during the campaign. Pundits echoed Clinton's surety. "Wisconsin looks like a blue wall there for Hillary Clinton?" a Milwaukee news anchor asked NBC's Chuck Todd three days before the vote. "It does," Todd replied. Or as Rachel Maddow said a few months earlier on MSNBC: "The Republican Party really, really, really wants Wisconsin to be a swing state—not true." She went on: "Even as Republican presidential candidates lose there year after year after year—I mean even Michael Dukakis won Wisconsin, right?—Republicans still have kept their hopes alive that Wisconsin could be theirs." If you looked at recent presidential elections, there was little reason to doubt the end result. In 2008, Barack Obama trounced John McCain in Wisconsin by fourteen points; four years later, he beat Mitt Romney comfortably by seven.

Some of Clinton's supporters were planning to gather on election night at a Marriott in Middleton, a Madison suburb, for a joint victory party with the Democratic Senate candidate Russ Feingold. Feingold had held one of the state's Senate seats for three terms before losing in 2010 to the Republican Ron Johnson, a wealthy political novice, in a shocking upset. In 2016, Feingold was heavily favored to win the rematch. His race tightened the week before the election, but he still led in every poll save one.

Feingold's campaign had asked Chris Taylor, a Democratic assemblywoman from Madison, to help with his press that evening. Taylor was not confident of the outcome. She had canvassed for Democrats in rural Iowa County the summer before the election and remembered the indifference, and sometimes hostility, she was greeted with. A few people slammed the door in her face. "These should have been easy doors for us: A lot of them were Democrats," she said. "It was worrisome."

Early on Election Day, Taylor, who was also on the ballot, took her two boys, Sam and Ben, to a busy intersection on Madison's Near East Side. The three of them wore "Chris Taylor for Assembly" T-shirts and held signs, waving at the cars honking their support. It was a clear and bright autumn day with a brisk wind blowing off Lake Monona a block away. Dozens of people had shown up to join Taylor and her kids. Someone brought doughnuts and hot chocolate for the volunteers, and the gathering turned festive. Taylor, though nervous, believed Clinton would pull it out.

In the afternoon, Taylor drove to the hotel for her press shift. Around seven, an hour before the polls closed, Feingold's staff began receiving unsettling reports of low turnout in Milwaukee, a Democratic stronghold. By nine o'clock, Feingold's prospects looked grim, and Clinton's chances in Florida and Pennsylvania were slipping away. "People were looking to me for reassurance," Taylor said. "They came up to me, crying: 'Oh my God, Chris. What are we going to do?'" Outwardly, Taylor maintained her calm, but she too started to worry that Clinton would lose Wisconsin.

Taylor tried to comfort people, telling them not to give up hope, that returns from heavily Democratic Dane County, which includes Madison, were still coming in. But the state's rural areas, including some of the towns and villages Taylor had canvassed, delivered strongly for Trump. Soon Taylor began panicking. Around ten, Feingold emerged into a large ballroom ashen-faced and visibly shaken. "Something is happening in this country tonight," he told his supporters in a brief concession speech. "I don't understand it completely. I don't think anybody does." People in the room started breaking down, crying.

Taylor left after Feingold's speech. She could no longer face the press. "I had been spinning Feingold was going to win," she said. "I just couldn't deal with it anymore. I ran to my car and called my husband. He and I just cried on the phone together." Taylor drove home and watched the returns in her living room. She saw Trump win Pennsylvania and Republicans make gains in both houses of the Wisconsin State Legislature. Democrats held on to a mere thirty-five of ninety-nine state assembly seats; in 2009, after Obama's election, they had fifty-two.

Around one in the morning, Taylor straggled to bed knowing Trump would win Wisconsin. A half hour later, the networks called it, awarding Trump Wisconsin's ten electoral college votes, which pushed him past the 270-vote threshold needed to win the White House. Wisconsin had just made Donald Trump president. "Wisconsin! *Wisconsin.* Wisconsin was barely in play!" Megyn Kelly said on Fox News. On CNN, Jake Tapper called the result "stunning."

Before she fell asleep, Taylor recalled a meeting she had with Democratic colleagues in the assembly months before the election. One of them assured Taylor that with Trump on the ticket, it would be a wave year for the state's Democrats. "I remember thinking to myself: 'You idiot! Republicans have a *network,* they have an infrastructure.' We don't. We might pick up a seat or two here and there, but until we have an infrastructure as strong as theirs, we're going to lose," she said. "Few people in the country are aware of the mightiness of their network, but *he* should have known."

DONALD TRUMP'S VICTORY may have shocked the Clinton campaign and media pundits, but the result merely heralded the final stage of Wisconsin's dramatic transformation from a pioneering beacon of progressive, democratic politics to the embodiment of that legacy's national unraveling. Powerful conservative donors and organizations across the country had Wisconsin in their sights years before the 2016 presidential election, helping Governor Scott Walker and his allies systematically change the state's political culture.

Wisconsin's history made it an especially attractive and important target. In the early twentieth century, native icons like the populist senator and governor Robert La Follette, who was known as Fighting Bob, and movements like Milwaukee's pragmatic "sewer socialism" forged a progressive tradition that withstood the most calamitous events of the twentieth century. La Follette instituted numerous reforms—direct primaries, a ban on corporate donations to political candidates, civil-service protections—to encourage citizen participation in government and help establish Wisconsin as a bastion of democratic ideals. "Democracy is a life, and involves continual struggle," he wrote in his autobiography. "It is only as those of every generation who love democracy resist with all their might encroachments of its enemies that the ideals of representative government can even be nearly approximated."

Throughout the twentieth century, Wisconsin led the country in devising pioneering legislation that aided the vast majority of its citizens. In 1911, the state legislature established the nation's first workers' compensation program, a progressive state income tax, and more stringent child-labor laws. The following year, President Theodore Roosevelt described Wisconsin as a "laboratory for wise, experimental legislation aiming to secure the social and political betterment of the people as a whole." The state's progressive spirit continued for generations, influencing the entire country: Wisconsin created the first unemployment-insurance program, and it was the first state to recognize collective bargaining rights for public employees. Indeed, much of Franklin D. Roosevelt's New Deal, including the Social Security Act, was drafted by Wisconsinites loyal to the Wisconsin Idea, an ethos that placed a moral obligation on the University of Wisconsin to serve the citizens of the state. More broadly, the Wisconsin Idea encouraged legislation, informed by the expertise of the university's faculty, aimed at creating a more equitable society. Its humanistic reach extended to Great Society programs like Medicare, designed by another Wisconsinite under its sway decades later. More than any other state, Wisconsin embodied Supreme Court Justice Louis Brandeis's hope that states might become "laboratories of democracy."

THE FALL OF WISCONSIN is the story of how the state went from a widely admired "laboratory of democracy" to a testing ground for national conservatives bent on remaking American politics. It traces the ways Wisconsin's century-old progressive legacy has been dismantled in virtually every area: labor rights, environmental protection, voting rights, government transparency. Those efforts have been wildly successful, culminating in Wisconsin's startling deliverance of the White House to Donald Trump.

By the time Speaker of the House Paul Ryan declared he would be returning home to Janesville rather than running for reelection, Wisconsin had seen one of the largest declines of the middle class of any state in the country. Its poverty rate had climbed to a thirty-year high; the state's roads were the second worst in the country; the University of Wisconsin–Madison had fallen, for the first time, out of the rankings of the country's top five research schools. A study estimated that 11 percent of the state's population was deterred from voting in the 2016 presidential election by Wisconsin's new voter ID law, one of the strictest in the nation.

How could this have happened?

To tell this story, I've relied on citizens who bore the brunt of the assault on long-cherished ideals and policies. They chose to fight back—and continue to do so in the face of enormous odds, a testament to their perseverance and a shared conviction that they might one day reclaim Wisconsin's progressive heritage.

But *The Fall of Wisconsin* is also a story about the direction of America as a whole. It explores whether the state's democratic ideals can persist in an era of increasing division and inequality. Wisconsin, after all, once had what any pragmatic citizen might admire, even covet: clean air and water, transparent government, good public schools, a world-class state university, and a strong tradition of supporting labor rights for its workers. Precisely because of those attributes, the state became a target for national conservatives. As Scott Walker boasted in his memoir, if he could change Wisconsin, he and his allies could "do it anywhere."

In the end, this is a story that addresses a concern central to every American: If conservatives cannot tolerate a state that offers what Wisconsin once did, what kind of future is there for the American citizen?

1

THE PEOPLE'S HOME

On April 8, 1837, Ole Knudsen Nattestad, his younger brother Ansten, and a mutual friend set out on skis from their home in Numedal, a valley in southeastern Norway, determined to immigrate to America. They took only the clothes they wore, knapsacks, and the equivalent of 800 dollars between them. "People looked at us with wonder and intimated that we must have lost our senses," Ole later wrote of his journey. "They suggested that we had better hang ourselves in the first tree in order to avoid a worse fate."

Ole had always dreamed of becoming a farmer, but while managing his family's property, he quickly discovered how difficult it was to survive by farming in Norway, where only 3 percent of the land is arable. "I entered upon my task cheerfully, worked with all my might and kept a careful account of income and disbursements," he later wrote. "To my great surprise, I soon found that in spite of all my toil and prudence, I did not make much headway. When the year was ended, I had little or nothing left as a reward for my labor." Ole abandoned the idea of farming to become a traveling merchant, but the

9

practice was illegal at the time, and he feared being arrested by local sheriffs. He tried to become a blacksmith, but here too he came into conflict with the law, which did not permit him to practice his trade in his hometown.

Over Christmas, a friend described to Ole an article he had read in a German newspaper, stating that no country gave citizens greater freedom than the United States. "This information had a magic effect on me as I looked upon it as an injustice that the laws of Norway should forbid me to trade and not allow me to get my living by honest work," Ole wrote. "Gradually I got to thinking of emigration and while considering the matter on my way home, the idea matured into a resolution. My brother Ansten did not have to be asked a second time."

When they left that April morning, the brothers and their friend traveled from Numedal across the Blefjell mountains to an adjacent valley, the site of a village called Tinn. Then they skied over hills and through forests to the port town of Stavanger, where they hoped to catch a boat to the United States. The travelers began telling everyone in Stavanger about their plans, but their excitement nearly cost them their journey. Local officials heard of their intention to emigrate and approached the men, asking for their papers. After inspecting the documents, the officials said the travelers' passports, which included a certificate from a pastor vouching for their "good habits and Christian conduct," would allow them only to stay in Stavanger.

Soon afterward, a stranger approached the migrants and told them he had heard that authorities planned to arrest them the following day and return them to their native valley. "The government here," the stranger told them, "was in a bitter rage against all emigrants and we could not count on any mercy."

He encouraged them to leave Stavanger at once. They departed in darkness to avoid being discovered and made their way to a nearby fishing village, where they persuaded a local skipper headed to Gothenburg, Sweden, to let them come along. There they paid the equivalent of fifty dollars apiece for passage aboard a ship. Thirty-two days later, they arrived in Fall River, Massachusetts.

From Fall River they journeyed to Detroit, and then Chicago, where they met up with other Norwegians, including Ole Rynning, the leader of a group who had immigrated to the United States earlier that year. Rynning and a few others, including Ole, inspected a piece of land for sale eighty miles south of Chicago, near a place called Beaver Creek. The group decided to purchase it and build a settlement there. Ole and another man stayed behind to construct a log house, while the others returned to Chicago to fetch their countrymen. About fifty people arrived, each of them picking a plot. The Norwegians managed to build enough housing to spend a comfortable winter, but in spring the settlement flooded, and a malaria outbreak devastated the community soon after. At least fourteen people died, including Ole Rynning. Most of the survivors fled to another Norwegian settlement elsewhere in Illinois.

Before he died, Rynning had written a comprehensive book that detailed his new country's government, soil, religious tolerance, and immigration opportunities. Ansten decided to journey back to Norway to try to publish it while Ole struck out on his own and headed north. On July 1, 1838, he arrived about five miles past the Illinois border, near a new hamlet called Clinton, in the Wisconsin Territory.

"No other Norwegian had planted his feet on Wisconsin

soil before me," Ole wrote. "For a whole year I saw no coun-
tryman but lived alone without friend, family, or companion.
Eight Americans had settled in the town before me but they
lived about as isolated as I did. I found the soil very fertile and
the monotony of the prairie was relieved by small bunches of
trees. Deer and other game were abundant. The horrid howl of
the prairie wolf disturbed my sleep until habit armed my ears
against annoyances of this sort." In September 1839, Ansten
returned to America, joining his brother in Wisconsin. He
brought several Norwegian immigrants with him, and soon
they established a colony they called Jefferson Prairie, the
fourth Norwegian settlement in the United States.

Other Scandinavians began leaving in great numbers too,
for similar reasons—a lack of social mobility, a desire for religious freedom—but above all to escape economic hardship.
Until the 1920s, waves of Scandinavian immigrants fled devastating crop failures and famines: One famine that swept
Sweden and Finland in the 1860s caused tens of thousands of
deaths and forced many people to survive on birchbark bread.
The largest population of Scandinavians to settle in Wisconsin
were Norwegians, whose migration rate soared in the 1840s,
when the Irish potato famine spread to Norway and caused
the deaths of some fifty thousand people. Many also fled for
political reasons—Norway emerged from four hundred years
of Danish rule in 1814, only to be taken over by Sweden later
that year. While class divisions persisted in Scandinavia, the
struggles of the region's people to survive their harsh environment helped forge a communitarian ethos many immigrants
brought to the United States.

The Norwegians were particularly grateful for the freedom they found in their new homeland. In the 1840s, Norwegian migrants founded a community in Muskego, Wisconsin, southwest of Milwaukee, and in 1845, they sent an open letter to the *Morgenbladet*, a newspaper in Oslo, proclaiming the greatest gifts of their new home. "We have no expectation of gaining riches," the letter read. "But we live under a liberal government in a fruitful land, where freedom and equality are the rule in religious as in civil matters, and where each one of us is at liberty to earn his living practically as he chooses. Such opportunities are more to be desired than riches."

Wisconsin would not become a state for another few years, but Ole and Ansten's settlement there would play a fateful role in the state's character, both demographic and political. Ansten had succeeded in getting Ole Rynning's book published in Norway. Called *A Truthful Account of America for the Instruction and Help of the Peasant and Commoner*, it captivated a desperate population, fueling a wave of Norwegian immigration to the United States. Ultimately, 800,000 Norwegians, 25 percent of Norway's entire population, emigrated to the United States between 1825 and 1925. Their top destinations were Minnesota, North Dakota, and Wisconsin.

AS SCANDINAVIAN IMMIGRANTS began to transform Wisconsin, the state began to transform American politics. On the evening of March 20, 1854, fifty-three abolitionist Democrats, Whigs, and Free Soilers (a short-lived party opposed to the Western expansion of slavery) gathered in a one-room schoolhouse in the little town of Ripon, seventy-five miles northeast of Madison, and declared themselves Republicans.

It was a cold night, and people huddled around the stove at the center of the little white schoolhouse, debating for hours whether to form a new party. Party allegiance, even to a party that no longer represents one's views, can die hard, and despite antislavery fervor, some opposed the idea. But eventually the faction supporting it prevailed, and the Republican Party was born.

The events that drove those citizens together went back six decades earlier, to 1793, when Congress passed the Fugitive Slave Act, one of the first of many untenable compromises that held the early United States together. The law provided a slave owner or a bounty hunter the right to capture a runaway slave in a free state and, with only a slaveholder's affidavit or oral testimony given to a local judge, return the fugitive to bondage. As antislavery sentiment grew in the North, so did defiance. Several states passed "personal liberty laws," which granted fugitives the right to a trial by jury and offered protection to free blacks, who were sometimes kidnapped by bounty hunters. In certain states, these laws forbade police to assist in the rendition of runaway slaves and even prohibited the use of local jail cells.

Half a century later, fissures over slavery had grown into a movement for Southern secession. Congress tried to appease the slaveholding states with an updated Fugitive Slave Act. The revised law imposed harsh penalties on citizens and police who refused to comply, fining law enforcement officials $1,000 for not cooperating and punishing a person caught aiding a fugitive with up to six months in jail. Abolitionists called it the "Bloodhound Law," for the dogs the slave catchers used to track down runaways. The law gave rise to a wave of political violence and one of the most fractious decades in American history, which culminated in John Brown's failed raid on Harpers Ferry.

The new Fugitive Slave Act passed in 1850. By then, Wisconsin had been a state for two years. Abolitionist sentiment, already strong, grew with an influx of immigrants known as '48ers, liberal revolutionaries who fled Germany after their 1848 rebellion failed at home. The Germans settled mostly in Milwaukee, but antislavery fervor ran throughout Wisconsin, including in Ripon. Founded in 1849 by David Mapes, a former steamboat captain from New York, Ripon's political temperament came from proximity to Ceresco, an 1,800-acre utopian farming commune that had been established five years earlier. Named for Ceres, the ancient Roman goddess of agriculture, the community operated under the pre-Marxist socialist principles of the French philosopher Charles Fourier, whose ideology was briefly in vogue. Fourier abhorred modern civilization and advocated sexual freedom, women's liberation—he coined the word *feminisme*—and collective ownership. He envisioned a society made up of "phalanxes," self-sustaining agricultural communities like Ceresco, which was also known as Wisconsin Phalanx.

Wisconsin Phalanx closed in 1850, and Ripon drew many former residents, as well as curious liberal reformers attracted by its legacy from the East Coast. Among them was a math professor and lawyer from upstate New York named Alvan Bovay, who arrived that year with his wife and their two-year-old son. Ripon had just thirteen houses then, but it grew quickly after Ripon College was established, in 1851, with Bovay's help. He would also prove instrumental in the rise of the Republican Party. Bovay had left New York a disaffected Whig angry at his party for not confronting slavery, the central issue of the day. The Whigs disbanded after failing to win the presidency, in 1852, and Bovay began dreaming of a new political party that could unite abolitionist Democrats, Free Soilers, and former Whigs to defeat the ruling, pro-slavery Democrats. Bovay wanted to call his new party "Republican," after *res publica*, Latin for "the common good." Initially, Bovay received little support for his idea, both in Ripon and from his close friend Horace Greeley, the influential editor of the *New-York Tribune*.

But two major events intensified the furor over slavery in Wisconsin. In January 1854, the Illinois senator Stephen Douglas proposed the Kansas-Nebraska Act, another attempt at a compromise on slavery, allowing settlers in new territories to determine whether they wanted to become a slave state or a free one. The next month, Bovay wrote to Greeley, urging him again to endorse a new party in his paper that would "advocate calling together in every church and schoolhouse in the free States all the opponents of the Kansas-Nebraska bill."

As he awaited Greeley's reply, Bovay called a community meeting on February 28 at Ripon's Congregational Church to agitate for his idea. The high-spirited gathering concluded with the passage of a resolution threatening to "throw old party organizations to the winds and organize a new party on the sole issue of the non-extension of slavery" if the Kansas-Nebraska Act passed the Senate. Four days later, it did. Bovay quickly began organizing another meeting with the intention of forming his new party. Among those he pressed to come were former members of Wisconsin Phalanx.

Eight days before Bovay's planned meeting, furor over the Fugitive Slave Act erupted nationwide when an abolitionist mob liberated a runaway slave named Joshua Glover from a Milwaukee courthouse jail. Glover had escaped from slavery on a Missouri farm and made his way to Racine, where he found work and built friendships in the city's small African American community. After two years, his former owner, Benammi Garland, tracked him down and, accompanied by federal marshals, knocked on Glover's cabin door. Glover did not open the door immediately—rumors of a slave catcher in town had been circulating—but a friend inside did. After a brief, violent struggle, during which a marshal beat Glover in the head with the butt of a whip, Glover was thrown, barely conscious and bloody, into the back of a wagon. Fearing that the small jail in Racine might be overrun by abolitionists, Garland and the marshals rode twenty-five miles north to the Milwaukee courthouse. Garland planned to transport Glover back to slavery the next day under the legal rights granted to slave owners by the Fugitive Slave Act.

A prominent abolitionist named Sherman Booth, who owned a Milwaukee newspaper, heard about Glover's capture. Riding his horse through the streets of Milwaukee, Booth shouted: "Free citizens who do not wish to be made slaves or slave catchers, meet at Courthouse Square at two o'clock!" Thousands of people answered Booth's call and assembled outside the courthouse. As the crowd swelled in size, it grew angrier. The protesters demanded Glover be given a fair trial and, after a tense standoff with a guard, stormed the building, breaking down Glover's cell door with a wooden plank. They quickly put Glover in a wagon that carried him to a safe house in Waukesha, a short ride away. From there, Glover spent more than a month traveling on the Underground Railroad, finally arriving safely in Canada. Sherman Booth was tried and imprisoned for violating the Fugitive Slave Act.

By the time of Bovay's second meeting, the Glover affair had enraged Ripon's abolitionists, and despite initial resistance, Bovay's idea prevailed. "We went into the little meeting held in a school house Whigs, Free Soilers, and Democrats," Bovay wrote afterward. "We came out of it Republicans." They were, Bovay noted, "the first Republicans in the Union."

MANY OF WISCONSIN'S Scandinavian immigrants quickly gravitated to the new Republican Party, identifying with its abolitionist founding principles. Egalitarian values led Scandinavian settlers to form agricultural cooperatives and disproportionately support the trade union movement. Finnish migrants, for example, were instrumental in organizing unions in northern Wisconsin's dangerous mines.

The Scandinavian political worldview, characterized by pragmatism and social modesty, was captured in Thorstein Veblen's landmark critique of American capitalism, *The Theory of the Leisure Class*. Published in 1899, Veblen's socioeconomic treatise introduced the idea of "conspicuous consumption," which defined American consumerism as morally corrosive and class-stratifying. Veblen was born to immigrant parents in Cato, Wisconsin, a Norwegian farming enclave near Lake Michigan. He did not speak English until he entered school, and his community in Cato, and later in Minnesota, emphasized modesty for the cohesion of the collective.

Those same norms were expressed in a more negative light in the Law of Jante, a series of dictates articulated in a novel by the Danish writer Aksel Sandemose that, while fictional, are widely accepted in Scandinavia as accurate descriptions of its mores. Two of Sandemose's most revealing edicts: "You're not to think you are anything special" and "You're not to convince yourself that you are better than we are."

This communitarian mind-set would foster an openness to the welfare state, which is viewed differently in Scandinavia. That difference is captured in the Swedish word *folkhemmet*, "the people's home," a nickname for the welfare state. "It implies that all people should feel safe, protected here," Julie Allen, a professor of Scandinavian studies at Brigham Young University, told me. "It's so different than how we view welfare, which is as handouts." The people's home, Allen said, is about "lifting everyone up."

Soon after the Republican Party's founding in 1854, Alvan Bovay again wrote to Horace Greeley, sharing the news, and this time Greeley embraced the new party, endorsing it with an editorial in the pages of the *Tribune*. "We should not much care whether those thus united [against slavery] were designated 'Whig,' 'Free Democratic' or something else," Greeley wrote. "Though we think some simple name like 'Republican' would more fitly designate those who had united to restore our Union to its true mission of champion and promulgator of Liberty rather than propagandist of Slavery." Word fanned out quickly, and within months the party had established itself as an important political outlet for abolitionists across the country.

On July 6, 1854, the Republican Party had its first state convention, in Jackson, Michigan. A week later, Madison hosted the second. The following year, the Wisconsin Supreme Court ruled the Fugitive Slave Act unconstitutional, making Wisconsin the first and only state in the nation to defy the federal law. Sherman Booth, the Milwaukee abolitionist, was freed from jail. In 1856, the Republican Party ran its first presidential candidate, John Fremont, who lost to the Democrat, James Buchanan, but won Wisconsin's five electoral college votes. Four years later, the state delivered them again to the Republican ticket and its candidate, Abraham Lincoln, who captured the presidency and then won the Civil War.

The commitment of Wisconsin's Scandinavian settlers to the Republican Party translated into the only non-English-speaking regiment in the Union Army. A year after the party's founding, a fervently antislavery immigrant named Hans Christian Heg joined the Republican Party, and two years later, he went to the state convention as a delegate. After the Civil War broke out, Heg organized a Norwegian regiment that included 115 men whose first name was Ole. Heg rose to the rank of colonel before Confederate soldiers killed him in 1863, during the Battle of Chickamauga, in Georgia. Wisconsin had become a Republican state, enamored with the party's dedication to the common good.

IN THE DECADE AFTER the Civil War, farmers in Wisconsin coalesced around the Grange, an agrarian populist movement that swept the Midwest. The Grangers battled monopolistic railroads that gouged them on the costs of shipping their crops. The railroad companies also demanded that municipalities pay for much of the capital costs needed to lay down new railroad lines. If farmers organized resistance, the companies often threatened to move the line elsewhere. At the same time, the Republican Party, which controlled the Wisconsin legislature, had become dominated by timber and railroad companies. Candidates did not run without the tacit approval of those interests. The corrupted process was made easier because candidates were chosen by party delegates at state conventions, not by voters in primary elections.

In 1873, however, the Grangers managed to elect a reform-minded Democrat named William Taylor as governor. The following year, Taylor mustered through a bill called the Potter Law, which established a commission overseeing the state's railroads. Most important, the commission had the power to regulate the rates railroads charged. Two months after the law passed, two railroad company presidents told Taylor they would not abide by it. They considered the law unconstitutional. Wisconsin's attorney general brought a suit against the railroads which was heard by the state supreme court, and decided in the state's favor. The chief justice of Wisconsin, Edward Ryan, a Taylor appointee, issued the majority opinion. Ryan noted that the companies had called the railroad commission an "act of communism," hyperbole that drew his outrage. "These wild terms are as applicable to a statute limiting the rates of toll on railroads, as the term murder is to the surgeon's wholesome use of the knife, to save life, not to take it," Ryan wrote.

In response, the railroads began a pressure campaign. They offered free travel to legislators, halted construction of new lines, and discontinued service to various towns. It worked. Taylor was defeated in 1875, and the Potter Law was repealed the following year. The Grange movement soon vanished, too.

But the Grangers and Chief Justice Ryan made a lasting impact on a young Robert La Follette, who was born on his family's farm twenty miles south of Madison, in 1855. "As a boy on the farm in Primrose Township I heard and felt this movement of the Grangers swirling about me," La Follette wrote in his autobiography. "I felt the indignation which it expressed in such a way that I suppose I have never fully lost the effect of that early impression." In 1873, La Follette, then eighteen, heard Ryan give a commencement speech to the graduating class of the University of Wisconsin Law School. "There is looming up a new and dark power," Ryan told them. "The accumulation of individual wealth seems to be greater than it ever has been since the downfall of the Roman Empire. The enterprises of the country are aggregating vast corporate combinations of unexampled capital, boldly marching, not for economic conquests only, but for political power." His talk issued a chilling warning that marked La Follette forever. "The question will arise and arise in your day, though perhaps not fully in mine," Ryan said. "Which shall rule—wealth or man; which shall lead—money or intellect; who shall fill public stations—educated and patriotic freemen, or the feudal serfs of corporate capital?"

La Follette matriculated at the University of Wisconsin in the fall of 1875. Five years later, after passing the Wisconsin bar, he ran for Dane County district attorney, challenging the party machine's incumbent. At the Dane County Republican convention, Eli Pederson, a Norwegian farmer La Follette had known since childhood, gave a passionate speech endorsing La Follette as "our boy." The Norwegians tended to vote as a block, and Pederson's speech delivered their votes to La Follette, who won a surprising victory and the enduring hostility of the party bosses. In 1884, the same rural voters helped propel La Follette to the House of Representatives, where he served three terms.

In the ensuing years, La Follette would become the most influential political figure in Wisconsin's history. Fighting Bob would go on to serve the citizens of Wisconsin as a Republican district attorney, congressman, governor, and senator—a tempestuous conduit and catalyst for the Progressive era.

Throughout his thirty-four years in office, La Follette was driven by an uncompromising moral vision: The purpose of government, he believed, was to alleviate economic suffering, foster equality, and encourage active citizenship to preserve American democracy. As he put it in an address to a group of citizens in the small mining town of Mineral Point, opening one of his campaigns for governor, "The basic principle of this government is the will of the people." And he recognized the emerging threat from corporate wealth and power:

> Since the birth of the Republic, indeed almost within the last generation, a new and powerful factor has taken its place in our business, financial and political world and is there exercising a tremendous influence. The existence of the corporation, as we have it with us today, was never dreamed of by the [founding] fathers. The corporation of today has invaded every department of business, and its powerful but invisible hand is felt in almost all activities of life.

La Follette closed by imploring the audience not to give up. "Think of the heroes who died to make this country free," he said. "Shall we, their children, basely surrender our birthright and say: 'Representative government is a failure?' No, never, until Bunker Hill and Little Round Top sink into the very earth. Let us here, today, under this flag we all love, hallowed by the memory of all that has been sacrificed for it and for us, dedicate ourselves to winning back the independence of this country, to emancipating this generation and throwing off from the neck of the freemen of America, the yoke of the political machine."

La Follette's class-based message forged an impregnable political coalition; in his 1910 reelection to the United States Senate, he won an astonishing 78 percent of the statewide vote and all but one of Wisconsin's then seventy-one counties. The apotheosis of Wisconsin progressivism was the 1911 legislature chronicled memorably by Frederic Howe, an Ohio politician, in his book *Wisconsin: An Experiment in Democracy*. Howe described how Progressives had transformed the state into "an experiment station in politics, in social and industrial legislation, in the democratization of science and higher education" in which "popular government is being tested in its reaction on people, on the distribution of wealth, on social well-being."

La Follette ran for president in 1924 on his own Progressive Party ticket, capturing his home state and 17 percent of the national vote. A measure of his influence can be seen in the fifty thousand people who came to pay their respects after his death one year later, when his body lay in rest at the state capitol, and in the condolences to his family from President Calvin Coolidge, Eugene Debs, William Randolph Hearst, and William Jennings Bryan.

In 1929, the sculptor Jo Davidson created a life-size statue of

La Follette for the National Statuary Hall in the United States Capitol, one of only two Wisconsinites honored there. Davidson also completed a bust of La Follette, a copy of which was purchased in 1977 by the state of Wisconsin and sits in the east wing of the state capitol. It became a tradition for every Wisconsin governor, Republican and Democrat alike, to be sworn in next to La Follette's bust.

SCANDINAVIAN-AMERICAN VOTERS and legislators helped win passage of the reforms first championed by La Follette and his fellow Progressives, and Wisconsin's pioneering workers' compensation law and unemployment insurance program both became models for New Deal initiatives. Franklin Roosevelt himself praised *Sweden: The Middle Way*, by the journalist Marquis Childs, at a news conference in 1936, singling out the country's cooperatives that flourished within a capitalist system. Childs's book made the case for Swedish social democracy as a workable, humanistic compromise between laissez-faire economics and Stalinist state planning.

With Roosevelt in the White House, Wisconsinites began migrating into Washington, and brought their political legacy, particularly their affinity for social insurance, to bear on the New Deal. Edwin Witte, an economics professor who studied under the political economist John Commons, left his Madison professorship in 1934 to lead Roosevelt's Committee on Economic Security in Washington. Roosevelt tasked the committee with drafting a program that would create security "against several of the great disturbing factors in life—especially those which relate to unemployment and old age."

Witte invited several other Wisconsinites to join the committee, notably Wilbur Cohen, who went on to design the Medicare program in the 1960s, and Arthur Altmeyer, later the commissioner for social security. Witte's committee studied Scandinavian, English, and German models and eventually drafted the Social Security Act. The law, which Roosevelt signed in 1935, included a framework for national unemployment insurance, based on Wisconsin's 1932 law. The New Deal demonstrated the Wisconsin Idea on a national scale, introducing the first real social welfare system in the United States.

Wisconsin's embrace of a social safety net was made possible, in part, by the region's hundreds of thousands of Scandinavian immigrants and their descendants, who tended to be receptive to it. La Follette's progressives forged a durable rural-urban coalition in Wisconsin, while Minnesota created the first Farmer-Labor Party, in 1918. Scandinavian immigrants in the United States followed progressive reforms in their home countries closely. When Norwegian women won a series of legislative victories in the early twentieth century, culminating in the right to vote, Norwegian-American women began agitating for suffrage in the United States. The interconnectedness went both ways; Scandinavian governments built welfare states that dissuaded many people from immigrating. That migration cut off abruptly in 1924, when the Immigration Act established a national-origins quota based on the 1890 census. "America must be kept American," President Coolidge said in his State of the Union address the previous year, ending the great wave of Scandinavian migration that had helped build a "people's home," both in the Upper Midwest and in Scandinavia.

Despite this, Wisconsin's progressive ethos was entrenched and often bipartisan. In 1967, Governor Warren Knowles and the Republican-controlled senate and assembly enacted legislation granting collective bargaining rights for all state employees. Even Governor Tommy Thompson, a conservative Republican, crafted a new state program in 1999 to provide subsidized health insurance for low-income families with children. But after the 1976 Supreme Court case *Buckley v. Valeo* outlawed limits on campaign spending, Wisconsin's politics, increasingly shaped by money, started becoming more like the politics of other states, a similarity that would be exploited by powerful national interests aligned with a new kind of politician.

WHEN SCOTT WALKER was two years old, his father, Llewellyn, moved the family from Colorado Springs to the little town of Plainfield, Iowa, to take a pastor's job at a small Baptist church. In Plainfield, Scott, Llewellyn's eldest son, started a "Jesus USA" club in elementary school, and once went door to door with an empty mayonnaise jar to collect money to buy an Iowa flag for the city hall. In 1977, when Walker was in third grade, Llewellyn got a new pulpit, at First Baptist Church in Delavan, a town of about six thousand in southeastern Wisconsin, and his family moved again. When his father was sick, Scott sometimes delivered the Sunday sermon to the church's eighty-odd congregants.

During high school, Walker became an Eagle Scout and was selected for a trip to Washington, DC, through the American Legion's Boys Nation program. After graduating, he entered

Marquette University, where he told Glen Barry, a fellow student, "God has told me I'm chosen to cut taxes and stop killing babies." His political ambitions became clearer when, as a freshman member of the student senate, he led an investigation into whether student senate leaders had billed their expensive homecoming dinner at Milwaukee's Pfister Hotel, as well as flowers and a limousine, to student government accounts. Walker endorsed impeachment for the accused, and was a dramatic presence at the trial before the student senate. "Did you know where these flowers for your corsage came from?" he asked one of the defendants. As a sophomore, Walker ran for student government president, though he lost badly. In the spring of 1990, he dropped out of school mysteriously to take a marketing job with the American Red Cross. Though he never released his transcript from Marquette, his staff has told reporters he left Marquette voluntarily, with a 2.59 GPA.

Later that year, Walker ran for state assembly against Gwen Moore, an African American congresswoman. It was the only race for elected office he has ever lost. Walker won a seat in the Wisconsin State Assembly in 1992, representing Wauwatosa, a conservative suburban enclave in Milwaukee County. He married his wife, Tonette, the following year, on February 6, a date he chose because it was Ronald Reagan's birthday. (The couple celebrate their anniversary by eating macaroni-and-cheese casserole and red, white, and blue jelly beans, two of Reagan's favorite foods.) As a freshman state representative, Walker cosponsored a "right-to-work" bill, which would forbid unions from requiring the workers they represent to pay dues. He joined the American Legislative Exchange Council, better known as ALEC, a national organization that pairs corporate lobbyists and conservative think tank fellows with state legislators to craft and disseminate model bills. But Walker attracted little notice during his time in the state assembly.

In late 2001, a pension scandal in Milwaukee County provided him with a political opportunity. County Executive Tom Ament, a Democrat, had cut a deal with the American Federation of State, County, and Municipal Employees (AFSCME), the public employee union representing Milwaukee County workers, that gave tens of millions of dollars in pension bonuses to county workers, most of it going to those with at least twenty years of seniority. The plan, which Ament helped create and then approved, included an enormous payout for Ament himself: a lump sum of $1.2 million when he retired, in addition to a $37,000 increase in his annual pension, a jump of 25 percent. Anger over the scandal led to a recall effort against Ament, who wound up forgoing the payout and retiring rather than facing the voters. In 2002, Walker ran for county executive in the Democratic-leaning county as an unabashed conservative, and won.

IN JANUARY 2010, the Supreme Court issued the *Citizens United* decision, allowing corporations and labor unions as well as other advocacy groups to spend unlimited sums on political advertising from their general treasuries as long as they did not coordinate that spending directly with a candidate. Despite an equal right to spend, the annual revenue of the companies in the Fortune 500 alone is hundreds of times larger than that of the entire union movement. *Citizens United* also struck down part of the 2002 McCain-Feingold campaign-finance law, which had prohibited corporations and unions from running campaign ads thirty days before a primary and sixty days before a general election.

The ruling emboldened conservative donors and advocacy groups. Americans for Prosperity, a political advocacy group founded and funded by the billionaire industrialists Charles and David Koch, vowed to spend $45 million on the 2010 elections. David Koch, who helped bankroll the Tea Party, personally donated $1 million to the Republican Governors Association. While the Republicans were well funded and energized, Wisconsin's Democrats were demoralized. In August 2009, a scandal engulfed Governor Jim Doyle, a two-term Democrat, when a reporter discovered that Doyle's chief legal counsel did not have a license to practice law in Wisconsin. Doyle's prospects were already doubtful. Wisconsin had lost 140,000 jobs since the beginning of the financial-crisis recession, forcing the governor to raise taxes and furlough state workers in the face of a $6.6 billion budget deficit. Confronting poll numbers below 40 percent, Doyle announced shortly after the scandal broke that he would not seek a third term. The day he dropped out, his lieutenant governor, Barbara Lawton, announced she was running. Lawton, a progressive, had some statewide appeal, particularly among women, but in late October she quit the race abruptly, citing only "very personal reasons."

In early November, a week after Lawton dropped out, Patrick Gaspard, Obama's political director, met with Milwaukee's mayor, Tom Barrett. That summer, Barrett had become something of a folk hero after intervening on behalf of a woman at the Wisconsin State Fair who called for help when she and her one-year-old granddaughter were being threatened by the baby's drunk, violent father. When Barrett came over to assist and began calling the police with his mobile phone, the man attacked Barrett with a lead pipe. One blow hit Barrett in the head and broke several teeth, while another permanently damaged his hand. Barrett was rushed to the hospital in an ambulance and required multiple surgeries: when President Obama and Vice President Biden heard about the incident, they called to commend him on his bravery. After Lawton dropped out, the White House reportedly pushed for Barrett to run, and shortly after meeting Gaspard, he announced his candidacy.

Meanwhile, Scott Walker had been courting working-class voters. As county executive, he embarked on an annual Harley-Davidson tour across the state. Ostensibly meant to promote tourism in Milwaukee County, the weeklong trip was seen by critics as little more than a taxpayer-funded junket for Walker's gubernatorial ambitions and an effort to cultivate his image as a blue-collar politician. But he also cultivated the support of national conservatives. In 2004, Walker held two fundraisers in Chicago, one of them attended by Karl Rove. Four years later, he spoke at the Milwaukee stop of the "Hot Air Tour," a rally opposing government efforts to mitigate climate change sponsored by Americans for Prosperity.

In April 2009, Walker announced his candidacy for governor. The Republican Governors Association spent $5 million on the Wisconsin election, and Walker also received more than $40,000—his second-largest donation—from KochPAC, the political action committee of Koch Industries. In September, he was given a prominent speaking role at a large AFP rally against the Affordable Care Act in Milwaukee. "I've never been so proud in my lifetime to be part of this angry mob," the conservative provocateur Michelle Malkin said during the rally's keynote address.

Walker's election strategy aimed at making inroads into the Democratic Party's labor base, and he scored an important union endorsement from one of the building trades, Operating Engineers Local 139, which had more than 9,000 members statewide and built many of the state's roads. "I sat down and I talked to Mayor Barrett, who was running for governor, and Walker," Terry McGowan, the union's president, told me, explaining the endorsement. "Mayor Barrett said we're good with the highway system we got, we just got to patch it, repair it. Walker said no, we got to get the highway fund back up, we got to build roads, continue to expand the infrastructure." Local 139 was the only statewide union to endorse Walker, but he also received contributions from the pipefitters' and carpenters' unions, and endorsements from unions representing the Milwaukee police and firefighters.

Barrett's campaign seemed to take labor for granted. Dave Poklinkoski, the president of IBEW Local 2304, a Madison electricians' union, didn't believe Barrett's heart was in the race. A few weeks before the election, the Utility Workers Coalition, a group of utility locals that includes Poklinkoski's, held a conference and invited Barrett to speak. The unions in the coalition represent 10,000 workers, but Barrett declined. "Here you are as an organized labor person trying to get out the vote," Poklinkoski said. "But he wouldn't come. It's October: How bad do you not want to be governor?" Poklinkoski described how unmotivated many of his members were to vote because of the Democrats' indifference to labor. "I call

Walker 'son of Doyle,'" Poklinkoski said, noting that during Doyle's first campaign for governor, in 2002, he promised to cut 10,000 state workers.

The Tea Party wave put Walker over the top. He beat Barrett by six points, his victory propelled by capturing more than a third of union households. Democratic disaffection contributed strongly to Barrett's defeat; he received 12 percent fewer votes than Doyle in 2006. For the first time since 1998, the Republicans would control all branches of state government.

Walker chose to stage his January swearing-in ceremony in the capitol's north wing, a deliberate break with Wisconsin tradition. In the north wing, a reporter noted, many of the attendees would have to turn their backs to the bust of Fighting Bob.

2

DIVIDE AND CONQUER

Randy Bryce has been an ironworker for more than twenty years, but he wasn't always a labor activist. He grew up in Milwaukee's "policeman's ghetto," a working-class neighborhood on the city's southwestern edge. His stepfather, Richard, was a beat cop, and his mother, Nancy, a doctor's secretary. Nancy's grandparents were immigrants from Poland, and Bryce attended Mass with his mother and his grandmother, Molly, at St. John Kanty, a Polish church on the South Side. Molly would reward him with a piece of candy if he spoke a Polish word for one of her friends. He still remembers the pungent smell of Molly's *czarnina*, duck blood soup, and how it made him flee the house and run out into the street.

Bryce's only memory of his birth father, a Mexican immigrant, is a box of crayons marked with "Enriquez," his father's last name. Richard adopted Bryce and, along with Nancy, raised him. A proud patrolman who never sought a promotion, Richard could be forgiving, like the time he pulled over a group of Bryce's teenage friends for speeding and let them go without a ticket. But he could also be severe. When Bryce was eleven, Richard took him into his precinct house, put him in a cell, and closed the door. "It was a warning to follow the right path," Bryce says.

Bryce attended Rufus King International High School, a magnet school on Milwaukee's north side, where he played trombone in the school orchestra alongside the violinist Gordon Gano, the future singer and guitarist of Violent Femmes. Bryce was a mediocre student, and a few months after graduating he enlisted in the army so he could pay for college. It was the early 1980s, and the Cold War was raging in Central America. Bryce trained to be a military policeman at Fort McClellan, in Alabama, and then became part of a rapid deployment force based at Fort Bragg, North Carolina. For several months, he was stationed at the Soto Cano Air Base in Honduras, then a launching point for American covert operations in Nicaragua and El Salvador.

"My dad was conservative," Bryce told me. "When I was in the army, I was, too. I was into Reagan, but it was more 'America first, USA, USA.' The Russians were the devil was the way I looked at it." His job in Honduras was to guard the air base's "secret square," where army officers reviewed intelligence collected by surveillance planes flying over the Nicaraguan border. The airplanes' microphones were sensitive enough to hear a whisper on the ground.

A few times a month, Bryce and the other soldiers got a pass to leave the base. They would go to Comayagua, the nearest town, where a group of impoverished children would be waiting when the soldiers' bus pulled up. They hoped to shine the Americans' shoes or show them the village and earn a bit of money for something to eat. Bryce picked out a boy named

George, who stood out from the crowd. Bryce felt bad for George because he saw the other kids pick on him for having big ears. George would take Bryce through the village, and Bryce would buy them a meal. Before he had to return to Soto Cano, Bryce would press a few dollars into George's hand.

For decades, Fort McClellan, the base where Bryce trained, had been used as a training site for chemical, biological, and radiological warfare. Mustard gas, Agent Orange, DDT, and other toxic materials had leached into its soil and water. Additionally, the base was adjacent to the town of Anniston, where, until the 1970s, a Monsanto plant poured millions of pounds of cancer-causing PCBs into the town landfill and creek. The company paid a settlement of $700 million to 20,000 residents of Anniston, which was once described in a *60 Minutes* report as "America's most toxic town." But the settlement did not include the soldiers who trained at Fort McClellan, a disproportionate number of whom were stricken with cancer at an early age. The army has maintained there were no adverse health effects from training there, but in 1999, the Environmental Protection Agency ordered the base to close. After his discharge, Bryce enrolled at the University of Wisconsin–Milwaukee, but he dropped out after one semester when he too was diagnosed with cancer.

Bryce lucked into an experimental trial at a medical college, which cured him, and eventually landed a job helping homeless veterans find shelter and medical care. One day a veteran who had been exposed to atomic testing during the Cold War showed Bryce his back. "It looked like someone had poured acid on it," Bryce said. Despite the soldier's wounds, the government wouldn't help because he couldn't prove the injury was caused by exposure to a nuclear test. Like many home-less vets, the man disappeared. "You don't know if you'll see them again," Bryce said. "When I saw that the government wouldn't help the brother, or even acknowledge that he suf-fered, I almost lost it." That encounter marked the beginning of a shift in Bryce's politics. "It couldn't have been made more clear to me that vets were disposable resources," he said.

When a federal grant funding his work with the vets ran out, Bryce moved on to a series of odd jobs. He was bartending and working security at a hospital when he heard about the apprenticeship program of Milwaukee Iron Workers Local 8. "I knew how to read a tape measure, that was about it," he remembers. The local's apprenticeship requires thousands of hours of on-site work and classroom training. Appren-tices earn 60 percent of full pay at the start, with their wages increasing as they gain experience. After four years of train-ing, Local 8 apprentices take a state certification test in weld-ing and then a journeyman's test to become full-fledged union ironworkers. Work could be spotty—it depended on the sea-son and the economy—and some years Bryce made as little as $30,000. But when work was plentiful he could make double that, and unlike non-union ironworkers, who learn the trade at a technical college, Bryce had no student loans to pay back.

Over the years, Bryce worked on many of Milwaukee's landmarks. He helped repair the elegant tied-arch Hoan Bridge, named for Daniel Hoan, a Socialist mayor and prag-matic visionary who ran Milwaukee from 1916 to 1940. From the bridge, you can see the Harley-Davidson Museum, another touchstone for Bryce. He worked on that too. When he drives by, he often remembers the Harley he owned for many years, which he loved riding on the county roads that crisscross Wisconsin's rolling farmland. "It was a way to reset myself," he said.

Gradually, Bryce became more involved in the union. He was grateful for what Local 8 had done for him—giving him direction, a real career. When there was a job action, a call to hold a banner outside a non-union job site or pass out union literature to non-union workers, he would be there. He also began to worry about Scott Walker, whose battles with the public-employee unions as Milwaukee county executive alarmed him. "I knew it was going to be bad," he said. "I just didn't know how bad."

In 2010, the year Walker ran for governor, Bryce stepped up his involvement, going to meetings of the Milwaukee Area Labor Council, an umbrella group of the Milwaukee-area AFL-CIO locals. Since the late 1960s, the building trades, which remain predominately white, had been partially cleaved off from the rest of the labor movement. But Bryce became one of the labor council's most active participants. "He came on his Harley with his mustache, and I thought, 'Oh my,'" Sheila Cochran, the longtime secretary-treasurer of the Labor Council, told me. Bryce's passion immediately won Cochran's respect, and she endorsed him when he ran for the council's executive board.

Bryce's work with the labor movement led to his showing up at rallies for immigrants' rights, Black Lives Matter, and a fifteen-dollar minimum wage. A few years ago, Bryce lent his hand to a unionization effort at Palermo's Pizza, one of the largest frozen-pizza makers in the country. Around the same time as the union drive, Palermo's terminated eighty-four workers who could not produce documents confirming their residency status. The company claimed the firings were unrelated to the union campaign, but the workers didn't see it that way. About a hundred of them went on strike, and Bryce, who was then the political coordinator for Local 8, joined them. He was the only member of the building trades to walk the picket line. "Whatever's been going on, I've usually been involved with," he said. "Just showing up and holding a sign and talking to people. It's a way of saying, 'I'm an ironworker, and I am with your cause.' It's something that keeps me going."

AS BRYCE BECAME more active in the labor movement, union membership in Wisconsin was withering, the economy was in steep decline in the wake of the Great Recession, and factories were closing throughout the state. In 2008, as Bryce was trying to organize non-union job sites, the General Motors plant in Janesville, one of the largest auto plants in the state, was closing. It was built in 1919, and when it closed, it was GM's oldest. In the late 1970s, seven thousand people worked there; by the end, there were fewer than twenty-five hundred. The standard wage then was $28 an hour, but many skilled tradespeople earned as much as $45 an hour.

"This is private property," a security guard told Tim Cullen outside a side entrance to the abandoned plant when we visited one summer day. Cullen briefly protested, explaining that he was the area's state senator for many years, that he had once gone to Detroit to try and save the factory. A Democrat, he had in fact served as cochair of the GM Retention Task Force, which included Paul Ryan, Janesville's congressman and native son. The group mustered $200 million in state and local money to entice GM to keep the plant open, but the company declined.

The guard was firm: We had to leave. Cullen backed his Buick out and pulled it around the corner to the front gate. The two-minute drive revealed the factory's mammoth scale, nearly five million square feet. Cullen parked by the front lot, which was empty, save for the weeds bursting through disintegrating pavement.

"Now the manufacturing jobs that are left in Janesville are almost all non-union," Cullen said. "They pay between twelve and seventeen dollars an hour with hardly any benefits."

Cullen's father worked at the plant from 1948 until his death, of a heart attack, in 1971. Cullen put himself through college, at the University of Wisconsin–Whitewater, by working summers here. GM had a special program for the sons of automakers, allowing Cullen to graduate with no student debt. "No one ever thought about it then," Cullen wondered as he pulled his car out of the entranceway. "Nor had I: What about the daughters?" We cruised along, Cullen admiring Janesville's egalitarian housing, where autoworkers owned homes that looked identical to those of local bankers and businessmen.

There were exceptions, however. "This is one of the few rich streets in Janesville," Cullen said, as he turned his sedan onto a quiet, pastoral block. We were on Paul Ryan's street, his house given away by the black SUV and a security agent posted in the driveway. The agent watched Cullen's car intently as we slowed down to take in Ryan's stately 1929 Georgian Revival mansion.

Ryan may have joined Cullen on the GM Retention Task

Force, but his home embodied his distance from the people he represented. It has six bedrooms and eight baths, befitting the previous owner, a scion of the Parker Pen family. Parker Pen was founded in Janesville in 1888. Until 1986, when new owners moved the headquarters to England, it was the second-largest employer in town, but after that buyout, jobs began migrating overseas. In 2009, Parker Pen closed its Janesville plant, ending the company's 121-year relationship with the town. The last 153 manufacturing jobs in Janesville were transferred to Mexicali, Mexico, a border town that boomed briefly after NAFTA passed, before fading as jobs moved to locations in Asia that promised even cheaper labor.

With the town stripped of these opportunities, Ryan would go on to wage war on Obamacare, the welfare state, and other critical pieces of the community's safety net. It hadn't always been that way, Cullen told me. "At the beginning," he said, "almost everyone thought Paul Ryan was this really good local guy."

Cullen has known the Ryan clan since before Ryan was born. One of his closest friends is Don Ryan, Paul's elderly uncle and a member of the road-building wing of the family. (Paul's father, who died when he was sixteen, was a lawyer.) "Paul was a very likable guy—he has great interpersonal skills," Cullen told me. "He was bright and young and wanted to represent Janesville, even though he left here when he was eighteen."

Later, running as Mitt Romney's vice-presidential candidate in 2012, Ryan would work to cast his upbringing as a working-class, up-by-the-bootstraps experience. "When I was growing up, when I was flipping burgers at McDonald's, when

I was standing in front of that big Hobart machine washing dishes, or waiting tables, I never thought of myself as stuck in some station in life," Ryan said at a campaign stop at a suburban Denver high school. Even after his father died in 1986, there was little reason Ryan would ever be "stuck": His family inherited a sizable estate from his father, a share of an Aspen ski condo, and an investment partnership from his maternal grandmother worth as much as half a milion dollars. When he needed work, he was able to get a job at his cousins' road-building company. He also received Social Security survivor benefits from his father's death, which he used to help pay for college.

"Paul grew up wealthy," Tuan Raphael, a friend of Ryan's from when they worked together at Camp Manito-wish, a YMCA camp in northern Wisconsin, told me. For half a summer, after Ryan's freshman year at Miami University in Ohio, Raphael and Ryan were roommates. After camp ended, Raphael went to Janesville to hang out with Ryan for a few days. "Nobody else was there," Raphael recalled. "We fired shotguns, drank beer, and went to his land. Their house was nice, old nice. There was a sauna." Ryan didn't discuss politics with him—"he was a frat boy"—but "he already seemed like a politician. You know, shake hands, kiss babies, kind of friendly networking." Raphael, the child of an African American serviceman and a Vietnamese mother, left Vietnam in 1975, on the last flight of Vietnamese orphans out of the country, and was adopted by a Jewish family in Oak Park, Illinois. "Janesville is a redneck town," Raphael said. "But Paul never came off as a redneck. His dad was a big name in that town, and Paul was willing to take a black Vietnamese Jew to his house."

After college, Ryan worked in Washington as a legislative aide in the office of Wisconsin Republican senator Bob Kasten. At night, Ryan waited tables at a Tex-Mex restaurant. After Kasten lost to Russ Feingold in 1992, Ryan took a speechwriting job with Empower America, a conservative think tank cofounded by former congressman Jack Kemp. When the congressional representative from Ryan's district, Mark Neumann, ran for senate in 1998, he encouraged Ryan to run for the seat. Ryan, then twenty-eight, won, largely because of his family's prominence.

"He said he was going to answer all constituent needs," Cullen told me over a BLT and lemonade at an old-school bar near Ryan's house. "Nobody saw the true conservative philosophy that he had." After the 2004 elections, Ryan began asserting that philosophy more aggressively, chiefly by pursuing a long-sought goal of the libertarian right: privatizing Social Security. The following year, Ryan authored a plan that would allow individuals to invest half of their payroll taxes in private accounts. Not only would it drain the Social Security Trust Fund, it would leave retirees' savings vulnerable to a market crash. The Bush administration pushed for a slimmed-down version of Ryan's proposal, one of the main reasons Republicans lost control of the House of Representatives in 2006.

Despite his party's wipeout, Ryan persisted with his attack on the welfare state. In 2008, he unveiled his "Roadmap for America's Future." The plan would replace Medicare with cash payments to seniors so they could, in theory, buy private insurance. Medicaid would be dissolved, and in its place lump sums would be given to states for them to spend however they wished. The "roadmap" also contained a scaled-down version of Ryan's Social Security privatization scheme. "Ryan became more vocal about his views, especially after Obama won," Cullen said. "When he was on the Romney ticket, he had a bigger national platform."

Projecting his narrative of hardworking, burger-flipping upward mobility, Ryan channeled his self-made mythology into an ethos of moral virtue and hatred of the welfare state, a philosophy rooted in the work of Ayn Rand, who had become his intellectual hero. "We don't want to turn the safety net into a hammock that lulls able-bodied people into lives of dependency and complacency," he said during a press conference in 2012, "that drains them of their will and their incentive to make the most of their lives."

Paul Ryan never pretended to appreciate Wisconsin's political past. "What I've been trying to do is indict the entire vision of progressivism," he told Glenn Beck in 2010, when he was ranking minority member of the House Budget Committee. Ryan called progressivism a "cancer," as well as "the intellectual source for the big government problems that are plaguing us today." His upbringing in Wisconsin, he told Beck, had given him an intimate knowledge of this disease. "This stuff came from these German intellectuals to Madison, University of Wisconsin," he said. The first progressives detached "people from the Constitution and founding principles to pave the way for the centralized bureaucratic welfare state." To Ryan this created "a culture of dependency on the government, not on oneself." Ryan described Wisconsin progressivism almost as an enemy within. "I grew up in the orbit of Madison, Wisconsin," he told Beck. "I know who these people are. I know what they think. I know what they believe."

IN 2011, with the economy showing signs of recovery, Bryce got a job building an addition at a Nestlé factory. "The iron we were working with was covered in ice," he told me. "It was the slipperiest stuff I ever dealt with. You had to take your gloves off constantly to feel where the bolt hole was." Despite the difficulty, Bryce was grateful for the work. Jobs had been scarce since the 2008 financial crash, especially in the winter, and Bryce was barely scraping by. He had been on and off unemployment, at one point relying on it for close to four months.

On the afternoon of February 11, as he pulled into his driveway after an eight-hour shift, he got a call from Colin Millard, the ironworkers' district business manager for Wisconsin and Michigan. Agitated, Millard told Bryce that Governor Scott Walker had just announced an assault on the labor movement unlike any other. Millard was planning to stage a protest in Horicon that Sunday afternoon, outside the home of Jeff Fitzgerald, the speaker of the state assembly. He asked Bryce if he could come. Bryce didn't hesitate. "I'll be there," he said.

A few hours earlier, Walker had held a press conference in an ornate room of the Wisconsin state capitol, where he announced his "budget repair bill," which would become known as Act 10. He began by praising the "good and decent people" who work in state and local government. But Wisconsin, he said, was in the throes of an economic and fiscal crisis. Sacrifice was needed. To avoid layoffs, furloughs, and children forced from the Medicaid rolls, he said, public workers would be required to contribute one half of the amount of their pensions and double the amount they had been paying toward their health care premiums. This drop in take-home pay would soon be estimated to approach $1 billion a year.

Walker eventually arrived at Act 10's distinguishing feature: the gutting of collective bargaining. Collective bargaining, which allows workers to have a unified voice in the conditions of their employment, would now be permitted only for wages, and then only for pay raises capped by the rate of inflation. No longer would public-sector unions have the right to address workplace safety, grievances, health care, or benefits. Union dues would be voluntary. The law required that union members vote to recertify their unions every year, and to win recertification they would need a majority of the entire bargaining unit, not just the workers voting. Walker exempted local fire and police departments, as well as the state patrol, owing to "longstanding tradition" of those services being treated differently. Critics noted that the Milwaukee police and firefighter unions, as well as the Wisconsin Troopers Association, had endorsed him.

Despite his hostility to unions, Walker had not campaigned on making radical changes to labor relations. During an interview with the editorial board of the *Oshkosh Northwestern* a week before the election, a board member asked him if collective bargaining would be used to negotiate the increase in pension contributions he was seeking from state workers. "Yep," Walker replied, nodding his head. "You still have to negotiate it. I did that at the county as well."

But eliminating collective bargaining rights may have always been central to his plans. Two weeks after he was sworn in, in a private exchange captured by a documentary filmmaker, a billionaire donor to Walker's campaign named Diane Hendricks asked the governor if there was "any chance we'll ever get to be a completely red state, and work on these unions." Walker assured her that Wisconsin would change. Hendricks then asked if Wisconsin would ever become a "right-to-work" state. Walker responded enthusiastically. "The first step is, we're going to deal with collective bargaining for all public-employee unions," he said, "because you use divide-and-conquer."

At certain points during the press conference, Walker adopted an authoritative tone. "This is what we have to offer," he said. "We are broke in this state. We have been broke for years. People have ignored that for years, and it's about time somebody stood up and told the truth." Officially called the "Wisconsin Budget Repair Bill," Act 10 was supposed to fix persistent budget shortfalls by making public employees pay more for benefits and all but eliminating collective bargaining rights. He described the bill's impact on the unions as "modest" eight times during the twenty-five-minute event.

Privately, Walker saw it differently. In a widely publicized prank phone call with a blogger impersonating David Koch, Walker described the dinner he held for his cabinet at his executive residence the night before his announcement. "It was kind of the last hurrah, before we dropped the bomb," he said to the faux Koch. At the dinner, Walker had held up a photograph of Ronald Reagan and told his cabinet that what they were about to do recalled Reagan's historic breaking of the air traffic controllers' union strike in 1981. He singled out the firing of the controllers as "one of the most defining moments" of Reagan's political career—a moment, he said, that "was the first crack in the Berlin Wall." Walker saw Act 10 in a similar light. "This is our time to change the course of history," he said.

BY THE TIME Walker announced Act 10, the first protest against it—the one Colin Millard had called Bryce about—was already being planned. Union leaders around the state had been tipped off early: The day before the announcement, Graeme Zielinski, the communications director of the Wisconsin Democratic Party, received a distressing phone call from a lobbyist for Wisconsin Energy, the state's largest utility company. He called to warn Zielinski and Mike Tate, the state Democratic Party chairman, that Walker planned an unspecified attack on unions. "This was the first strike we knew was coming," Zielinski said. "We just didn't know how radical it would be." After the lobbyist's call, Zielinski immediately alerted a list of activist union leaders and rank-and-file members. "Graeme was the Paul Revere of Act 10," Bryce told me.

One of the first union leaders to hear from Zielinski was Millard. The pair had been outraged by Walker's fights with the public employee unions during his tenure as Milwaukee county executive. Zielinski and Millard had followed Walker along his final Harley-Davidson tour "across Wisconsin"—a tour that also took in parts of Iowa, the host of the first presidential caucus. The image Walker promoted, as a champion of the working class, offended them. At many of the stops, Millard would be waiting, holding an enormous banner for hours. Don't let Walker do to Wisconsin what he did to Milwaukee County, it warned.

They planned a protest that would take place just two days after Walker's announcement, in Horicon, a town an hour northwest of Milwaukee that is home to a unionized John Deere plant. Horicon sits in Dodge County, where three state prisons are staffed by unionized corrections officers. Millard, who lived in the town, estimates that close to 30 percent of the county's work force was unionized, twice the statewide rate. He deliberately scheduled the protest for Sunday, when people wouldn't have to miss work, and contacted all the local unions in the area and several others from farther afield. But both he and Zielinski encountered intense pressure from their superiors in the Democratic Party and the AFL-CIO to call the protest off.

On the Friday before the protest, just after he talked to Bryce, Millard got a call from Phil Neuenfeldt, the head of the Wisconsin AFL-CIO, telling him to cancel it. "They were going to phone-bank instead, and try to convince a couple of Republican legislators," Millard said, laughing. "It was obvious calling these guys was not going to change their minds; they wouldn't have announced it if they didn't have the votes." Millard told his supervisor he would hold the protest with or without his approval.

Mike Tate, Zielinski's boss, ordered him to call it off too. "The big boys were saying they were going to ride this out," Zielinski said. "I had a discussion and I was told no." Zielinski worried he might be fired, but he took inspiration from Millard. "Colin said, 'Fuck it—this is an emergency. It's time to break the glass.'" Zielinski had been committed to labor since he was a child, growing up in a union household on the South Side of Milwaukee. His father, mother, and both sets of grandparents all had worked for Ladish, a tool-and-die manufacturer nearby. He can still recall the tremors that shook the area around the plant when the 375,000-pound forging rams of Ladish's five-story counterblow hammer, the largest in the world, were dropped. He also remembers his father's union hall, a community center for the working-class, largely Polish neighborhood, and the social-justice sermons of labor-friendly Catholic priests.

Zielinski visited the picket lines during a Ladish strike in the late 1970s and those of the bitter, twenty-eight-month strike at the Patrick Cudahy meatpacking plant a decade later. The company brought in minority workers as strikebreakers to try and break the union, and when the Cudahy strike finally ended, the union had to accept significant wage and benefit concessions. That outcome further diminished the willingness of the state's workers to go out and strike. "We had no conception of what kind of muscle memory there was in Wisconsin—or anywhere—for any kind of labor action," Zielinski said. "I didn't think there would be a lot of people at the protest on Sunday. I was expecting twenty or thirty, and there were several hundred. It caused our jaws to drop."

The protesters gathered at the hall of the machinists' Local 873, the home of the John Deere workers. From there they marched through the snow-covered town carrying American flags and placards with messages like "Scott Walker = Too Extreme" and "Don't Let Politicians Take Away Your Union," written below a drawing of two hands, one black and one white, clasped together over a map of Wisconsin. After the march, they gathered on the driveway of a union member's home, across the street from Fitzgerald's house. Fitzgerald had been warned about the protest and wasn't home, but the protesters remained for more than an hour. They ended with a chant of "Unity." Millard stood in the middle of the street, with a bullhorn attached to his belt, gazing at the spirited crowd. "This is what we got to do," he told them. "We've got to stand together."

Millard saw the attack on labor as inevitable. "In 1983, during a strike at Kohler plumbing, two guys were literally run over on the picket line with a car," he said. "The labor peace we got lasted for a generation. Look at my grandma, who retired from Oscar Mayer in the early eighties. My cousin's husband worked there as a maintenance mechanic in 2001, but Grandma made more on the assembly line than he did because they destroyed the meatpackers' union. Now they say it's a job no American wants. Well, that's because they destroyed the wages. When my grandma retired, it was still owned by the Oscar Mayer family. She had health insurance until she died. You have to make your own deal when it gets to your generation's turn."

On Monday, the day after the protest in Horicon, a thousand protesters, led by the University of Wisconsin's teaching assistants' union, marched on the state capitol. It was Valentine's Day, and they delivered Valentine cards for Walker with a plea that read: "We ♥ UW: Governor Walker, Don't Break My ♥." On Tuesday morning, eight hundred students from Madison's East High walked out of school and marched down East Washington Avenue to the capitol to show support for their teachers. They were soon joined by thousands of citizens, union and non-union alike, who began flooding the rotunda. A troop of firefighters marched through the capitol, playing bagpipes in a dramatic show of solidarity, and a contingent of police officers held "Cops for Labor" signs. It seemed that Walker's effort to divide the unions had backfired.

Protesters inside the capitol began their unplanned occupation of the building with a campaign to stall the bill by getting as many people as they could to deliver two-minute testimonies—as much time as the rules allowed—to the Joint Finance Committee, trying to delay passage until the public could be mobilized to bring pressure on Republican senators. The occupation, on the heels of the Arab Spring, prompted the *New York Times* to wonder if Madison was "the Tunisia of collective bargaining rights." Pizzas for the protesters arrived from a nearby restaurant, ordered by supporters in all fifty states and sixty-eight countries. Paul Ryan, then the Republican chairman of the House Budget Committee, characterized the Madison protests as "riots."

THE PROTESTS IN MADISON were the first significant resistance to the ascendant Tea Party and helped set the stage for Occupy Wall Street. For many of the participants, it was a hopeful moment. That first week, Bryce began taking off from work to go to the capitol, driving early in the morning to Madison and then returning at night. "I was very optimistic just seeing how many people were there," he said. "The community in the capitol grew organically, there were stations set up for medical needs, food. People were cleaning. I remember all the Post-its on the walls, little messages of encouragement: 'Don't do this.' 'Kill the Bill.'"

The first Tuesday of the capitol occupation, hundreds of people waited through the night to testify before the Joint Finance Committee and register their opposition to Act 10. One Republican senator on the committee, Randy Hopper, had won his last election by only 163 votes, but he seemed unconcerned about his support for the bill. He was seen texting or speaking to an aide almost constantly through the endless stream of outraged testimony. But after midnight, a woman began her testimony by saying, "My parents live in Senator Hopper's district, my family goes back over 100 years in his district, and my father voted for him." Hopper stopped texting, looked up, and began to listen.

Each day brought ever-larger crowds to the capitol to protest Act 10. The senate had a rule requiring a quorum of twenty members to vote on fiscal measures, and Republicans then had nineteen senators. On Wednesday, February 16, the fourteen Democratic state senators fled to Illinois to deny the chamber a quorum, allowing more time for public opposition to build. Inspired by the walkout of the high school students and their own anger over Walker's attack on the unions, Madison Teachers, the local representing the three thousand teachers and professional staff who worked in Madison's public schools, staged a "sickout" that Wednesday. Many of the city's teachers continued the action through the rest of the week. Teachers in Milwaukee and Racine began following suit, but despite the teachers' demonstrated willingness to defy the law, which forbids public employees from striking, statewide union leaders and the leadership of the state's Democratic Party firmly opposed any kind of work stoppage.

Other union officials across the state issued similar messages. The day after Walker announced Act 10, AFL-CIO officials and Wisconsin union attorneys held an emergency meeting at the Teamsters building in West Milwaukee, where Paul Secunda, a professor of labor law at Marquette University, urged them to call a general strike. Secunda was told that it was not an option, because it was illegal. "It was technically illegal for the Selma marchers," Secunda later told me, vent-ing his frustration. He believed history showed such strikes could work. Though Reagan's firing of the air traffic controllers in 1981 loomed frighteningly large, during the 1960s and '70s, many public-sector unions had staged successful, illegal strikes, including a wildcat strike of US postal workers in 1970 that involved more than 200,000 people. Besides, Secunda wondered, at this point, what was the alternative? "Collective bargaining will become collective begging," he said.

The protests at the capitol continued for nearly three weeks. Walker took to entering the building through a secret tunnel, as did most of the Republican legislators. In early March, Walker tried to order the Dane County police to stand in front of the capitol doors to bar protesters from entering. (They would be permitted to leave.) The Dane County sheriff, Dave Mahoney, declined to do so. "I refused to put deputy sheriffs in a position to be palace guards," Mahoney told reporters.

With the Democratic senators still in Illinois, senate Republicans decided to separate the collective bargaining measure from the budget bill and vote on it immediately. Within a couple of hours, the senate majority leader, Scott Fitzgerald, called a meeting of the senate and assembly leadership to move the bill forward. During the meeting, a heated argument erupted between Fitzgerald and Peter Barca, the assembly's minority leader. Barca had been handed a thirty-seven-page summary of the bill, not the bill itself.

"I said I wanted an explanation of what's in this document, so I can at least know what I'm voting on," Barca told me. Fitzgerald ignored his request. Barca then began reading a 2010 memo from the attorney general outlining Wisconsin's open meetings law, which generally requires a government body to give twenty-four hours' notice to the public before it meets; Fitzgerald had called the meeting with less than two hours' notice.

"Clerk, call roll," Fitzgerald interrupted.

"No! Excuse me!" Barca shouted. "This is clearly a violation of the open meetings law, you have been shutting people down . . ." As Barca spoke, the Republicans murmured "aye," and, by a 4–0 vote, the committee separated the collective bargaining measure from the budget bill. Barca's exchange was captured on WisconsinEye, a local version of C-Span, and went viral, further enraging the protesters, many of whom were as upset about the unprecedented process as the bill itself. "I felt like I was flying by the seat of my pants," Fitzgerald told me when I asked if he had regrets. "Sometimes it was a spot decision that was made, so I don't want to second-guess a lot of what we did."

The new collective bargaining bill passed both houses within hours.

AFTER SIGNING ACT 10, Governor Walker told a reporter for The Associated Press that the bill was "progressive," a word with special resonance in Wisconsin. Wisconsin's Progressive movement, a coalition of workers, farmers, and academics, flourished in the early twentieth century. It emphasized a democratization of politics, economic equality, labor rights, improving public education, and the protection of natural resources. More broadly, Wisconsin's Progressives championed the public sector against encroachment by the private one. Though the political movement itself eventually faded, it established a set of traditions that persisted in the state's institutions and the public's imagination.

Walker's description marked a fealty to this tradition, a recognition of its importance to voters, and a perversion of its meaning. Some of Walker's opponents noted the irony of enacting Act 10 during the centenary of Wisconsin's 1911 legislature, arguably the most progressive legislative session in American history. The primary inspiration for the 1911 legislature was the Wisconsin Idea, whose moniker came from the title of a book about that legislative session. But the origins of the Wisconsin Idea go back decades earlier, to the work of John Bascom, the University of Wisconsin's president from 1874 to 1887.

Bascom saw society as a living thing, a type of organism. To maintain its health, the state needed to foster social, moral, and economic harmony. If the rich grew too rich, if workers became impoverished, if women were subjugated, society fell out of balance, and the whole of it suffered. Bascom believed in activist government to foster balance—levying taxes on corporations and the rich, accepting the right of workers to form unions and to strike, and supporting women's suffrage and the right to a university education, to prevent their subservience to men. "Protection is admitted by all to be the first duty of government," he wrote. "But this protection is not that of the productive classes against the depredative classes simply, is not of society against criminals merely, but is also the protection of the weak, universally and broadly, against the strong."

The year Bascom arrived in Madison, 1874, was the year before his most renowned pupil would enroll: Fighting Bob

La Follette. An indifferent student but even then a brilliant orator, La Follette owed his graduation to Bascom's tie-breaking vote on the faculty committee deciding his fate. Bascom's strong support for women's rights, labor unions, and the idea of service to the citizens of the state made a deep impression on La Follette. "During my terms as governor I did my best to build up and encourage the spirit which John Bascom in his time had expressed," La Follette wrote in his autobiography. For La Follette, Wisconsin's entire Progressive legacy would not have been possible without the mentoring of his former teacher to so many of the animating protagonists of the Wisconsin Idea. "The guiding spirit of my time," La Follette said of Bascom. "The man to whom Wisconsin owes a debt greater than it can ever pay."

Though Bascom disliked socialism, he was more contemptuous of laissez-faire capitalism and the corrosive effect he felt it had on the common good. "Wealth means power, and power and wealth combined mean the relative subjection of the many," he wrote. "The let-alone policy in America is little more than an irrational conviction that public interests will take care of themselves with no watchfulness on the part of the people; that public prosperity is necessarily included in private gains." Bascom's belief in the need to restrain corporate wealth and power left the strongest mark on La Follette.

The bond between the university and state government, the core tenet of the Wisconsin Idea, began in 1901, when La Follette, the state's newly elected governor, established what would become the Legislative Reference Bureau, a small agency providing nonpartisan technical assistance to legislators. The bureau would also facilitate the involvement of university experts, whose work would help shape the drafting of legislation. La Follette chose Charles McCarthy, a political scientist and Wisconsin alum, to lead the agency, which was located in an attic room in the state capitol. McCarthy energetically expanded its scope and reach, scouring the world for legislation to inform his research. He and his staff began drafting bills themselves, reforming an ad hoc process that had been corrupted by lobbyist-lawyers. McCarthy wanted legislation well wrought enough to withstand the kinds of court challenges that had stymied progressive efforts in other states.

His skill was apparent in Wisconsin's income-tax bill. Since the seventeenth century, sixteen attempts had been made in colonies and states to try and institute a successful income tax. All of these efforts failed. Most of them managed to collect only a few thousand dollars, because people would lie about their earnings and politicians were too fearful of voter backlash to enforce the law. In 1908, however, Wisconsin voters overwhelmingly approved a referendum to implement a state income tax on both individuals and corporations. A senate committee began a long drafting process, producing a bill that finally came up for hearings in 1911. Delos Kinsman, a professor from a nearby teachers' college, came to testify before the legislative committee; he had written his dissertation on the failures of previous income-tax efforts. Kinsman delivered a withering critique of Wisconsin's bill, prompting McCarthy to try and persuade Kinsman to rewrite it.

"The long story of failure beginning with the Massachusetts Colony in 1643 caused me to hesitate," Kinsman recalled in an interview decades later. "But Dr. McCarthy declared that a measure would be passed anyway and it ought to be the best possible." Kinsman agreed to try. His college gave him three months' leave to rewrite the bill and persuade legislators of its merits. His version included appointed, rather than elected, tax commissioners and a progressive tax rate that placed the largest burden on the wealthy, and it returned most of the collected revenue to local governments. The tax was widely accepted, popular even, because of its fairness and the improvement of services that the revenue provided. The tax also mitigated the rampant economic inequality that pervaded Wisconsin at the time, and by 1920, eleven states had followed suit.

Even more influential was the 1911 legislature's workers' compensation law. Drafted by John Commons, the University of Wisconsin economist, the bill offered workers and their families redress for injury or death on the job. In 1900 alone, more than 2,500 railroad workers in the United States were killed while working. (A century later, there were fewer than twenty.) Companies barely considered worker safety, in part because, for them, workers' lives were cheap. Before the law, the only option a worker or his family had after an injury or death was to sue the company, an almost insurmountable expense. Over time, the law prompted Wisconsin's owners and bosses to make working conditions safer. The Wisconsin workers' compensation program became a model for other states too. Nine additional states passed similar laws that year; thirty-six more did by the end of the decade.

John Commons's most important mentor was Richard Ely, a progressive political economist who taught Commons at Johns Hopkins University. In 1892, the University of Wisconsin wooed Ely to Madison to become the director of its new

School of Economics, Political Science, and History, but just two years later, Ely was put on trial by the Board of Regents—with his job on the line—after the state superintendent of education accused Ely of supporting labor strikes, boycotts, and socialism. The regents ultimately acquitted Ely, and their report exonerating him came to be called the "Magna Carta of Academic Freedom." A quote from the report is engraved on an iconic plaque at the top of the university's Bascom Hill quadrangle. Known as the "sifting and winnowing" plaque because of its inscription, it reads: "Whatever may be the limitations which trammel inquiry elsewhere, we believe that the great state University of Wisconsin should ever encourage that continual and fearless sifting and winnowing by which alone the truth can be found."

Ely's verdict established the University of Wisconsin as a haven for progressive economists, many of whom Ely brought to Madison. Commons, for example, came to the university in 1904, at Ely's invitation, after his dismissal by administrators at Syracuse University, which accused him of harboring radical economic views and scaring off donors. (Some of Ely's and Commons's other views, on race, for example, were abhorrent: like many progressive and conservative elites, they supported eugenics.) Ely was an economic advisor to Bob La Follette when he was governor, and his ideas influenced Woodrow Wilson (a student of Ely's at Johns Hopkins), Teddy Roosevelt, and Franklin Roosevelt. A driving force in the social gospel movement, Ely believed capitalism could produce great wealth, but that government intervention and strong labor unions were needed to counterbalance its power and alleviate suffering.

Ely and Commons helped transform the University of Wisconsin's multidisciplinary economics department, which Ely directed until 1925, into a center for "institutional" economics. Institutionalists challenged the previously dominant neoclassical theory of laissez-faire capitalism associated with Adam Smith, which they saw as irrelevant in an era when large corporations, not small farmers and entrepreneurs, dominated the economy and exploited workers. To remedy this power imbalance, Commons advocated for the workers' compensation law, a minimum wage, unemployment insurance, and child-labor laws. He was also a proponent of a "living wage," a term that was codified in a Wisconsin state statute Commons drafted, which passed in 1913. The minimum wage, the law read, "shall be not less than a living wage," sufficient to permit an employee to maintain herself or himself "in reasonable comfort, reasonable physical well-being, decency, and moral well-being." (Scott Walker's 2015 budget struck the "living wage" language from Wisconsin's books.)

Like the other Progressive milestones of the 1911 legislature, the passage of workers' compensation was aided by the twelve assemblymen and two state senators who were members of the Milwaukee Socialist Party. In 1910, after a corruption scandal in Milwaukee had tarred both Republicans and Democrats, the Socialists swept into power, winning the state legislative offices, the mayoralty (which they would hold, off and on, until 1960), and a congressional seat. The party's electoral victories in 1910 pushed the progressive Republicans to the left, prompting them to make bolder reforms to compete for voters. "The only way to beat the Socialists is 'to beat them to it,'" Charles McCarthy wrote.

Milwaukee's Socialist Party grew out of the enormous number of German immigrants who began pouring into the city in the late 1840s. Many of those migrants were fleeing the failed 1848 revolution in Germany and had been members of the *Turnverein*, or Turners, a physical-fitness movement focused on gymnastics that also encouraged intellectual development and liberal, sometimes revolutionary, politics. The Turners established strongholds across the Midwest and were especially active in Milwaukee. Like many of Wisconsin's Scandinavian farmers, they held strong antislavery views, and the movement passionately supported Abraham Lincoln's 1860 presidential campaign. Prominent Milwaukee Turners included Carl Schurz, a '48er who went on to become a Union Army general, a United States senator, and the secretary of the interior, and Mathilde Franziska Anneke, a journalist, socialist, and friend of Karl Marx who settled in the city in 1849 and three years later started *Deutsche Frauen-Zeitung*, the first feminist journal founded by a woman in America.

The Turners built several centers in Milwaukee that offered gymnastics equipment as well as beer halls, meeting rooms, and auditoriums for social and cultural events. The facilities also became incubators of radical politics. In 1897, the Social-Democratic Party, the precursor to Milwaukee's Socialist Party, was cofounded by a Romanian Jewish immigrant named Victor Berger, a brilliant tactician and organizer who developed what became called the "bundle brigade." An army of volunteers that swelled to a thousand members, it could print flyers and pamphlets in twelve languages and deliver literature in the appropriate language to every home in Milwaukee within forty-eight hours.

In 1895, Berger, who would later become a United States

congressman, visited the labor organizer Eugene Debs in an Illinois prison, where Debs was serving a sentence for leading a railroad strike. Berger brought Debs a copy of Marx's *Capital*, introducing Debs to socialism. In 1901, Berger, Debs, and another comrade founded the Socialist Party of America; Debs would go on to become the party's presidential candidate in four elections, winning 6 percent of the vote in 1912. But even as Berger shaped the broader movement, his strand of socialism was democratic and reformist, focused not on revolution but on achieving concrete gains for Milwaukee's working class through the electoral process. "In America for the first time in history, we find an oppressed class with the same fundamental rights as the ruling class—the right of universal suffrage," Berger wrote in the *Social Democratic Herald*, a Socialist weekly. "It is then nonsense to talk of sudden bloody revolutions here, until the power of the ballot has been at least tried."

A woodcarver named Emil Seidel captured Milwaukee's mayor's office in 1910, becoming the first Socialist mayor of a major American city, while the party also won majorities on the city council and the county board. The party's victories that year were owed largely to its reputation for being incorruptible. ("They never were approached by the lobbyists, because the lobbyists knew it was not possible to influence these men," William Evjue, a progressive Republican legislator, once said of the Milwaukee Socialists.) Two years after Seidel's victory, Democrats and Republicans conspired to defeat him, but in 1916 another Socialist, Daniel Hoan, won the mayor's office and held it for the next twenty-four years. Hoan fashioned a transparent city government and won a higher minimum wage for city workers, while investing in "public enterprise"—libraries, schools, and one of the country's most extensive park systems. While the party's strength would never match its 1910 peak, its influence on Milwaukee, and the state as a whole, persisted. In 1924, despite a sometimes fractious alliance with La Follette's progressives, the Milwaukee Socialist Party endorsed La Follette's presidential bid, helping make Wisconsin the only state his Progressive Party would win.

While Victor Berger is credited as the architect of Milwaukee socialism, it was Emil Seidel who captured the spirit of its idealistic pragmatism. "Some eastern smarties called ours a Sewer Socialism," Seidel wrote in his memoirs. He went on:

> Yes, we wanted sewers in the workers' homes; but we wanted much, oh, so very much more than sewers. We wanted our workers to have pure air; we wanted them to have sunshine; we wanted planned homes; we wanted living wages; we wanted recreation for young and old; we wanted vocational education; we wanted a chance for every human being to be strong and live a life of happiness. And, we wanted everything that was necessary to give them that: playgrounds, parks, lakes, beaches, clean creeks and rivers, swimming and wading pools, social centers, reading rooms, clean fun, music, dance, song and joy for all. That was our Milwaukee Social Democratic movement.

JESSE BARNES, a wiry, bearded, sixty-four-year-old retired autoworker, was an enthusiastic participant in the demonstrations against Act 10. He considers himself a socialist—partly,

he said, from the legacy of Milwaukee socialism. When I visited him at his house six years after the Act 10 demonstrations,
the first things he wanted to show me were two posters, which
he had mounted on a storage cabinet in the entranceway. One
was a reproduction of an iconic photograph of black sanitation
workers on strike in Memphis in 1968, holding picket signs
that read "I Am a Man." The other carried an image of his
state capitol's rotunda overflowing with protesters fighting
Act 10. It read: "From Memphis to Madison."

The two signs traced the arc of public-employee unions
from their apex to their death throes. But they also embodied something else: the collaborative strength of the labor
and civil rights movements, an alliance that the Memphis
strike stood for more than any other in American history.
The indifference of Memphis officials to the deaths of two
black sanitation workers, Echol Cole and Robert Walker, who
had been crushed by a malfunctioning garbage-truck com-
pactor, had sparked the strike, but its origins lay in decades
of mistreatment. Two weeks after their deaths, 1,100 Memphis sanitation workers refused to go to work. They sought
an end to poverty wages—40 percent of the workforce quali-
fied for welfare—and recognition for their union, which the
city refused to accept. The sanitation workers' union, Local
1733, was an affiliate of AFSCME, which had been founded
more than three decades earlier in Madison, out of fear that
Roosevelt Democrats might turn Wisconsin's nonpartisan
civil service system into a patronage one. Having succeeded
in safeguarding the civil service rules, AFSCME had grown
as the Wisconsin legislature recognized its right to represent
municipal workers and later state workers, and it added new

locals across the country. Its support of Local 1733—hesitant at first, then full-throated—was crucial to sustaining the Memphis strike. Nonetheless, by mid-March of 1968, the strike was faltering.

It was then that Dr. Martin Luther King Jr. revived the strike with his support. The Memphis walkout became central to King's Poor People's Campaign, which he launched a year earlier in the hope of uniting impoverished Americans of all races to address poverty throughout the country. King believed that racial and economic injustice were inseparable. He outlined that view to striking workers and their supporters in his "I've Been to the Mountaintop" sermon, which he delivered at a Memphis church. "You know, whenever Pharaoh wanted to prolong the period of slavery in Egypt, he had a favorite, favorite formula for doing it," King said. "What was that? He kept the slaves fighting among themselves. But whenever the slaves get together, something happens in Pharaoh's court, and he cannot hold the slaves in slavery."

The labor and civil rights movements had been a united force in American politics at least since the Montgomery bus boycott began in 1955; the United Auto Workers (UAW), which supported the boycott, paid the defendants' bail and court costs, and its president, Walter Reuther, grew to be one of King's most loyal and devoted supporters. (The law "prohibiting conspiracies" that was used to charge Rosa Parks, King, and eighty-seven other African Americans who voluntarily turned themselves in to the authorities had been originally written to break Alabama's trade unions.) In the years that followed, King became a central figure in the alliance, arguing that the fates of the civil rights and labor movements were deeply connected.

"The coalition that can have the greatest impact in the struggle for human dignity here in America," King wrote in a 1962 letter to the Amalgamated Laundry Workers, a New York union, "is that of the Negro and the forces of labor." But King warned against the dangers of narrow self-interest. Three years later, in a speech to a New York public-employees' union, he said that "the strength of labor will fail if it does not become a social force pressing for greater dimensions of wealth for all those who labor."

King was assassinated in Memphis the day after delivering his "I've Been to the Mountaintop" sermon. Four days later, more than forty thousand people, including Coretta Scott King, Reuther, and AFSCME's national president, Jerry Wurf, marched through the Memphis streets and demanded that the city negotiate with the striking workers and recognize Local 1733.

Wurf declared that the strike would last "until we have justice," but Henry Loeb, the segregationist mayor of Memphis, continued to refuse even to meet with the union's local leaders, arguing that their strike was illegal. President Lyndon Johnson demanded that his undersecretary of labor step in as a mediator, and on April 16 Loeb finally caved to national pressure. Union negotiators settled the strike with the city, paving the way for recognition of the sanitation workers' union, and with it a new contract that offered better wages, a pension, and a grievance procedure. That victory, in the virulently anti-union South, was the most prominent example of a great wave of public-sector militancy that swept across the country, with people staging strikes that won better wages, working conditions, and benefits for millions of public workers.

Ultimately, despite lingering racism in many trade unions, the alliance between labor and civil rights would have another impact: It is likely that no group has benefited more from the labor movement than African Americans. Between 1948 and 1979, the period with the greatest union density in the United States, hourly compensation for the average American worker rose by 93 percent, which contributed to a decreasing wage gap between African American and white workers. In 1935, the year the Wagner Act was signed, less than 1 percent of all union members were black; by the 1970s, 40 percent of African American men and a quarter of African American women were union members. In the heavily industrialized Midwest, as many as 60 percent of black men in the private sector were in a union. (Later, as unionization rates began collapsing, the racial wealth gap spiked. Jake Rosenfeld, a sociologist at Washington University, estimates that if unionization rates had remained at 1970s levels, black men would be earning roughly $2,600, or nearly 10 percent, more a year.)

Barnes is grateful for what the union did for him. On his front lawn, he displays a "Proud Union Home" sign, and he told me his immaculate beige 1976 Corvette in the driveway was bought with his first union wages. He owes his yellow two-story corner house with trimmed hedges and an attached garage to those wages too. But Barnes also expressed gratitude for the nonmaterial benefits the union brought him. "If you have a good, strong union, race doesn't matter," he said. "I had white friends that I worked with every day. Some I disagreed with, some I got along with."

Barnes joked that his job was nothing like Upton Sinclair's *The Jungle*, but it wasn't easy either. Barnes worked the third shift, 10 p.m. to 6 a.m., inspecting catalytic converters on an assembly line at a Delphi Automotive plant outside Milwaukee. His job, as he put it, was "unskilled labor"—picking up the converters from a conveyor belt, inspecting a weld, and then flipping them back over, all within six seconds. He did that five days a week for thirty years. "I never tried to get overtime," he said. "This was a marathon." Ten years into the job, he started experiencing carpal tunnel syndrome, and eventually he had to wear braces at work and at home. "The worst time is when you go home trying to sleep," he said. "When you're relaxing, that's when it's really intense throbbing pain. It wouldn't go away." Barnes's plant closed in 2008, a casualty of NAFTA, four years after his retirement.

As I was leaving, Barnes wanted to show me a memento. It was a picture of his son, Mandela, taken in the summer of 1990, when Mandela was three and Barnes won a family scholarship to attend Walter Reuther's UAW camp in Black Lake, Michigan. Reuther had founded the camp as an educational and recreation retreat for the UAW's members and leadership. The picture of Mandela showed the small boy surrounded by other three-year-old children of autoworkers— black, white, Latino—a tangible relic of King's dream for unity among Pharaoh's "slaves." "We were all working basically for the same thing," Barnes said. "A safe workplace, being treated humanely, adequate wages, the opportunity for growth and development through apprenticeships."

When I asked what his family did at the camp, Barnes told me they swam in the clean lake, enjoyed leisure time together, and were given a history of labor. "They showed us how labor's role in politics—especially local politics—makes a difference," he said. "They talked to us about solidarity, and the 1937 sit-down strike in Flint that made the UAW what it was. They wanted us to know that the company doesn't just give us these benefits: They're *won*."

THE PASSAGE OF ACT 10 did not stop the protest movement that arose to defeat it. The day after Walker signed Act 10 into law, the crowd at the capitol swelled to more than a hundred thousand people. Speakers addressing the protesters emphasized that the battle would turn, focusing on overturning Act 10 by removing Governor Walker and several Republican senators through a recall process—another Progressive reform introduced by the 1911 legislature. If enough signatures were gathered, a new election would be triggered.

Some union leaders, though, felt uneasy about the strategy. "The AFL-CIO leadership is scared of the masses," Dave Poklinkoski, the electricians' union president, told me. "They had more than 100,000 people out there, and then they tell people to go home."

At the Act 10 signing ceremony at the capitol, a reporter asked Walker if he had any comment on the protests raging at that moment in the rotunda. "Governor, we can hear thousands of people in the hall screaming 'shame, shame, shame,'" the reporter said.

"I think we've had a good civil discussion," Walker replied. "They have a right to be heard, but the countless numbers of taxpayers, the millions and millions of people who live in this state, the middle-class taxpayers of this state also have a right to be heard, and there is no point should their voices be drowned out by the protesters here and around the capitol. Because in the end they are the ones that have had to pay the higher taxes and the higher burden of excessive government."

A month later, Walker testified in Congress before a special panel of the House Committee on Oversight and Government Reform. Called "State and Municipal Debt: Tough Choices Ahead," the panel included the president of the anti-union National Right to Work Legal Defense Foundation, two "resident scholars" of the conservative American Enterprise Institute, and an economist from the University of Rochester School of Business. "We are going to give local governments the tools they need to balance their budgets for many years to come," Walker told the committee. "In Wisconsin, we are going to pursue a truly progressive option." Representative Dennis Kucinich challenged the premise that restricting collective bargaining saved money. He noted that Act 10 required unions to hold annual votes to continue representing their own members. "How much money does this save your state budget?" Kucinich asked. "It doesn't save any," Walker acknowledged.

After Act 10 passed, the decimation of labor came quickly. In 2010, Wisconsin's union density was 14 percent; six years later, it was 8 percent. WEAC, the teachers' umbrella union, plummeted from 98,000 members to 36,000 in the same period. "Act 10 was a political attack," Tim Cullen, the former state senator from Janesville, told me. Cullen, the most moderate member of the Democratic caucus, had been a member of Republican governor Tommy Thompson's cabinet. While hiding out in Illinois, Cullen and Bob Jauch, another moderate Democrat, were secretly negotiating with Walker's aides at a McDonald's in Kenosha and at a Beloit motel, both just inside the Wisconsin border. Cullen and Jauch tried to win concessions, including an allowance for collective bargaining on workplace safety. "Walker's chief of staff said to us, 'There is only one item in the bill which is nonnegotiable, and that is getting rid of the automatic dues check-off,'" Cullen said. "That was the funnel of money from public employees to their unions. That was the core issue; that was what Walker wanted more than anything."

"It's illegal for the public employees to strike," Colin Millard said, taking stock of the aftermath of Act 10. "But if they're going to repeal the law, and take away your right to bargain, don't you think at that point you should think about collective action? Writing postcards isn't going to do it. If correctional guards would have just sat down on the job, not even gone out on strike, this thing would have been over and Walker would have lost. But he made the correct calculation that they wouldn't do that."

Millard noted how far union density had fallen in Wisconsin since 2010, but it didn't seem to ever be enough for Walker and the state Republicans, who continued to try to drive it down further. "At eight percent of the population, or even fifteen, what makes us such an enemy? I'll tell you: Labor is the enemy of capital. They really won't be happy until we're starving on the street."

For Randy Bryce, the most painful memory of the battle of Act 10 was watching Walker's success in dividing labor against itself. "It's hard when you don't have people showing up regularly to the union meetings," he said. "What happened with the public-sector unions is a lot of people showed up and made a point. It took a while for it to get out to the rest of the country, but after it was all said and done, everybody went back home. Nothing really happened."

He saw the division even among his fellow ironworkers in Local 8. "We had guys in our local supporting Act 10," he told me in disbelief. "Not all unions are the same, they'd tell me— it's a good thing. They see themselves as separate. All these years I've been telling them: But they're going to come after you, too. *You're* going to have a turn, and the longer you wait, the fewer people are going to be able to stand up for you."

3

THE LAST DEER
ON EARTH

Eighteen thousand years ago, the Laurentide Ice Sheet, covering much of what is now Wisconsin, began melting. Water accumulated in an enormous lake, encompassing more than eighteen hundred square miles, which was enclosed by an ice dam. As the glacier retreated, the sand in its meltwaters added to the vast sand deposits already in the lake. Temperatures continued warming until the dam burst, suddenly and violently. The waters carved out the unique rock formations and tributary canyons of the Wisconsin Dells, a five-mile-long scenic gorge along the Wisconsin River. The flooding fused the upper and lower parts of that river and drained the lake, exposing a vast sand-laden lake bed that spanned ten present-day Wisconsin counties. Today, these are known as the sand counties.

Ten miles south of the Dells, in Sauk County, one of the sand counties, there is a particularly lush patch of land: an eighty-acre farm that Aldo Leopold, then a professor of game management at the University of Wisconsin, bought in 1935 for the bargain price of eight dollars an acre. At the time, it was completely deforested, except for a few sickly trees lining the side of a gravel road. The sandy soil, already poor and thin for agriculture, had become further eroded by drought and overfarming, and after years of unpaid taxes by a delinquent owner, the farm had been abandoned and taken over by the county. The farm's decimated condition thrilled Leopold, who saw his acquisition as a laboratory for land restoration.

Rural life always appealed to Leopold. He grew up in the small Mississippi River town of Burlington, Iowa, where his father taught him to love hunting and the outdoors. When Leopold was a teenager, President Theodore Roosevelt named Gifford Pinchot to be the first director of what later became the United States Forest Service, launching a national conservation movement. Pinchot had helped found the Yale Forest School, the first graduate school of forestry in the nation, from which Leopold graduated in 1909. He then began a career at the Forest Service, working as a ranger and administrator in Arizona and New Mexico, where he led the effort to designate the Gila National Forest as the country's first wilderness area. He was transferred to Wisconsin in 1924, the year Bob La Follette ran for president on the Progressive Party ticket, and the peak of the La Follette family's influence on the state.

In 1933, when Leopold started his game-management position at the University of Wisconsin, FDR's new Soil Erosion Service also recruited him for a large-scale restoration effort in Coon Valley, a farming community in west-central Wisconsin. Some eight hundred farmers, most of them Norwegian immigrants, had watched their livelihoods vanish after erosion, caused by overgrazing, excessive logging, and poor agricultural practices, ruined the soil. Chunks of steep hillside might break off and crumble into the creek below after a single bad storm. The fallen earth would fill in streams, which became too shallow and warm for the trout that once thrived in them. "Great gashing gullies are torn out of the hillside," Leopold wrote in "Coon Valley: An Adventure in Cooperative Conservation," an essay about the project. He saw the problems of Coon Valley as endemic to American agriculture: "Coon Valley, in short, is one of the thousand farm communities which, through the abuse of its originally rich soil, has not only filled the national dinner pail, but has created the Mississippi flood problem, the navigation problem, the overproduction problem, and the problem of its own future continuity."

Leopold and the other University of Wisconsin faculty had been recruited by Hugh Hammond Bennett, the Soil Erosion Service's first director. Coon Valley was the first watershed restoration project in the United States, a demonstration meant to show private landowners the need for conservation and the value of the federal government's assistance. The Coon Valley project offered farmers free labor (provided by the Civilian Conservation Corps, another New Deal program), seeds, and planting stock if they agreed to commit to the full length of the five-year trial, which included planting trees by the hillsides, relocating crops and cows to flat areas, and repairing gullies and stream banks. A slim majority of the valley's eight hundred farmers signed on to the plan. Within a year, the number of quail spotted in Coon Valley doubled. Today it is one of Wisconsin's most bucolic locations, with a premier trout stream.

As he worked on Coon Valley, Leopold also began transforming his barren sand farm, though with only his family's help. Leopold began by planting pine trees, and with his wife,

Estella, and their five children, he eventually planted forty thousand trees on the property. The family spent weekends and summers on the farm, whose only building was a 350-square-foot dilapidated chicken coop that Leopold refashioned into rustic living quarters—bunk beds, a fireplace, a make-shift kitchen.

The land, and the effort to restore it, became an inspiration for *A Sand County Almanac*, a collection of Leopold's essays published a year after his death. The book received critical acclaim at the time of publication and later took a place along-side Rachel Carson's *Silent Spring* and Henry David Thoreau's *Walden* as a touchstone for the environmental movement. One of the reasons for its endurance is a biographical essay called "Thinking Like a Mountain." In it, Leopold describes his passion for killing wolves while he was working as a Forest Service ranger on public lands in Arizona. One day, he was eating lunch with fellow rangers on the edge of a plateau. They spied what looked like a deer below, fording a white-water river. They soon realized the deer was in fact a wolf, and they watched it greet a half-dozen grown pups. The wolves writhed playfully beneath them. "In those days we had never heard of passing up a chance to kill a wolf," Leopold wrote.

In a second we were pumping lead into the pack, but with more excitement than accuracy: how to aim a steep downhill shot is always confusing. When our rifles were empty, the old wolf was down, and a pup was dragging a leg into impass-able slide-rocks. We reached the old wolf in time to watch a fierce green fire dying in her eyes. I realized then, and have known ever since, that there was something new to me in those eyes, something known only to her and to the mountain. I was young then, and full of trigger-itch; I thought that because fewer wolves meant more deer, that no wolves would mean hunters' paradise. But after seeing the green fire die, I sensed that neither the wolf nor the mountain agreed with such a view.

Today the gravel road to Leopold's farm is lined with towering white and red pines that he and his family planted in the 1930s. In the autumn of 2017, Curt Meine, a conservation biologist and a biographer of Leopold, met me at the Aldo Leopold Foundation, an environmental nonprofit headquartered there. Meine, a trim, gray-haired expatriate from the Chicago suburbs, led me to a pair of wooden benches in front of the center's low stone-and-wood meeting hall.

"Leopold appreciated the Wisconsin Idea," Meine said. "He understood it and became a living example of it. He saw himself as an academic serving the public." Leopold took his first appointment at the University of Wisconsin in the Department of Agricultural and Applied Economics, a role that led him to speak out about the dangers facing rural economies. He believed that conservation had to include the entire landscape, Meine explained: "You can't treat the human community as something separate from the soils, waters, plants, and animals." In a 1945 article called "The Outlook for Farm Wildlife," Leopold warned that the industrialization of agriculture was "generating new insecurities, economic and ecological, in place of those it was meant to abolish." He saw two possible paths for farmers: the farm as a place to live, in which wildlife could be accommodated, or the farm as food-factory, which demanded ever-increasing yields. The latter, he said, was "humanly desolate and economically unstable."

After the Second World War, the federal government began promoting a "cheap-food" policy that pushed, above all, for higher yields. In 1948, for example, the US Department of Agriculture partnered with A&P, then the country's largest supermarket chain, to sponsor the "Chicken of Tomorrow" contest, whose goal was to breed a bigger bird that had a "superior meat-type." Large agricultural corporations began swallowing up family farms, which could no longer generate enough revenue to survive. When Leopold issued his warning, there were roughly 150,000 dairy farms in Wisconsin; today there are fewer than 9,000.

"We're producing even more than we did then," Meine said. "But we're doing it with fewer people, and so the depletion of small-town rural life and community has been enormous. There's bitterness in the rural communities, especially young people. These places are unsustainable. The economic trends in America over the past eighty-year period have created this chasm between urban people and rural people."

Meine gestured toward the west, where the Driftless Area, the anomalous hill-and-valley country untouched by glacier, begins. Unique in the Midwest, it covers twenty-two Wisconsin counties as well as parts of Iowa, Minnesota, and Illinois. It is also unusual politically; besides Vermont, the Driftless Area is one of only a few rural regions in the entire country that tends to vote Democratic. In 2008 and 2012, a majority of the Driftless counties voted for Barack Obama. Meine believes that is because the unusual topography has allowed agriculture to remain smaller-scale, helping rural life maintain cohesion. "It has relatively few thousand-acre corn or soybean fields," Meine said. "It doesn't have four-thousand-herd dairies. Quite the opposite. It's home to one of the greatest concentrations of certified organic growers in the country."

Meine noted that historically the state has alternated politically. "You have these deep channels of Wisconsin political culture that weave back and forth," he said. "There's a tension, which has often been a healthy tension, between social responsibility and individual responsibility, government action and individual action. We've been able to use that tension in Wisconsin in a positive way for generations." Efforts like Coon Valley's restoration, whose success depended on collaboration between the government and private landowners, influenced Leopold. "He was a tireless defender of public lands and the role of government agencies," Meine said. "But he understood the limits of what government can do, especially in conservation. He was a pragmatist, not an ideologue. Is there such a thing as a progressive conservative?" Meine wondered. "It's someone like Leopold who understood rural culture and life."

Leopold's work incorporated ecological concerns into economic analysis, an idea that maintained currency in Wisconsin's government until Governor Walker. "Walker is representative of a cohort of politicians who are unaware of this tradition and its nuances," Meine said. "It's now been undermined, and done away with in many cases." Nowhere had this been more apparent than in the Republican effort, on behalf of Chris Cline, a billionaire coal magnate in Florida, to facilitate the construction of an enormous iron-ore mine in a pristine section of northern Wisconsin called the Penokee

Hills. "The proposal seemed to wrap up in one package all that was going south," Meine said. "The influence of corporate money and political corruption, narrow, short-term thinking about economic value, and an active disinterest in science and a fair and transparent public process."

Since Walker introduced the mining proposal in 2011, the Bad River Band of Lake Superior Chippewa, whose reservation sits a few miles from the site, have led a fiercely determined opposition to it. In their response Meine saw hope that Wisconsin's legacy of environmental stewardship might yet be revived. "Just at the time when political authorities in Wisconsin no longer espoused or defended the land ethic, the Native communities and voices were there," he said. "They were the ones who spoke for the land and water, for the plants and animals, for future generations. They were the true conservatives."

MIKE WIGGINS JR., the chairman of the Bad River Band, has a stocky build and short black hair, and often wears a colorful beaded medallion with a starlike design his mother gave him. A former game warden, he grew up on the Bad River Reservation, where like other Chippewa—or Ojibwe, as they are also known—he learned to fish, hunt, and gather wild rice from the Chequamegon Bay sloughs, which are sacred to the Ojibwe. One afternoon when Wiggins was ten, he wandered into the reservation's social-services building to get a drink of water. Inside he saw Walt Bresette, a member of the Red Cliff Band and a celebrated environmental activist. Bresette wore a vest and hat over long black braids, and he turned to Wiggins and smiled at him. Bresette said nothing, but to Wiggins he seemed to be glowing.

In the 1980s, Bresette led the fight to affirm the Ojibwe's treaty rights in federal court. After that victory, Ojibwe began spearfishing off-reservation, in the "ceded territories," a large portion of northern Wisconsin designated by the treaties. Spearers were often confronted by angry—and sometimes violent—mobs at boat landings. In response, Bresette cofounded Witness for Nonviolence, a coalition of Native and non-Native treaty rights supporters. Members from the group would gather at the landings to support the Ojibwe fishermen and to document some of the racism directed at them, which included an effigy of an Indian head with a three-pronged spear rammed through it and signs urging protesters to "Save a Walleye, Spear an Indian." Wiggins, who has drawn inspiration from Bresette, has recalled that brief childhood encounter often since he began leading the fight against the proposed mine in the Penokees.

I first met Wiggins in March 2012, in the parking lot of a Shell station in Mellen, Wisconsin, a town close to the mining site. He told me about a series of dark and premonitory dreams he had two years earlier. "One of them was a very vivid trip around the North Woods and seeing forests bleeding and sludge from a creek emptying into the Bad River," Wiggins said. "I ended up at a dilapidated northern log home with rotten snowshoes falling off the wall. I stepped out of the lodge, walked through some pine, and I was in a pipeline. There was a big pipe coming in and out of the ground as far as I could see.

"I had no idea what the hell that was all about," Wiggins continued. But he said the dream became clearer when a stranger named Matt Fifield came into his office several months later and handed Wiggins his card. Fifield was the managing director of Gogebic Taconite (GTac), a division of Cline's Florida-based mining company. He had come to Wiggins's office to discuss GTac's desire to build a $1.5-billion open-pit iron-ore mine in the Penokee Hills, about seven miles south of the Bad River Reservation. The proposed mine would be several hundred feet deep, roughly four miles long, and a half mile wide; the company estimated it would bring 700 long-term jobs to the area. Fearing contamination of the local groundwater and rivers, Wiggins told Fifield he planned to oppose the mine. He didn't know at the time that the company's lawyers were working hand-in-hand with Republican legislators to draft a bill that would gut Wisconsin environmental law to expedite the permitting process.

Over the following year, the mining bill that Wiggins was intent on stopping became increasingly significant to the Walker administration. During his campaign for governor, in 2010, Walker had promised to create 250,000 private-sector jobs. In 2011, Wisconsin lost more than 12,000 jobs, more than any other state in the nation. After Walker rejected $810 million in federal stimulus money for a high-speed rail link between Madison and Milwaukee, anger grew over the loss of potential jobs. (The state Department of Transportation estimated that the construction of the link would have created nearly five thousand jobs.) Aligning himself with the Tea Party's categorical opposition to stimulus spending, Walker balked at the $7 million Wisconsin would need to contribute annually for the train's maintenance. During the opening months of 2012, as the economic situation in the state continued to deteriorate, the mining bill became a top priority for Walker's jobs program. It also managed to create a rare split in his broad-based opposition.

After GTac promised that most of the mining equipment would be built in Milwaukee with union labor, many of the large private trade unions backed the bill. Even Randy Bryce, then political coordinator of Milwaukee Iron Workers Local 8 and already one of Walker's most tenacious opponents, reluctantly supported the legislation. "They're trying to divide us," he told me, "but my members need work." (Bryce later recanted his support.) In March 2012, the capitol was flooded with hard hat–wearing union workers from the building trades lobbying for the mining bill at the behest of Walker and Republican legislators. Just a year earlier, some of them had been protesting the same politicians, who were in the process of demolishing collective bargaining rights for public employees.

To Wiggins, a large open-pit mine in the Penokee Hills was a life-or-death matter for his tribe. The headwaters that feed the Bad River would be in the footprint of the mine, and his tribe's reservation lay downstream. Wiggins also worried about the tribe's sensitive wild-rice beds, which lie on the coast of Lake Superior. Cyrus Hester, a scientist working for the tribe's Natural Resources Department, told me that sulfuric acid might contaminate the groundwater and ravage fish populations in the area's rivers and streams.

Wiggins and his allies organized educational trips to the mining site for journalists and state legislators. The only Republican to participate, however, was Dale Schultz, the moderate state senator from southwestern Wisconsin, who had voted against Act 10. Schultz also held two listening sessions with

Democratic colleagues in towns near the mining site and visited some of the natural sites in their footprint, such as Caroline
Lake, the source that feeds the Bad River. Two questions posed
by a high school student named Tyler Jaeger made a lasting
impression on Schultz. "What are we going to gain from the
mine?" Jaeger asked. "What are the impacts that we are going
to be left with?"

"There's a very good reason this area has never been
mined," George Meyer, the director of the Wisconsin Wildlife
Federation and former head of the Wisconsin Department of
Natural Resources (DNR), told me. "A lot of mining companies
looked at it and walked away." One of the biggest problems
with the site is that the ore there sits at an angle, a position
that generates a larger-than-usual amount of "overburden"—
waste rock—that needs to be discarded. The low-grade ore
and expensive process for removal led many observers to
wonder what was motivating GTac, especially given that the
company was formed in 2010 and had no previous taconite
mining experience.

Wiggins told me about several meetings he had with Walker
in which he tried to convey how dire the mine would be for his
reservation and the surrounding environment. One meeting,
in September 2011, turned particularly acrimonious. Before-
hand, Wiggins held a news conference inside the capitol outlining his opposition to the mining legislation. The assembly
bill would allow the company to fill in streams and ponds with
mine waste. It imposed a 360-day deadline for the permit-
ting process, where before there had been none, and it would
eliminate hearings in which citizens or organizations could
question mining or government officials under oath about the

safety of the mine. Many of the key provisions in the assembly bill were drafted by lawyers working for GTac.

"Walker saw the news conference as disingenuous," Wiggins said. "When we got to the meeting, he was fixated on his anger with me." Leaders from all eleven Wisconsin tribes also attended that meeting. After some heated back and forth, Walker told Wiggins he didn't see the need for the meeting to continue, because he had a copy of the Bad River Band's news release. "So the Bad River had a press conference," Tom Maulson, the chairman of the Lac du Flambeau Band, told Walker and his aides. "We have to quit this crying and get down to business." Wiggins got angry. "You know, governor," he said, "some of the things that are proposed in the mining initiative represent a catastrophic destruction for my reservation, health impacts to my people, and you think everything that you and I have to talk about is contained on one piece of paper right there?"

Marvin DeFoe, a tribal elder from the Red Cliff Band, then told a story that momentarily broke the tension. DeFoe explained to Walker and his aides that he had recently taught a young boy how to skin a deer, demonstrating on an animal that would be used to feed several families. "The boy asked me," DeFoe said, "'What if that deer was the last deer that ever lived? What would you do?'" DeFoe looked at the boy and thought for a moment. "If this was the last deer on Earth? And there would be no more? Well, I'd go right with that deer."

DeFoe was trying to convey how inseparable the Ojibwe are from the land, water, and wildlife that sustain them, but he also wanted Walker to understand the different way they see the world. "One of my responsibilities is stewardship of the land, air, and water," DeFoe told me later. "If you have a Western set of values, those values say: jobs. Our challenge is how do you—or can you—do both." In the Ojibwe tradition, a decision is made based on how it will affect people seven generations forward. By contrast, the company's optimistic estimate for the lifespan of the first phase of the mine is thirty-five years. "This wasn't just about stopping a mine in northern Wisconsin," DeFoe said. "This was looking through the eyes of our children."

After DeFoe told his story, Wiggins noticed a change in Walker's aides. "I could see some of his staffers break," Wiggins said. But Walker remained impassive and would not budge.

IN SEPTEMBER 1963, President John F. Kennedy flew in a Marine helicopter over Madeline Island, the largest of a twenty-one-island archipelago in Lake Superior called the Apostle Islands. Martin Hanson, a prominent Wisconsin conservationist who was part of an effort to win federal protection for these primeval islands, rode a couple of seats behind Kennedy. He had asked everyone he knew with a sailboat to bring it out that day, at the hour the sailboat-loving Kennedy was scheduled to fly over. There was a storm looming, and bald eagles soared above the islands. The wind was blowing in just the right direction for unfurling brightly colored spinnakers. When Kennedy initially failed to notice, Hanson got up from his seat, tapped Kennedy on the shoulder, then pointed down. Kennedy saw the Apostles surrounded by the sailboats and a surprised and joyful look came over his face.

The helicopter landed in Ashland, a coastal town where Kennedy was to give a speech as part of a nationwide tour he had undertaken to promote conservation. "This section of Wisconsin," Kennedy said, "which in the past depended upon a few natural resources, has known what economic distress can do when those resources are exhausted or when indifference lays them waste." He described the area, a vast water-rich ecosystem that includes the Penokee Hills, as "a central and significant part of the freshwater assets of this country."

The idea for the conservation tour belonged to Gaylord Nelson, Wisconsin's senator and former governor, who prodded Kennedy to undertake it. Nelson was born in Clear Lake, Wisconsin, in 1916 to Anton Nelson, a country doctor, and Mary, a nurse who taught her son about the area's rich wildlife. His parents were deeply involved in Wisconsin's Progressive movement; as medical students in Milwaukee, they stood rapt through a five-hour speech given by Bob La Follette that concluded at 1 a.m. Anton would later serve as county chair and delegate to the 1946 state convention of the Wisconsin Progressive Party, spearheaded by the sons of Fighting Bob, who opposed the increasingly conservative Republican Party.

In 1958, Nelson had paid homage to La Follette's progressive legacy in his campaign for governor, promising voters he would revive "the philosophy and the purpose of the Wisconsin Idea as old Bob La Follette envisioned it." Nelson was the person largely responsible for Wisconsin's outsized role in the modern environmental movement. As governor, he launched a program to buy private land for conservation and recreation, financed by a tax on cigarettes, a penny per pack. Over its twenty-year lifespan, Nelson's initiative delivered 450,000 acres of formerly private land to the citizens of Wisconsin, much of it wetlands and wildlife habitat threatened by development. (The effort also included funding for youth conservation camps and for cities to expand parkland, which fostered bipartisan, urban-rural support, easing the initiative's passage despite Republican control of Wisconsin's legislature.) Other states began copying the idea, earning Nelson national renown, but he took the most pride in how the public land-buying effort elevated the environment from its second-class status in American politics.

After Kennedy's conservation tour, Nelson spearheaded legislation in the US Senate that saved the Appalachian Trail and created a vast new network of national trails. Over the objections of several Midwestern governors, he secured funding for an extensive cleanup of the Great Lakes, which were heavily polluted by industrial waste. For his home state, Nelson, along with Senator Walter Mondale of Minnesota, created the St. Croix National Scenic Riverway, which preserved 250 miles of wild rivers and streams in upper Wisconsin and Minnesota. After a decade-long campaign, Nelson also won protective National Lakeshore status for the Apostle Islands and twelve miles of Lake Superior coastline.

Nelson didn't, however, merely champion legislation behind the scenes: he kept searching for a way to galvanize the public. In 1969, he visited Santa Barbara to witness what was then the largest oil spill in American history, which dumped three million gallons of crude oil into the ocean, created a six-inch-thick, thirty-five-mile-long oil slick along the coast, and devastated fish and wildlife populations.

On the flight to Berkeley, where he was giving a speech, he

read an article in *Ramparts,* a counterculture magazine, about the campus teach-in movement's success in mobilizing opposition to the Vietnam War. Nelson thought the general idea could be transferred to environmental causes, and he decided to stage a national teach-in. His determination grew in June, when Cleveland's Cuyahoga River caught on fire after decades of local steel mills and chemical plants dumping their waste in it. On April 22, 1970, Nelson's teach-in came to fruition in the form of Earth Day, which boasted twenty million participants, the largest secular event in American history.

Nelson's view of the "environment" was comprehensive. "Earth Day can—and it must—lend a new urgency to solving the problems that still threaten to tear the fabric of this society, the problems of race, of war, of poverty," he said in a speech in Denver on the first Earth Day. "Environment is all of America and its problems. It is rats in the ghetto. It is a hungry child in a land of affluence. It is housing that is not worthy of the name; neighborhoods not fit to inhabit. . . . Our goal is not just an environment of clean air and water and scenic beauty. The objective is an environment of decency, quality, and mutual respect for all other human beings and all other living creatures."

Nelson's daughter, Tia, was only seven years old when her father flew with Kennedy over the Apostle Islands. She stayed behind in suburban Washington with her mother, and doesn't recall her father speaking of the trip, which was overshadowed by Kennedy's assassination two months later. But when Tia turned eighteen, she took a job waitressing at a ski lodge coffee shop in Cable, Wisconsin, an hour south of the Apostles, and visited the archipelago for the first time. "I found it to be the most magical of places," she told me. "It's when I first understood the significance of my father's effort to protect it."

Tia lives in a small ranch house in Maple Bluff, a Madison suburb, which is also the location of the governor's mansion, where she lived from 1959 until 1962, when her father was elected to the United States Senate. Her home office doubles as a shrine to her father. The walls in the small room are covered with portraits of a lost era of American politics: Harry Truman laughing heartily with Nelson and his wife, Carrie Lee; Bobby Kennedy wearing a pinstriped suit, his eyes frozen in a penetrating gaze; a head shot of Eugene McCarthy, which McCarthy autographed twice for ten-year-old Tia. She put on black reading glasses and picked up a framed letter Bobby Kennedy wrote to her. "I had this big crush on Bobby Kennedy," she explained, before reading the letter aloud. "For Tia," Kennedy had written. "I enjoy working with your father on the labor and education committee. He is the senator who is closest to me in seniority and that is not good."

She moved on to another cherished image, a portrait of her family standing on the rear platform of a train in 1968 during a campaign stop for her father's reelection. It was taken in Amery, a town of less than three thousand in northern Wisconsin, ten miles from Clear Lake, the even smaller community where Nelson grew up. The train photo was part of a reenactment of Robert La Follette Jr.'s whistle-stop tour of 1926, which included a stop in Amery. Nelson's father, Anton, took Nelson to hear "Young Bob," the eldest son of Fighting Bob La Follette, on that tour. La Follette Jr. had recently been elected to fill the vacant Senate seat of his father, who had died the year before. "Driving home after the speech, my grandfather asked my father what he thought," Tia said. "My father went so far as to say there in the car, when he was ten years old, that when he grew up he wanted to be a US senator and help people like Bob La Follette was helping people. But he had one fear: La Follette would have solved all the problems by the time he was grown up."

EARLY ONE MORNING, not long after I met Mike Wiggins, I picked him up at his small house. It was still dark outside, but dawn was just beginning to break. We drove to a nearby Lake Superior beach. Wiggins brought along a jar of maple sugar and tobacco to make an offering to the Great Spirit. When we parked, Wiggins asked me to leave my recorder and notebook behind. He wanted to sit in silence, separate from each other, as he made his offering at the lake, which the Ojibwe call *Gichi-gami*, "the Great Sea."

The interconnectedness of human beings with the natural world is the cornerstone of Ojibwe belief, and it demands of them humility toward that world. In the 1940s, Aldo Leopold posited a similar idea. "A land ethic changes the role of *Homo sapiens* from conqueror of the land community to plain member and citizen of it," Leopold wrote. "It implies respect for his fellow members, and also respect for the community as such." As I looked out into Superior, my thoughts drifted to an inscription from a psalm above the altar in my parents' synagogue. "Know Before Whom You Stand," the words read in Hebrew. Those words had terrified and fascinated me as a child, but when I thought of them here, before Lake Superior, the psalmist's demand seemed less severe, more fitting.

More than five hundred years ago, before Columbus sailed from Spain to the Caribbean, the Wisconsin Ojibwe arrived at the Great Lakes from their home on the Atlantic Coast. According to their prophecy, they were returning home. The Great Spirit, *Gichi-manidoo*, had placed them in the Great Lakes originally, but after fighting among themselves and forgetting the teachings the Great Spirit had given them, they were told to leave. They settled near the "Great Salt Water," but their prophecies foretold that they would one day return.

Their migration would include seven stops, and their path would be guided by a vision of a sacred cowrie shell. That led them to their first stop, a turtle-shaped island near present-day Montreal, where they stayed for a time. They continued down the Saint Lawrence River, past Niagara Falls, the Detroit River, and eventually to the Great Lakes Basin. Many of them stayed along the way. The prophecy had told the Ojibwe to seek "the place where food grows on water," and those who continued on finally arrived at the wild-rice beds of Chequamegon Bay in Lake Superior. They settled on a nearby island they called *Moningwunakawning*—"The Home of the Golden-Breasted Woodpecker"—later known as Madeline Island. I could see it in the distance. The Ojibwe consider it the center of the world.

After about forty-five minutes on the beach, I wandered over to Wiggins. He picked up a nearby stick and ushered me close. He used the stick to draw a series of animal shapes in the sand. The animals were lined up in a row, each connected to the next by thin lines at the heart and head levels. Wiggins sketched a thick line underneath the animals and then four

small ovals beneath that line. He drew another line connecting the first animal to the four ovals. Wiggins told me his sand
drawing was a re-creation of a nineteenth-century Ojibwe
pictograph. The first animal represented Chief Buffalo, the
leader of all the Ojibwe clans at the time. The animals behind
him were the leaders of the individual clans. The thick line
represented Lake Superior, while the ovals were the wild-rice
beds the Ojibwe depended on for food. The lines connecting
the clans were meant to show they were all of one mind and
one heart. The lines to the ovals were the inland trails that led
to the wild-rice beds. The drawing signified the inseparability
of the Ojibwe from their home.

The original pictograph was an Ojibwe petition, drawn in
1849, to the United States government, in which they pleaded
not to be forcibly removed from their land. The treaties of 1837
and 1842 affirmed the Ojibwe's right to hunt, fish, and gather
wild rice in the territory they ceded to the United States. As
long as they did not make war on the settlers, they had the
right to occupy the land. Nevertheless, by 1848, as logging and
mining activity in the area increased, rumors had begun circulating among the tribes that they were to be relocated. In
1850, President Zachary Taylor signed a removal order for the
Ojibwe to be resettled in the Minnesota Territory. To coerce
them, the government moved the Indian agency that made
annuity payments the Ojibwe depended on from Madeline
Island to Sandy Lake, Minnesota, 150 miles away. Nonetheless, in the fall of 1850, nearly three thousand men from nineteen bands made the perilous journey as the north-country
cold set in.

When they arrived at Sandy Lake that October, the agency

had been burned down. Some suspected it was an act of treachery. Snow and cold had settled in already, and the only food that survived the fire were barrels of pork, government rations that had become tainted. Starving, the weary Ojibwe ate the pork. At least 150 Ojibwe died—some from food poisoning, others succumbing to hunger, measles, and exposure. Many of the survivors chose to return home, despite the winter conditions. On that journey back, 250 more Ojibwe perished. The following year, Chief Buffalo wrote to the Commissioner of Indian Affairs, pleading to rescind the removal order. "We wish to . . . be permitted to remain here where we were promised we might live, as long as we were not in the way of the Whites," he wrote. That plea and others were ignored, and many of the young Ojibwe warriors began talking of making war on the United States. Instead, Chief Buffalo called the other chiefs together. They decided to journey to Washington to appeal to the president in person.

In the spring of 1852, Chief Buffalo, then ninety-three years old, led an entourage that included his deputy, O-sha-ga, four braves, and a white translator named Benjamin Armstrong. They set out for Washington in a twenty-four-foot birchbark canoe, and later traveled by steamboat and railroad. In Michigan, they were stopped by an Indian agent accompanied by American soldiers. The agent asked if they had permission for their trip. They didn't. Armstrong attempted to persuade the agent to let them pass. They were trying to avoid a war, Armstrong told them as he presented documents from a local mining company, which affirmed the Ojibwe were peaceful neighbors. "To give up this trip would be to abandon the last hope of keeping that turbulent spirit of the young warriors in bounds," Armstrong wrote in his memoirs.

When the group finally arrived in Washington, eleven weeks after leaving northern Wisconsin, they were rebuffed by staff at the Office of Indian Affairs and the White House. As despair began to set in, Armstrong befriended Congressman George Briggs, who happened to be eating with several members of President Millard Fillmore's cabinet in the hotel dining room. (Zachary Taylor had died in office two years before.) Intrigued and impressed by the delegation, Briggs offered to get them an audience with the president. When Chief Buffalo met President Fillmore, he brought out a new pipe, filled and lit it, and then passed it to Fillmore. Fillmore took a few puffs, smiled, and, according to Armstrong, asked: "Who is the next?" The pipe was passed around the room and smoked by all, from the secretary of the interior to the young braves accompanying Chief Buffalo.

After a subsequent meeting, Fillmore agreed to rescind the order and made provisions for their journey home. But he told the Ojibwe chiefs that they had one more treaty to negotiate. That treaty, signed in 1854, established the small reservations Wisconsin's Ojibwe live on now. Where they had once held millions of acres, their combined reservations would shrink to 300,000 acres. But the treaty did include a provision, ignored for generations, until Walt Bresette and others fought for it to be honored, that the Ojibwe "shall have the right to hunt and fish" in the territory ceded.

"After they smoked the pipe, and Fillmore lifted the removal order, the story is that Chief Buffalo broke the pipe," Wiggins told me. "He said it was to honor what was done here today."

Chief Buffalo died a year after the treaty was signed, at the age of ninety-six, and the pieces of his pipe are now held by one of his descendants, Marvin DeFoe, the Red Cliff tribal elder who had once challenged Scott Walker to imagine a world without deer.

DALE SCHULTZ FELT tremendous pressure to vote for the assembly's mining bill. Walker and the Republican leadership knew Schultz believed it gave GTac too much, and Schultz's concerns only deepened after he visited the mining site and heard the fears of Mike Wiggins and other local citizens. The state senate held a one-vote Republican majority—if Schultz defected, the bill would die. "All kinds of people tried to exert pressure on me," Schultz said, without disclosing names. "They would say this is a terrible blow to the governor's economic program and we need this mine for political purposes."

The pressure had an ugliness that felt unfamiliar to the courteous Schultz, and foreign to his thirty years in Wisconsin politics. It disturbed him. "We have this whole industry in politics that is there to—" He paused. "It's like thuggery. No, that's too strong a word. *Political* thuggery, where they'll do robocalls across the whole district and leave misinformation. Or they'll gin it up on talk radio so you get fifty phone calls from heaven knows who, which are unbelievably abusive." Schultz sighed. "The world has changed now, politically. We now hear everybody talk about the base all the time. What that means is we want fifty percent plus one of the electorate and we're going to do whatever we can to hang onto that, and the hell with everyone else. The idea now is let's obliterate all these people in the middle."

We were sitting in the kitchen of his farm about sixty miles west of Madison. The land has been in Schultz's family for six generations. His father grew up on the farm, and Schultz, as a boy, spent his summers there. Schultz is an avid hunter, and he poured me coffee and described some of the animals—grouse, wild turkey, even a bear—that he has hunted throughout Wisconsin. A few days earlier, he gave a reading at an event honoring Aldo Leopold. "I'm a guy who believes that the Leopold land ethic makes sense," Schultz said. "It's about stewardship, but using resources wisely is OK."

Leopold's land ethic, which is included in *A Sand County Almanac*, has proven its durability to a wide range of environmentalists including those, like Schultz, who are more open to development. "A thing is right when it tends to preserve the integrity, stability and beauty of the biotic community," the ethic asserts. "It is wrong when it tends otherwise." The organizers of the event had asked Schultz to read from "Sky Dance," Leopold's appreciation of the springtime rites of woodcocks. "The woodcock is a living refutation of the theory that the utility of a game bird is to serve as a target, or to pose gracefully on a slice of toast," Leopold wrote. "No one would rather hunt woodcock in October than I, but since learning of the sky dance I find myself calling one or two birds enough. I must be sure that, come April, there be no dearth of dancers in the sunset sky."

Wisconsin's largest deposit of iron ore is the GTac site. The second-largest deposit is in the Baraboo Hills, which lie in Schultz's district. "As I'm making these decisions about the mining bill, I know that these changes could directly affect my constituents," he said. "A few years ago, there was a big amount of anger in the country that legislators didn't read bills. Now it's 'I don't care if you read the bill, you got to vote for this.' Either you're on the team, and on the team one hundred percent, or I'm just going to be angry with you. In terms of the mining bill, I would say to people: 'Do you realize that this allows for the filling of navigable rivers and streams and lake beds?' They'd say: 'I didn't see that in there.'"

Unemployment around Mellen, where the GTac mine would be located, was significantly higher than the statewide average. Despite this, during Schultz's town-hall meeting there with state senator Bob Jauch, who represented the area, a majority of the attendees registered their opposition to the assembly bill. "We want the mine; we fear the mine," Mellen's mayor, Joseph Barabe, said at the meeting. "We have the most to lose." Schultz believed that a mine in the area would be feasible, but that radically changing long-established environmental law would be unwise and contrary to the state's ethos. He and Jauch developed a compromise bill that sought to strike a balance between the state's conservationist traditions and the accommodations GTac sought. Notably, it preserved the hearings that allowed citizens and organizations to question mining officials under oath. But it was described by Scott Fitzgerald, the senate majority leader, as a "nonstarter" and never brought up for a vote.

In March 2012, the senate narrowly voted to reject the assembly's mining bill, 17–16. Schultz joined the sixteen Democrats in voting against the bill. After the vote, GTac issued a brief statement to say it was abandoning its interest in the Wisconsin mine. Before he took the vote, Fitzgerald thought he had one Milwaukee Democrat lined up to support the bill, and he still hoped he could persuade one. "I would not rule out calling an extraordinary session," Fitzgerald said, "if we could get a signal from the corporation and a seventeenth senator. I just need one more vote."

TIA NELSON HAD encouraged me to see Clear Lake, where her father grew up and which forged his politics and ecological awareness. When I arrived in late September, the ferocious heat felt unnerving. Despite Clear Lake's location in Wisconsin's North Woods, the temperature that day reached a high of eighty-eight degrees. The fall heat wave would have alarmed Nelson, who warned of the dangers of global warming as far back as the 1980s. But the surroundings—red barns adorned with cupolas, grassy hills that hinted at the Great Plains to the west—seemed timeless.

When Norwegian and German farmers first arrived in Clear Lake in the 1860s, the land was dense wilderness, with no roads, so the settlers carried food and supplies on their backs. Before settlement, white-pine forests blanketed the region, but by the end of the nineteenth century the forests were decimated—"cut-over" country, as the timber companies called it. Along with the railroad interests, the big timber companies controlled the Wisconsin State Legislature. But their power waned after deforestation was complete, and in 1910, Wisconsin voters approved a constitutional amendment promoting forest and water conservation.

Parked outside the high school, I left a message with Charles Clark, an old family friend of the Nelsons. After getting his answering machine, I mumbled where I was parked, adding that I would be leaving town momentarily. Two minutes later, a Buick roared up the quiet street and screeched to a halt next to my car. "Hop in," a voice said. It was Clark, eighty-three years old and eager to take me on a whirlwind tour of Nelson's Clear Lake.

Nelson died in 2005. Like La Follette's funeral, eighty years earlier, Nelson's was held at the state capitol. But he was buried in Clear Lake, and Clark's first stop was the graveyard, where Nelson's stone is engraved with the Presidential Medal of Freedom, which Bill Clinton awarded to him in 1995. "The stone was all done," Clark explained. "Then when he got the Presidential Medal of Freedom, I called him up and I said 'Gaylord, there's room for that right on the bottom.' It looks like it belongs there. The monument guy took it back and redid it." (Clark also wanted me to see the gravesite of Clear Lake's other famous son, Burleigh Grimes, the last legal spitball pitcher in major-league baseball.)

Next Clark showed me the ninety-five-foot-deep lake the town is named for, forged during the Ice Age. As a kid, Nelson grew fascinated by the three-day migration of turtles from Clear Lake across town—and over a highway—to Mud Lake, where they hibernate for the winter. Nelson would pick them off the middle of the road and carry them the rest of the way. Sometimes he and a friend would spin them half a dozen times and point them back in the direction of Clear Lake. The turtles would stick their heads out of their shells and immediately turn around and head for Mud Lake, even when Nelson put them behind a tree or in tall grass so they couldn't see. The turtle migration sparked his boundless love of nature.

Before I left Clear Lake, Clark made sure I saw the Nelsons' modest two-story house, which had a wraparound porch and a spacious lawn that Clark used to mow for fifty cents. Parked in front of the house, Clark recalled the generosity of Nelson's father, who viewed his medical practice more as a service mission than a career. "As a doctor in hard times, he'd go out and deliver babies, and they'd give him a chicken or something," Clark said. "Gaylord's father didn't have any money, and he didn't care about money. That wasn't what he was interested in."

After saying goodbye to Clark, I passed over the Namekagon River. I recalled a film I had seen of Nelson's last battle, which took place on this river. In 2003, the Lac Courte Oreilles Chippewa asked Nelson to help them fight a utility company that wanted to put a power line over the river. In the 1960s, Nelson had saved the Namekagon when he passed legislation to preserve the St. Croix and its tributaries.

He could barely walk, and he could barely speak then, but he went. Tribal members put Nelson in a canoe on the Namekagon, and he made a declaration that he would fight with them until his last breath to prevent the river from being diminished. After they led him out of the canoe, he sat down and they had a pipe ceremony, and he began breaking down, weeping. A blanket was wrapped around him, and though he was struggling for breath, he began quoting a passage from *Moby-Dick*. "The moot point is, whether Leviathan can long endure so wide a chase, and so remorseless a havoc; whether he must not at last be exterminated from the waters, and the last whale, like the last man, smoke his last pipe, and then himself evaporate in the final puff."

AFTER DALE SCHULTZ sank the mining bill in March 2012, Scott Fitzgerald admitted that perhaps the mining company, whose operations were mostly in West Virginia and Illinois, had pushed too far for Wisconsin. "I think the corporation and their attorneys drafted a bill that may have been acceptable in other states," he told me.

But Schultz believed GTac's announcement that the company would leave was a feint. "I know they've *said* they're pulling out," he told me. "That's designed to increase pressure." Schultz's vote had given opponents a one-vote majority. The company needed to flip just a single senator to win passage, and the 2012 elections were only seven months away. The state Democratic Party focused its efforts on two goals: keeping Wisconsin in Barack Obama's column and electing Representative Tammy Baldwin to the Senate. In that regard, the outcome was a stunning success. Obama beat Mitt Romney by seven percentage points, despite Paul Ryan's presence on the ticket, and Baldwin defeated former Wisconsin governor Tommy Thompson by a slightly smaller margin. But that focus also had a cost: in the state legislature, Democrats lost three senate seats and made no gains in the assembly. The results highlighted the party's fundamental weakness, but also the strength of the Republican grip on power.

GTac's role in those senate losses was pivotal—and revealing. Walker had met with GTac lobbyists to discuss the mine shortly after his inauguration in 2011. The company's owner, Chris Cline, had donated to his campaign, and GTac increased its financial support during Walker's recall election the following year, three months after Schultz's vote had defeated the bill. According to the Wisconsin Democracy Campaign, a nonpartisan campaign-finance watchdog, within a span of two years, GTac executives and other supporters of the mine had donated a total of $15 million to Walker and his Republican allies in the legislature, outspending the mine's opponents by more than six hundred to one.

One of the primary targets was Jessica King, a Democrat from Oshkosh, who had narrowly defeated a Republican incumbent in a senate recall election held in August 2011. When King sought a full term in the election the following year, mine proponents funneled nearly a million dollars in donations to both Wisconsin Manufacturers & Commerce, the state's most powerful business lobby, and the Wisconsin Club for Growth, an arm of the libertarian-leaning national group. In the last three weeks of the campaign, those organizations ran close to two million dollars in attack ads against King. King lost to the newcomer Rick Gudex, a production manager at a manufacturing plant, by fewer than six hundred votes.

In January 2013, a new mining bill, even more industry-friendly than the first, was introduced. It included all the changes to Wisconsin environmental law proposed in the earlier bill, such as allowing GTac to pay taxes solely on profit, not on the amount of ore removed, raising the possibility that the communities affected by the mine's impact on the area's roads and schools would receive only token compensation.

Marcia Bjornerud, a geology professor at Lawrence University in Appleton, testified to the legislature that samples she had taken from the mine site revealed the presence of sulfides both in the target iron formation and in the overlying rock that would have to be removed to get to the iron-bearing rocks. (When exposed to air and water, sulfides oxidize and turn water acidic, which can be devastating to rivers and streams, along with their fish populations.) Sulfide minerals, Bjornerud said, would be an unavoidable by-product of mining, but the bill only addressed "ferrous" iron mining and did not mandate a process for preventing the harm from the sulfides that mining would unleash. "The legislation was scientifically nonsensical," Bjornerud told me. "You can't distinguish between ferrous and non-ferrous mining." Equally troubling was the discovery by Tom Fitz, a geology professor at Northland College, in Ashland, of a highly carcinogenic asbestos-form mineral at one of GTac's sampling sites. The fibers of the mineral, which would be dispersed in blasting, are like tiny, breathable needles.

Nonetheless, the new mining bill passed 17–16. "They made it even worse than the earlier bill in terms of wetlands protection," Schultz said. "It was particularly disappointing how they went after legislators when they didn't produce a bill the industry wanted." With the exception of Schultz, all the senate Republicans, including the three new members, voted in favor.

ON A SUNNY AFTERNOON in September 2013, several hundred people gathered on the grass outside the John F. Kennedy Memorial Airport, in Ashland, to commemorate the speech Kennedy had given there fifty years earlier. The event included a preamble by the Ashland High School Band, reminiscences by elderly observers like former House appropriations chairman David Obey, and the replaying of Kennedy's address over loudspeakers. "Lake Superior, the Apostle Islands, the Bad River area are all unique . . . and we must act to preserve these assets," Kennedy's voice boomed out over the crowd. It took seven years after Kennedy's assassination, until

Gaylord Nelson finally won protective status for the Apostle Islands.

While the speakers celebrated that victory, and other achievements of the past—the Wild and Scenic Rivers Act, the Clean Air Act, the Clean Water Act, the Endangered Species Act—there was an undercurrent of anxiety. "I have a suspicion that we're also here yearning for the kind of politics than we had in those days," Obey said. Though Obey did not mention GTac directly, the company had recently begun bulk sampling iron ore at the site.

Still, the mine faced many hurdles before it could be permitted. The company had filed incomplete sampling applications with the state's Department of Natural Resources. GTac's president, Bill Williams, was facing a criminal inquiry in Spain. The charges stated that runoff from an open-pit mine where he once worked as an executive had contaminated local groundwater. (Williams was eventually convicted, fined, and given a one-year suspended prison sentence.) Most important, the Bad River could challenge the mine in federal court.

One of the event's last speakers was Mike Wiggins. The previous summer, Wiggins had played Governor Walker a recording of Kennedy's Ashland speech. Wiggins told me that the governor appeared indifferent to Kennedy's words; Walker has never wavered in his support of the mine. A month before the Ashland event, Wiggins and five other Ojibwe tribal leaders had begun seeking redress from the federal government. They sent President Obama a letter asking him to direct the Interior Department to prevent the construction of GTac's mine, citing their claims that the mine would infringe on their treaty rights. Though the letter did not mention it, in 2009

Obama told nearly four hundred Native American tribal leaders, "We have a lot to learn from your nations in order to create the kind of sustainability in our environment that we so desperately need." The president said that the tribes "deserve to have a voice" and "will not be forgotten as long as I'm in this White House." Wiggins never received an answer from the president.

That evening, after the airport speeches, Wiggins drove me to a dinner in Ashland celebrating JFK's speech. In 2011, Wiggins had delivered the State of the Tribes address, an annual speech given by the head of one of Wisconsin's eleven tribes to the governor and state legislature. That day, on his way to Madison, he was about to listen to Bresette's speeches in his truck when suddenly a giant bald eagle, an animal sacred to the Ojibwe, swooped in front of his windshield. He thought it was a powerful sign. As we drove to Ashland, Wiggins, who calls Bresette by his Ojibwe name, *Makoons* ("Little Bear"), put on the same CD. We listened in silence as a thin, searing voice unspooled the Chippewa philosophy of the Seventh Generation. I watched Wiggins lean forward over the wheel, clinging to every word. Bresette began by describing the Great Spirit's creation of the earth, waters, vegetation, and animals.

"And the world was complete," Bresette said. "But the creator didn't stop," Bresette continued:

> He said, we'll create one more, one more people we will create. The Anishinaabe [Ojibwe]—the people—you. We are dependent on all of those first three creations. If we lose the vegetation, we will die. If we lose the animals who give us our spirit, who give us our name, who come to us in the sweat

lodge and say 'you will be Makoons,' we will lose our identity, we will lose our spirit. . . . We are in a crisis situation. Not because the earth will die. The earth will be happy. Because some day, some day our children are going to rise up and they're going to say '*Where were you?! Where were you when you poisoned my river?! Where were you when I can't eat the fish no more?!*' . . . They will remember who sat idly by. They will remember that. And as we poison their bodies, and as we poison their minds, they will turn on us. And we will not have a happy old age. The Seventh Generation is something of a good philosophy. But we must not forget this generation. It is that close."

As we drove, Wiggins mentioned an earlier mining fight against Exxon, which wanted to mine precious metals in Crandon, Wisconsin, near the Mole Lake Chippewa Reservation. Bresette had won that battle by forging an alliance between the Ojibwe and white fishermen, an alliance that helped win the passage of a mining moratorium law in 1998. The law mandated that companies seeking to mine sulfide ores such as copper, zinc, and gold need to prove that similar mines had operated for ten years, and been closed for ten years, without causing pollution. (The Mole Lake and Potawatomi were later able to buy the Crandon site, and vowed never to allow mining there.)

The victory highlighted the value of alliances, which Bresette tried to cultivate. "Even as the Chippewa spearers and white anglers were in conflict over treaty rights, Walt understood that they really had more in common than they had differences," Zoltan Grossman, a friend of Bresette's, once said. "He felt the people of northern Wisconsin had to defend their clean environment and their mom-and-pop businesses together, or both would be lost to outside corporations."

Wiggins has followed that strategy, forging a wide coalition with non-Native mining opponents across the state. As corporations like GTac exerted greater control over the Wisconsin State Legislature, the tribes, Wisconsin's first conservationists, became the last hope, the only group with any power to stop the dismantling of the state's environmental heritage.

BEFORE I LEFT Aldo Leopold's old farm, Curt Meine wanted to show me "the shack" where Leopold and his family lived. On our walk over, he mentioned a new law Governor Walker had signed a few days earlier to give Foxconn, a Taiwanese company, $3 billion in taxpayer subsidies to build an LCD-screen factory in Racine. Meine noted that the law gave Foxconn unprecedented court privileges. Unlike other litigants, the company would receive multiple appeals of unfavorable trial court rulings in a single case. In addition, Foxconn was granted the right to appeal an unfavorable ruling directly to the conservative-controlled Wisconsin Supreme Court. To Meine, it showed how corporations such as GTac and Foxconn may be engineering a more permanent shift in Wisconsin politics than previous watershed events like Joe McCarthy's defeat of Bob La Follette Jr. in the Republican primary for the United States Senate in 1946.

"That shows us how far down we've gone," Meine said. "And we haven't apparently hit bottom yet. Can we reclaim our culture of conservation and civic value in Wisconsin? Sure, anytime we want to. Anytime we resist those who prefer to divide and conquer. But it takes something we have not yet tried to do before, because we haven't had to."

As we approached Leopold's shack, Meine pointed out some of the wildlife surrounding it. In front of us were prairie dropseed, a musky-smelling native grass, gray-headed coneflower, and big bluestem. The building was locked, but I peeked inside a window to catch a glimpse of a rustic, cozy room, with pots hanging on the wall, a big table for writing, and a fireplace. On the walk back to our cars, Meine began telling me how Leopold died.

"It was springtime, so it was the time for brush burning and burning trash piles if you're a farmer," Meine said. A neighbor was burning a trash fire that got out of control. "Aldo Leopold is a forester, he sees smoke, he does what every forester does, he goes into action," Meine said. "He's sixty-one years old. He gets a can full of water. He tells his wife and daughter: 'I'm going out to check out the fire and suppress it.' And he has a heart attack and dies while fighting the fire.

"He was kneeling down on the grass. The fire burned over the grass, so he died symbolically. He was helping a neighbor and also protecting his own landscape, his young trees, maybe even his own family. That balance of self-interest and community interest. That's what rural life is about, or has been about. It doesn't mean it's been perfect, but it means that rural communities, or maybe every community, can only survive that way."

4

THE MODEL FOR
THE COUNTRY

Since 1926, Wisconsin law has allowed for the recall of elected officials who have served at least one year in office. If petitioners can gather signatures equaling one-quarter of the votes cast in the previous election, a new election is triggered, typically within a few months. Until 2011, there had been only four recalls of state officials in Wisconsin. But that fall, anger over Governor Walker's attacks on labor unions, environmental regulations, public education, the university system, and voting rights forced the recall elections of nine state senators—six Republicans, and, after a Republican counteroffensive, three Democrats. Two of the state senators (both Republicans) lost, while seven others (three Democrats and four Republicans) held on. The following June, four more Republican senators faced recall elections.

That June would also include the recall election against Walker himself. Petitioners gathered nearly a million signatures, almost twice what was needed to trigger the election. Their effort fixed the national spotlight on Wisconsin, demonstrating continuing resistance to the growing strength of the Tea Party. If Walker lost, he would be only the third governor in American history to be recalled. More important, while he was campaigning to hold on to the governor's mansion, his recall was a national proxy for his battle with the unions, whose defeat would be secured only if he won. For Walker's wealthy donors, his victory was paramount. "What Scott Walker is doing with the public unions in Wisconsin is critically important," David Koch told the *Palm Beach Post* in February 2012, three months before the recall election. "If the unions win the recall, there will be no stopping union power." Koch added: "We're helping him, as we should. We've gotten pretty good at this over the years. We've spent a lot of money in Wisconsin. We're going to spend more."

Nearly $140 million dollars would ultimately be spent on the 2011 and 2012 recall races, including $81 million for the governor's race alone. That was more than double the total for the 2010 governor's race, which was the first contest after the Supreme Court's *Citizens United* decision and, until the recall, the most expensive in Wisconsin history. *Citizens United* allowed corporations and labor unions to spend unlimited sums on political advertising and other "issue advocacy," as long as they did not coordinate their spending directly with a candidate. An unprecedented $10 million was spent during the recall race of Alberta Darling, a Republican state senator. Darling, whose district covers parts of Milwaukee and its wealthiest suburbs, raised $1.4 million in direct contributions, more than double what her opponent raised. The job itself pays $49,000 a year.

Darling's trajectory suggests the rising influence of conservative donors and organizations on the Wisconsin GOP.

She received support for her recall campaign from Wisconsin Right to Life as well as Tea Party groups including the Wisconsin Club for Growth and Americans for Prosperity. Earlier in her career, she had been a moderate on reproductive rights, even serving on the board of the Wisconsin chapter of Planned Parenthood from 1986 to 1995. But in 2011, she voted to defund the organization. Three years earlier, Darling had received an 85 percent rating from the Wisconsin League of Conservation Voters. In March 2011, five months before her recall election, Americans for Prosperity sent out a press release praising Darling for signing the group's No Climate Tax Pledge, a promise to oppose any legislation to combat climate change that includes a net increase in tax revenue. Darling held her seat.

Walker's recall did not provoke a similar urgency from national Democrats, many of whom saw it as an unwelcome distraction from the upcoming presidential race. The week before the June election, President Obama made fundraising trips to nearby Minneapolis and Chicago, but he declined to make even a brief stop in Wisconsin to campaign for Walker's opponent, Tom Barrett, despite Barrett's plea for help. "This is a gubernatorial race with a guy who was recalled and a challenger trying to get him out of office," Stephanie Cutter, the deputy campaign spokeswoman for Obama's 2012 campaign, told NBC News. "It has nothing to do with President Obama." Walker gloated over Obama's absence, spinning it as a smart political calculation. "He knew a significant number of his supporters were also backing me in the recall," Walker wrote in his memoir, *Unintimidated*.

But Obama's decision was also rooted in an earlier, more fundamental political calculation, made by the Democratic Party a generation earlier, to move rightward and support Republican priorities such as welfare reform and school vouchers. Bill Clinton had pushed for charter schools "run by private corporations," whose teachers would be non-union, in an early State of the Union address, two years before signing a welfare reform bill based on the model advanced by Governor Tommy Thompson of Wisconsin. Clinton embraced the Republicans' framing of the measure, which stated that welfare recipients lacked "personal responsibility" and would be required to work within two years of receiving any assistance, while ignoring the precipitous decline in good-paying jobs for people without a college degree. Obama allowed states to loosen the work requirements under welfare reform, but he never repudiated the concept. More important, he and his education secretary, Arne Duncan, promoted linking standardized test scores to teacher pay and teacher tenure, and expanding charter schools, all of which were anathema to many of the same unions spearheading the recall effort. A few months after Act 10, Duncan appeared at an event at a Milwaukee school with Scott Walker. "You've done some things we agree with, and you've done some things that we don't agree with," he said. He gave Walker only a tepid rebuke, telling the governor that stripping collective bargaining rights was "not the right way to go."

A few days before the first wave of recalls, in 2011, I visited the state capitol in Madison to witness a "solidarity sing-along." The daily noontime gathering featured some of the activist elements of the Democratic base—teachers, firefighters, students, and other union sympathizers—singing labor songs and standards with revamped lyrics to reflect Wisconsin's union fight. Toward the end of this gathering, the singers delivered their version of "My Bonnie Lies Over the Ocean." ("Though we may be 'God's frozen people' / We bask in the warmth of our plea / Don't bury my rights in a snowbank / Oh, bring back Wisconsin to me.") After the song, one of the members announced that it was President Obama's birthday. A few boos erupted, but mostly there was silence. There were no cheers.

But if an erosion of support for Obama and the Democratic Party reflected neglect of the party's base, it was also tied to the failure of progressives to build the vast infrastructure conservatives had created over the past forty-five years. Conservative institutions such as the Wisconsin Club for Growth; Americans for Prosperity, the Koch brothers' political advocacy arm; and the Bradley Foundation, a Milwaukee-based organization focused on a state-based strategy to move the country to the right, played a crucial role in attacking Wisconsin's progressive legacy and supporting Walker and his allies in the recall elections.

The Bradley Foundation, headquartered in an antebellum mansion known as the Lion House (for the two enormous carved lions that gaze east into Lake Michigan from the building's portico), is a tax-exempt charitable organization with assets now worth nearly $850 million. It specializes in what the *New Yorker* writer Jane Mayer has called "weaponized philanthropy." Each year the foundation distributes tens of millions of dollars in grants to think tanks, litigation centers, opposition research firms, and other organizations promoting a spectrum of conservative causes including voter ID laws, school vouchers, the curtailing or elimination of safety-net programs, and anti-union measures like right-to-work laws.

The foundation was created in 1942 by a Milwaukee industrialist named Harry Bradley, and owes its existence to the fortune Harry and his brother Lynde made from the Allen-Bradley Company, an electronic-controls manufacturer Lynde started under a different name in 1903. The company's first product was based on a toy rheostat Lynde designed when he was only fourteen. A high-school dropout, Lynde devoted his working hours to improving his inventions as well as crafting new ones. He claimed fifteen patents before he turned forty—six of which he shared with Harry, also a high-school dropout, who worked as a draftsman, electrician, mechanic, designer, and company manager. Allen-Bradley floundered until the First World War, when demand for ships, planes, and weapons fueled the need for electronic controls to run mass-production machinery. The company grew quickly, buying a factory on South 2nd Street in Milwaukee, which the brothers expanded over several decades until it encompassed four city blocks and 1.8 million square feet of manufacturing space.

Harry Bradley lavished perks like marble bathrooms, a rooftop sundeck, and Tuesday-afternoon jazz concerts on his employees. But his generosity came with a paternalism that grew to rankle the company's workers. The largesse was also meant to keep unions out, and Allen-Bradley employed a consultant to break up any unionization drive and pledged loyalty to "the open-shop principle." Organizing was made easier, however, by the passage of the Wagner Act, and even Allen-Bradley could not resist the tide. In 1937, a majority of the company's employees voted to form Local 1111, a chapter of the

United Electrical, Radio, and Machine Workers. Two years later, punch-press operators initiated a company-wide strike over the presence of non-union employees in their department. More than 90 percent of the workforce went out on a twelve-week strike, which included violent skirmishes with strikebreakers and the arrests of twenty-four people. According to Allen-Bradley's official corporate history, written by the Milwaukee historian John Gurda, Lynde Bradley looked out the window at the picket line and said: "What do they *want*?" What the strikers wanted was a union shop, and though their strike ultimately failed to achieve it, Harry was booed by workers on the picket line, fueling his animus toward unions and the New Deal.

World War II, and the enormous expansion it brought for Allen-Bradley, temporarily ended some of the acrimony. The war also brought the brothers great wealth, and Lynde began to explore the idea of a foundation to lower his inheritance tax. Lynde died in 1942, before he managed to create one, but a few months after his death, Harry established the Lynde Bradley Foundation, a charity focused on helping needy families in Milwaukee and supporting local colleges and hospitals. The foundation's politics would soon become clear when it began distributing grants to conservative groups like the Christian Anti-Communist Crusade and the Committee for Constitutional Government.

In 1965, when Harry Bradley died, his foundation remained small by national standards. Twenty years later, Allen-Bradley was sold to Rockwell International, a defense contractor, for an astounding $1.65 billion. Proceeds from the sale swelled the Bradley Foundation's budget from $14 million to nearly $300 million. Wanting to make a national impact, the board recruited Michael Joyce, a fiery neoconservative activist who had grown a similar organization, the John M. Olin Foundation, into a powerhouse. At the Olin Foundation, Joyce had helped fund the creation of the Federalist Society, a conservative legal group, and beachhead centers for conservative economics at prestigious universities like Yale and Harvard. When Joyce came to the Bradley Foundation, in 1985, the vast majority of its funding still went to traditional institutions like Marquette University, the Milwaukee Art Museum, and the Milwaukee Repertory Theater. By 1990, 60 percent of the foundation's grants went toward public policy.

Joyce's advocacy and the Bradley Foundation's funding of the Wisconsin Policy Research Institute helped launch the school-voucher program in Milwaukee, in 1990, which was the first in the country. "Perhaps more than any other person, he was responsible for the voucher legislation under which Wisconsin became the first state providing public dollars for private schools," a prominent Milwaukee-based education writer named Barbara Miner would write of Joyce. Wisconsin's voucher program has been replicated by thirteen states and Washington, DC; in doing so, they weakened countless public-school systems, as well as teachers' unions, by draining public-school budgets. Joyce funded other efforts with national impact, too—under him, the Bradley Foundation directed $1 million in grants to Charles Murray to coauthor *The Bell Curve*, the 1994 polemic attributing the intelligence of African Americans and other minorities partly to a genetic inferiority to whites.

When Joyce retired in 2001, the foundation's board selected a Milwaukee corporate attorney named Michael Grebe, a

Republican Party activist, as its new president. Grebe would become Scott Walker's most important adviser, opening the door to a network of national conservative donors. Grebe had known Walker since the 1980s, when Walker was a student at Marquette and they both volunteered at events for President Ronald Reagan. Grebe donated to Walker's first campaign for state assembly in 1993 and when Walker was elected county executive, Grebe was a member of Walker's transition team. And in 2010, Grebe signed on to lead Walker's gubernatorial campaign. Walker was not the only powerful Wisconsin Republican Grebe would mentor. At a 2009 Bradley Foundation dinner in Washington, Paul Ryan called Grebe "virtually my political godfather."

THERE WAS ANOTHER key institution, almost unheard of before Walker's election, that was essential to the effort to remake Wisconsin, and states across the country, in a conservative mold: the American Legislative Exchange Council, also known as ALEC.

On a clear June evening, five months before the 2016 presidential election, Chris Taylor, a Democratic assemblywoman, drove to New Glarus, a former Swiss settlement forty miles southwest of Madison. A reddish sun set over bucolic farmland and prairie as Taylor wended her way along county roads. She was on her way to give a talk to a group of citizens about how ALEC brings together corporations, conservative think tanks, and state legislators to draft and distribute model bills. Versions of these bills are then passed in state legislatures across the country.

ALEC is a nonprofit public charity whose major donors include ExxonMobil, Koch Industries, and PhRMA, the pharmaceutical trade organization. The group describes itself modestly as a "forum for experts to discuss business and economic issues facing the states," but to its critics, ALEC is one of America's most powerful corporate lobbies. It was part of that same infrastructure that Taylor had lamented on election night, and as an unlikely ALEC member herself, she knew its intricacies better than any of its critics.

Taylor had joined ALEC to learn what was coming next for Wisconsin. She became ALEC's most intimate foe, slogging through countless hours at the group's task force meetings, workshops, and panels, which are open only to ALEC members. She writes about the group's initiatives for left-leaning outlets like *The Progressive* magazine, Madison's *Capital Times* newspaper, and the website of the Center for Media and Democracy, a Wisconsin-based watchdog dedicated to tracking corporate influence on government. "I see my role as exposing what they do," Taylor said.

Since 2010, when Republicans gained more than seven hundred seats in state legislatures across the country and control of all branches of government in twenty-six states, ALEC has been extraordinarily successful. Dozens of states have passed versions of ALEC model laws that diverted public-school budgets to private education, restricted voting rights, and decimated labor unions and environmental regulations. ALEC claims nearly one-fourth of all the state legislators in the country are now members; the group boasted of passing two hundred bills based on its models in a single year. ALEC has also spearheaded campaigns for states to obstruct the EPA's Clean

Power Plan and to reject Medicaid expansion under Obamacare, which paved the way for President Trump's destruction of those programs.

Since 2010, Wisconsin has enacted a statewide school voucher program, a right-to-work law, and one of the country's strictest voter ID laws. An ALEC member introduced each of these bills in the legislature. Many of the provisions were inspired by models ALEC devised, and some were word-for-word copies. ALEC's model right-to-work bill, for example, reads: "No person shall be required, as a condition of employment or continuation of employment . . . to become or remain a member of a labor organization." The Wisconsin version: "No person may require, as a condition of obtaining or continuing employment, an individual to . . . become or remain a member of a labor organization."

"ALEC defines the parameters of what's possible," Taylor said. She outlined a "three-legged stool" that, in addition to ALEC, includes the State Policy Network, a constellation of conservative state-based think tanks that amplify ALEC's work by supplying slanted research and talking points to state legislators. The third part of the stool—and the junior partner in Taylor's view—are the state legislators, who return from ALEC's conferences armed with bills they dutifully introduce, often without much regard, or sometimes even a basic understanding, of what they are and what their effect on their constituents will be.

When the state's right-to-work bill was introduced, in 2015, Scott Fitzgerald, the senate majority leader and the bill's sponsor, denied that "outside groups" were involved. "All of that scuttlebutt about other groups—no, we did it right here," he told me the day before the bill was voted on. I then asked if Wisconsin's bill was modeled on Michigan's, and he answered without hesitation that it was. He failed to mention that Michigan's law was based on ALEC's model, or that in 2013, the year after Michigan passed right-to-work, ALEC published a State Policy Network "toolkit" titled *You Can Too!* It included an article offering advice on how a state could replicate Michigan's success. Fitzgerald's bill was a copy of a copy.

Taylor grew up in Van Nuys, California, forty-five minutes north of downtown Los Angeles, and was raised by moderate Republicans who voted for Ronald Reagan. Her mother, Pat, taught elementary school and when she became pregnant with her first child, Taylor's older sister, she tried to conceal it out of fear of losing her job. It was eventually discovered, and Pat was fired, a common practice at the time. "That sent such a strong signal to me as a young girl," Taylor said. "I really resented that she had to choose between being a teacher and being a mother." Taylor's father, Jack, cleaned swimming pools. "My dad barely graduated with a GED," Taylor said. "He was always outside working. If you look at his hands, you can tell how hard he worked. His skin is like tissue paper from all the sun and chlorine." Pat, who returned to teaching when Taylor was in sixth grade, became active in her union. When Reagan broke the air traffic controllers' union, in 1981, she and Jack left the Republican Party.

When Governor Walker signed Act 10, inspired by Reagan's action, Taylor was on maternity leave from her job as a public policy director of Planned Parenthood. Like tens of thousands of others, she protested at the state capitol. After the protests failed, she agonized over what to do, ultimately running for office out of anger at Walker's attack, as well as gratitude for the role unions had played in lifting her family into the middle class. "I had a four-month-old and a four-year-old," Taylor said. "I had never contemplated running for office, but my family survived because my grandma and mom were in unions." Taylor's grandmother, a single mother to three children, managed to get a union job as an administrative assistant to the lead colorist at Technicolor after years of selling purses on commission at a department store. "She finally made a decent wage and could send her kids, who all became teachers, to college," Taylor said.

Equally motivating was Governor Walker's budget that year, which cut funding for public schools by $850 million—the largest such reduction in the history of Wisconsin. "I remember going to register my son for kindergarten at his little school," Taylor said. "My heart sank looking at these kids. That school is the heart of our community." During the six-way primary, Taylor emphasized her work for Planned Parenthood, the need for living wages, and the fact that she was the only mother of schoolchildren in the race. She won with 30 percent of the vote. "I was not prepared to win," she said. "I was in the shower when the AP called me to tell me. My hair was dripping wet. I was in shock. I had just been so focused on knocking on doors."

Shortly after she won, Republicans moved her district's lines, requiring Taylor to run against a legislator she admired, Mark Pocan. But Pocan wanted to run for Congress and abandoned his seat. During a meeting they held before Taylor took office, Pocan encouraged her to assume his role and join ALEC. Pocan had become a member in 2003, after an assembly hearing about a bill to overturn a statewide ban on bail bondsmen and bounty hunters. The state's for-profit bail companies had been barred because the bipartisan legal community—judges, district attorneys, defense lawyers—was almost unanimously opposed to them, arguing the practice led to corruption. The same bipartisan legal coalition came out against the new bill, which was based on an ALEC model, introduced by an ALEC member, and supported by testimony from an industry lobbyist from California, who was also an ALEC member. The presence of the out-of-state lobbyist piqued Pocan's curiosity, prompting him to join the organization, which cost state legislators like him the same as it costs Taylor now—$100 for a two-year membership. (Corporate members pay a minimum of $7,000.) "That bill was the first connection for me, because it was something no one in Wisconsin was asking for," Pocan, now a congressman, said.

At the time, Pocan could access ALEC's model legislation with a password through the group's website: "I thought it would give me the road map of what they were going to work on." Pocan gave his password to other liberal organizations, and he began filing dispatches from ALEC meetings for *The Progressive*, pioneering the undercover legislator-reporter role that Taylor later took on.

At the 2011 ALEC conference, in New Orleans, Pocan learned about the Special Needs Scholarship Program Act, a bill that provided children with disabilities taxpayer-funded scholarships to attend private schools. It was introduced in Wisconsin's first legislative session after the conference by Michelle Litjens, an ALEC member, and of its thirty-six sponsors, twenty-five were ALEC members. Before the legislature voted, Pocan delivered a floor speech detailing how he first learned of the bill in New Orleans. "I remember going to a workshop and hearing a little bit about a bill they did in Florida and some other states . . . to dismantle public education," Pocan said. "There was a proposal to provide special-needs scholarships. Lo and behold, all of a sudden I come back to Wisconsin, and what gets introduced?" he asked. "A bill to do just that." He started reading something at random from ALEC's model bill. "'Section 6, accountability standards for participating schools.'" He then switched to the Litjens bill. "What's here? 'Section 6, accountability standards for participating schools.'" The bill passed.

The next day, Pocan outlined for me a strategy ALEC advises its members to use: "You have to introduce a fourteen-point platform," he said, "so that you can make it harder for them to focus and for the press to cover fourteen different planks." He pointed to several bills introduced in the past two sessions, including one that would allow more children to enroll in virtual charter schools. "It sounds good," Pocan said. "Kids could access virtual schools for homeschooling. But again," he emphasized, the real purpose is "taking apart public schools. You do it drip by drip, and this is one of those bills that will do just that."

Like many of ALEC's bills, this one shared two distinguishing features: draining public budgets and taking an attritional approach. In 1984, ALEC released its first model bill promoting school vouchers. Its stated purpose was to "introduce normal market forces" into education. Six years later, Governor Tommy Thompson of Wisconsin, a former ALEC member, established the first voucher program in the country that allowed public-school funding to be given to private schools. The program was initially limited to three hundred low-income Milwaukee students. But soon similar programs aimed at struggling school districts were replicated across the country. While Thompson has denied that ALEC had anything to do with the Milwaukee voucher program, a speech he delivered at ALEC's 2002 annual conference is suggestive. "I always loved going to [ALEC] meetings because I always found new ideas," he said. "Then I'd take them back to Wisconsin, disguise them a little bit, and declare that 'That's mine.'"

ALEC'S MOTTO, "Limited Government, Free Markets, and Federalism," is rooted in the long backlash to the New Deal, whose prolabor stance and social welfare programs were seen by many wealthy industrialists as an unwelcome disruption of American capitalism. Some of them began organizing against it. As early as 1934, Irénée du Pont, an heir and former president of the DuPont company, warned that the country was losing the "freedom granted by the Constitution." Two years later, Roosevelt himself warned his supporters of his adversaries in an address at Madison Square Garden, three days before his second election.

> We had to struggle with the old enemies of peace—business and financial monopoly, speculation, reckless banking, class antagonism, sectionalism, war profiteering. They had begun to consider the government of the United States as a mere appendage to their own affairs. We know now that government by organized money is just as dangerous as govern-

ment by organized mob. Never before in all our history have these forces been so united against one candidate as they stand today.

On November 8, 1954, President Dwight Eisenhower wrote a letter to his brother asserting the New Deal was indestructible. "Should any political party attempt to abolish Social Security, unemployment insurance, and eliminate labor laws and farm programs, you would not hear of that party again in our political history," he said. Eisenhower was responding to the ongoing effort of prominent conservative businessmen like Lemuel Boulware, a virulently anti-union vice-president of General Electric, to unravel Roosevelt's legacy. As part of his campaign, Boulware gave every GE plant supervisor a copy of John Flynn's *The Road Ahead*, a national bestseller that argued New Deal programs were turning citizens into serfs and that America was in the first stage of totalitarianism.

Even more hostile was William Grede, a Milwaukee foundry owner and the president of the virulently anti-union National Association of Manufacturers. (Grede later became a founding member of the John Birch Society.) As early as 1933, Grede had railed against the New Deal, and he had succeeded in keeping his foundries free of unions, even during the Depression. He used his supervisors as strikebreakers and called the police both for protection and with a threat that they would be held liable for any damages. When Grede eventually instituted shorter working hours at his foundries, he insisted that it was not "out of consideration for the men or for humanitarian reasons," but only because "it was the most efficient way to operate."

But perhaps no company and its leadership epitomized the backlash to the New Deal more than Milwaukee's own Allen-Bradley Company, which by the end of World War II was taking in $200 million in annual revenue in current dollars. With the onset of the Cold War, Harry Bradley became increasingly active in far-right politics. In January 1959, he attended the second recruitment meeting of the John Birch Society, a two-day event in Milwaukee that Bradley called "the most rewarding experience of my life." Afterward, Bradley began inviting the society's founder, Robert Welch, for regular speaking appearances at Allen-Bradley sales meetings. The company's equally conservative president, Fred Loock, distributed John Birch Society literature to employees. Loock also wrote a memo to company staff equating social spending with totalitarianism, a common linkage among many of the industrialists who never accepted the New Deal. "At the rate our government is spending—and we are paying—it won't be long before all money in excess of bare living will be taken away from us in Taxes," he wrote. "Except for the bureaucrats, you and I and everyone else will have become 'slaves of the state'—a title no one should be proud of. It will be the end of 'Free Americans.' Fact is that we in this country are much further along on the road to complete socialism than most of us are aware of."

Harry Bradley shared Loock's view. One of the conservatives Bradley admired was Clarence Manion, a former Notre Dame Law School dean. The *Manion Forum of Opinion*, Manion's weekly radio and television program, was an early recipient of Bradley Foundation funding. One episode attacked "the murderously oppressive Marxist Federal Income Tax; gigantic and unnecessary subsidies of tax money for fantastic highway and housing projects; Federal aid to education which would inevitably be followed by Federal Socialist control; tyrannical control of American workers by politically and ruthlessly ambitious union czars; appeasing and fraternizing with Communist mass murderers, thugs, and slave masters."

Shared prosperity and high union density marginalized the strength of the New Deal's postwar opponents, but by the early 1970s, anger in corporate America reached a boiling point, galvanized by the unlikely figure of future Supreme Court Justice Lewis F. Powell Jr. Until his nomination to the court in October 1971, Powell worked as a corporate attorney in Richmond, Virginia. He sat on the boards of eleven companies, including Philip Morris, and represented the Tobacco Institute, the industry's trade group. Over lunch one day in the spring of 1971, Powell discussed his fears for the future of corporate America with a friend and neighbor, Eugene Sydnor, the chairman of the education committee of the United States Chamber of Commerce. Sydnor asked Powell if he would draft a memo for the chamber outlining his views and recommendations.

On August 23, 1971, Powell mailed Sydnor a manifesto titled "Attack on the American Free Enterprise System." In it, Powell blamed the media, clergy, academia, and government for trying to destroy American capitalism through "bureaucratic regulation of individual freedom." But just as troubling was the business community's passivity. "One of the bewildering paradoxes of our time is the extent to which the enterprise system tolerates, if not participates in, its own destruction," Powell wrote. He implored corporate America to conduct "guerrilla warfare with those who propagandize against the system" and called for funding a counterrevolution in every forum—courts, universities, think tanks, government, the press. "The time has come—indeed, it is long overdue—for the wisdom, ingenuity and resources of American business to be marshaled against those who would destroy it," Powell wrote. "Political power is necessary . . . it must be used aggressively and with determination."

The confidential memo was never mentioned in Powell's confirmation hearings; it circulated only to a few of his friends and a small number of people at the chamber. Sydnor told Powell his committee received it "like a lead balloon," for fear it might require an increase in members' dues. But in September 1972, a Chamber of Commerce employee leaked the memo to the *Washington Post* columnist Jack Anderson, who wrote two columns criticizing it. Many corporate executives responded by writing Powell fawning letters, detailing their plans to fulfill his call to arms.

"The Powell memo was never as simple as: 'Let's implement this directly,'" Jason Stahl, a historian at the University of Minnesota, told me. "But it got people thinking in new ways about what they could do with their own position." Stahl's book, *Right Moves*, details the evolution of William J. Baroody Sr., the president of the American Enterprise Institute during the 1960s and '70s, who transformed AEI from a technocratic institution into an unabashedly partisan one.

Powell's memo also inspired conservative activists to begin creating new organizations aligned with its combative spirit. The most dynamic builder of the new infrastructure was Paul Weyrich, press secretary to the Colorado senator Gordon

Allott. Weyrich grew up in a working-class neighborhood in Racine. His father, Ignatius, immigrated from Germany in the 1920s and tended the boilers at Racine's St. Mary's Catholic Hospital, where his mother, Virginia, worked as a nurse. Ignatius imparted to his son a religious fervor that Weyrich would fuse with his conservative political activism, which began in college when he joined the Racine County Young Republicans. In 1964, he volunteered for Barry Goldwater's campaign, and after dropping out of college, he found work as a city hall reporter for the *Milwaukee Sentinel* and a political reporter for local radio and TV stations. In 1966, he moved to Denver to take a job as a radio station news director, and the following year he moved to Washington to work for Allott.

"All of a sudden lobbyists were telling me how smart and wonderful I was," Weyrich told the *New Republic*. "No one had ever been very nice to me before. Back home [in Wisconsin] they'd cross the street before they'd talk to me." In 1969, Weyrich attended a meeting of congressional Democratic aides, lobbyists, lawyers, and Brookings Institution fellows to orchestrate a pressure campaign to get President Nixon to sign fair housing legislation. "All I did was sit there with my mouth open, watching the system being orchestrated," he said in an interview with the *Washington Post*. These included "getting outside demonstrators, when to get the op-ed piece in the newspaper so it would coincide with the demonstrations, when to have personal lobbying, who was going to speed up the timetable at Brookings to get their study out. It was magnificent. I said, 'Thank you, Lord, I have needed this insight.'"

After Allott lost his seat in 1972, Weyrich began fashioning the conservative infrastructure outlined in Powell's memo. In

1973, Weyrich persuaded Joseph Coors, the anti-union beer magnate, to fund the creation of the Heritage Foundation. Around the same time, at the direction of the Illinois state representative Donald Totten, a Republican activist named Juanita Bartnett started ALEC as a low-key educational forum for conservative state legislators. An early funding solicitation from Bartnett reached Weyrich, who organized a large donation from the foundation of Richard Mellon Scaife, the principal heir to the Mellon fortune. That contribution gave Weyrich de facto control of the group. Weyrich moved it from Chicago to Washington, and Bartnett was fired soon after. She was told a man had to run the organization. (Bartnett sued for sex discrimination and settled out of court.)

"The original idea was low-budget or no-budget," said Nick Surgey, the former director of research at the Center for Media and Democracy, who interviewed Bartnett in 2013. "Share a few bills and then go out and get drunk. It was a noble concept at the beginning, trying to get state representatives to share good ideas in a way that undercut the lobbyists. But after Weyrich seized control, ALEC got taken over by corporations."

Weyrich helped create much of the infrastructure of what was then called the New Right. Besides ALEC and the Heritage Foundation, he helped found the Moral Majority, in 1979, with the Reverend Jerry Falwell. They hoped it would sway evangelicals to back Ronald Reagan's presidential bid. In 1980, Weyrich gave a speech to a convention of Christian conservatives in Dallas, which revealed his approach to politics. "So many of our Christians have what I call the goo-goo syndrome: good government," he said. "They want everybody to vote. I don't want everybody to vote. Elections are not won by a majority of people. They never have been from the beginning of our country, and they are not now. As a matter of fact, our leverage in the elections quite candidly goes up as the voting populace goes down." The Moral Majority, a name Weyrich coined, succeeded in delivering the evangelical vote to Reagan, a decisive factor in his 1980 victory.

In his first inaugural address, Reagan affirmed his support for federalism, the means by which ALEC planned to transform the states. "All of us need to be reminded that the federal government did not create the states; the states created the federal government," he said. In 1986, Reagan gave a private briefing to ALEC at the White House. "I want to congratulate you on your outstanding program of drafting model legislation covering everything from tort reform to juvenile justice and to balanced budgets and to drugs," he told the legislators. "Power has stopped flowing to Washington and begun to flow back where it belongs—to the states."

That same year, Reagan urged a wealthy South Carolina businessman and Heritage Foundation trustee named Thomas Roe to push for conservative policy at the state level. Roe started by founding the South Carolina Policy Council, envisioning his tax-exempt group as a mini–Heritage Foundation for his state. Soon after, Roe linked his new organization with other like-minded state-based think tanks to form an association called the Madison Group. In 1992, he launched the State Policy Network, a more ambitious umbrella group, which now boasts sixty-five think tanks, at least one in every state (except North Dakota) and Puerto Rico. (Wisconsin has three: the MacIver Institute, Wisconsin Institute for Law & Liberty, and the Badger Institute.)

Many of these organizations, as well as the SPN itself, are members of ALEC.

The scope of Roe's ambition was revealed in an exchange with Robert Krieble, a fellow Heritage trustee, in the 1980s. "The evil empire can be dissolved—I'm going to go out and help do it," Krieble told Roe. "You capture the Soviet Union," Roe replied. "I'm going to capture the states."

THE RECALL EFFORT against Walker and the Republican senators officially launched at midnight on November 15, 2011, when groups organizing the effort filed an electronic petition, beginning the sixty-day countdown. They had until January 14 to collect at least 540,208 signatures, a quarter of the total vote in the last gubernatorial election. Walker had already responded by purchasing a $300,000 ad that began airing that night during a big *Monday Night Football* game pitting Wisconsin's beloved Green Bay Packers against the Minnesota Vikings. Running in the Green Bay, La Crosse, Madison, and Wausau markets for the entire week, the ad proclaimed the benefits of Act 10. "We were worried when the state budget meant there was going to be less money for our school district, and we have twenty-five schools," the Waukesha School Board member Karin Sue Rajnicek said in the ad. "But Governor Walker—he gave us options that reduced our biggest costs so that we could put more money back into our classrooms."

Wisconsin election law allowed individual donors to make contributions up to $10,000, but a quirk in the law permitted an elected official to collect unlimited sums from the time a recall petition was filed until the election was authorized.

Diane Hendricks, the billionaire donor whom Walker confided his "divide-and-conquer" strategy to, quickly wrote him a check for $500,000. But documents leaked to the *Guardian*, which came from a secret criminal investigation into alleged campaign-finance violations by the Walker campaign, showed that Walker's advisers had already begun pursuing less conventional fund-raising strategies. The materials, which came from a grand jury–like "John Doe" investigation launched by the Milwaukee County district attorney's office, contained an email dated September 7, 2011: A fund-raising consultant named Kate Doner had sent Walker and some of his senior aides an urgent message. It dispensed a series of bullet points distinguished only by their venality. "Corporations," she wrote. "Go heavy after them to give." Other suggestions include: "Take Koch's money" and "Get on a plane to Vegas and sit down with Sheldon Adelson. Ask for $1 million now."

"The governor is encouraging all to invest in the Wisconsin Club for Growth," Doner wrote in a note to R. J. Johnson, Walker's top campaign adviser, in another of the leaked emails. "Wisconsin Club for Growth can accept corporate and personal donations without limitations and no donors disclosure." The governor, she said, wanted all of his advertisements "run thru one group to ensure correct messaging."

Early one spring morning, I drove west from Madison to the village of Spring Green to meet with Eric O'Keefe, one of Wisconsin Club for Growth's directors. O'Keefe had suggested we meet at the Taliesin Visitor Center, which was built by Frank Lloyd Wright. The land, covered in radiant greenery, is at turns gentle and roughhewn. It marks the eastern edge of the Driftless Area, whose craggy hills inspired Wright. Born in nearby Richland Center, Wright built his home and studio, Taliesin, in Spring Green, as well as the visitor center, a low, beguiling building that spans two hills and houses a restaurant overlooking the Wisconsin River. Wright was a model for the architect Howard Roark, the protolibertarian hero of Ayn Rand's *The Fountainhead*. It's a curious choice given that Wright's work pays tribute to nature, while Roark had little use for natural beauty, a view Rand shared. ("I would give the greatest sunset in the world for one sight of New York's skyline," Roark announces.) But the landscape of southwestern Wisconsin managed to touch even Rand, who described it fondly in *Atlas Shrugged*.

O'Keefe, a trim sixty-two-year-old, greeted me with guarded warmth. He grew up in a wealthy suburb of Detroit, where his father was an anti-Communist stockbroker; his mother raised O'Keefe and his six brothers and sisters. Politics was a favorite dinnertime topic, and his older brother subscribed to *Human Events* and *National Review*, which O'Keefe devoured as a teenager. He joined a conservative book club and, under the spell of the Austrian neoclassical economists Friedrich Hayek and Ludwig von Mises, became a libertarian.

O'Keefe was a committed autodidact. "I just wanted to get out of high school," he told me, picking at his salad. "I hated school." In June 1973, he skipped the graduation ceremony to head for Michigan's Upper Peninsula in a Chrysler he bought for $270. He wanted to try and survive in the woods eating fish and blueberries. He lived in a canvas tent, but ultimately could not survive on his own. "I had to buy things," he said. "I did go to bars," he added, "but only on weekends."

O'Keefe lasted until Thanksgiving in the wild. He moved

back home and took a job running a drill press in a machine shop in Detroit. In 1974, United Steelworkers, his union, rejected their contract. O'Keefe reluctantly went on strike, even walked the picket line. After the strike ended, he poured his wages, which he had saved assiduously, into a stock that took off in 1975. He then quit his job, moved to Detroit, and devoted himself to reading, becoming a self-described "radical libertarian." In the run-up to the 1980 election, O'Keefe headed to Los Angeles for the Libertarian Party convention that nominated David Koch for vice-president. ("A great guy—likes politics, Charles doesn't.") O'Keefe volunteered in Michigan, Indiana, Ohio, and West Virginia to collect signatures to put the Libertarian Party on the ballot in those states.

O'Keefe believes that any campaign-finance law violates the first amendment. "Limits on campaign contributions are not constitutional," he said. During the 2011 and 2012 recall elections, O'Keefe's Wisconsin Club for Growth, a nonprofit whose primary purpose, according to the IRS, is "social welfare," spent more than $21 million on different races. The money bought late advertising blitzes, which usually came a week or two before the election, often overwhelming the intended target.

O'Keefe has defended the flood of dark money into Wisconsin politics, disputing the idea that it crowds out the voices of ordinary citizens. "We don't spend nearly enough on politics," he told me, comparing the amount with the much larger figures Americans spend on sports and marijuana. O'Keefe spoke proudly of his role as an equalizer, "countering" familiar shibboleths of the right—George Soros, unions—as though they were an equivalent force. "Wisconsin politics did become nationalized," he said unapologetically. "And I helped nation-alize them."

LAMPPOSTS IN DOWNTOWN New Glarus are adorned with Swiss and American flags. There are street signs written in both English and German, in an elaborate Gothic script. The small town (population 2,172) is a regional tourist attraction whose residents remain proud of its founding, in 1845, by 131 immigrants from Canton Glarus, Switzerland. The odyssey of the colonists, driven to emigrate by economic desperation, was recorded in a two-volume diary by a tinsmith named Mathias Dürst. Dürst's journal traces an arduous 124-day voyage that cost the lives of eight migrants, including a six-month-old girl and an unnamed baby, who was born at sea and died the next day. The party had collectively purchased land in advance of their arrival, intending to settle and farm even though only four had been farmers in Switzerland. On August 8, Dürst finally laid eyes on the 1,200 acres the group had bought, describing it as "beautiful beyond expectation."

Taylor pulled her car into a parking spot on Rüti Strasse. Tall and thin, she wore an orange sleeveless dress and fixed her long, beige-blond hair in the rearview mirror before entering Tofflers Pub and Grill, the site of the meeting. She ordered a Spotted Cow, a prize-winning local beer, then headed upstairs, welcomed by a burst of applause from fifteen or so elderly Wisconsinites. "They all know about ALEC," Debbie Fairbanks, who works at Lands' End and organized the gathering, told me. "My big question of the night is: How do you know if your local representative is joining?" Another participant, Jeanette

Kelty, learned about ALEC after Act 10. "I started doing some research about ALEC and saw they were part of this very long effort to take away rights from working-class folks," she said. Kelty had retired early from her job as a nurse at the University of Wisconsin hospital, part of a wave of veteran state workers who chose to get out rather than accept the draconian pay and benefit cuts levied by Walker's law.

The attendees settled in around long folding tables, most nursing pints of beer and a few eating plates of meatloaf topped with bacon. Many knew something about ALEC, but they grew rapt listening to Taylor describe infiltrating it. "It costs me a hundred dollars per legislative session to be a member of ALEC," Taylor told them. "We don't have to pay much because we're really the foot soldiers, we're the ones that go to the conferences, hear about the policies that we're supposed to push out in our states." Taylor described how isolated she felt as the only progressive among a sea of conservatives. "It's a very strange circumstance, to go into an organization you fundamentally disagree with," she said. For Republicans with national aspirations, like Scott Walker, who had been an ALEC member when he was in the Wisconsin State Assembly, the conferences can be pivotal networking opportunities. "The rumor is Walker met the Koch brothers at an ALEC conference," Taylor said. "But I don't know if that's true or not." In the summer of 2015, during Walker's short-lived presidential campaign, he gave a keynote address at ALEC's conference in San Diego. "He was the belle of the ball," Taylor said.

ALEC's role in Wisconsin first gained notoriety on March 15, 2011, a few weeks after Walker announced Act 10. At the time, few people inside the state, or out of it, had heard of the group.

But William Cronon, a world-renowned professor of environmental history at the University of Wisconsin, speculated in the first post of his new personal blog, *Scholar as Citizen*, that ALEC might have played a role in writing Act 10, along with other new measures like the voter-ID bill, which Wisconsin Republicans had also just introduced. Cronon's entry included a brief history of ALEC and encouraged citizens to pay attention to it. Within two days, the post had attracted a half-million views and enraged Wisconsin's Republican leaders. The party's state director, Stephan Thompson, sent a letter to the university's legal office, demanding that the university release all of Cronon's emails on his school account, since the beginning of the year, that contained words such as "Republican," "Scott Walker," and "rally." Thompson argued that a UW professor is a state employee, and thus subject to Wisconsin's expansive open records laws. A national outcry over academic freedom erupted, and despite the opposition of the chancellor, the university was forced to turn over a portion of Cronon's emails. A pervasive chill has settled over the University of Wisconsin ever since. "I don't know if I want to be quoted by name," one University of Wisconsin employee told me while we were discussing the origins of the Wisconsin Idea.

Taylor emphasized ALEC's success with preemption laws, now on the books in forty-three states. These laws bar local governments—cities, counties, villages—from setting their own ordinances, such as taxing plastic bags or requiring employers to give their workers paid sick leave, both of which are addressed in ALEC model bills. Wisconsin has enacted 162 of these laws since 2011, according to the Legislative Fiscal Bureau. They include versions of the ALEC model bills outlawing plastic-bag taxes and voiding requirements for paid sick leave; paid sick leave had passed in 2008 in Milwaukee, by voter referendum, and was upheld in the state court of appeals. Taylor told the crowd that a few months earlier, Koch Industries had registered to lobby in Wisconsin to support a bill to prohibit local communities from banning plastic bags. "It subverts our democratic tradition," she said. "The ability of people like you to influence policy."

After nearly two hours, Taylor wrapped up her talk to another round of applause. She gave Fairbanks a hug and headed outside. Toward the end of the New Glarus gathering, Taylor had gotten into a polite back-and-forth with a citizen angry at the Democratic Party, and some of its donors, for their support of charter schools, one of ALEC's priorities. Taylor and the rest of the audience admonished the man, urging him to stop complaining and work to elect the kind of people he would like to see in office. In the privacy of our drive back to Madison, Taylor shared some of the same misgivings about her party's failings and lethargy. "Democrats are not a very courageous bunch," she told me.

Despite her disappointment in her party, what burned in her, what kept her traveling all over the state to speak to small groups like the one we had just left, was a memory. She recalled the citizens who had woken at 4 a.m. to drive five hours from Hayward, in the state's far north, to speak to the powerful Joint Finance Committee, of which she was a member, about Walker's devastating cuts to their rural schools. Their two-minute testimonies, which they had waited hours to deliver, were ignored, barely tolerated by many of her Republican colleagues. For Taylor, they were a testament to the faith Wisconsin's citizens still held that their government might listen to

them. "That's the saddest thing to me," she said. "This legislature is doing everything in its power to shut them out."

Part of her dreaded the upcoming ALEC conference the
following month in Indianapolis. At her office earlier that
day, I had seen her shudder when she described being chased
through the Adler Planetarium by a drunk Republican legislator during ALEC's Chicago conference in 2013. But no matter how exhausting, draining, and occasionally frightening
the ALEC conferences could be for her, Taylor knew she could
never abandon the people of Hayward, or Debbie Fairbanks
and the neighbors she gathered together at Tofflers. Taylor felt
obligated to try and restore the frayed bond, once so strong in
Wisconsin, between citizen and representative.

WHILE WALKER'S RECALL drew the most passion and media
attention, the transformation of Wisconsin's politics could be
seen more clearly in the recall effort started by Lori Compas, a
wedding photographer and mother of two. With no assistance
from the state Democratic Party, Compas led an unlikely drive
to recall the senate majority leader, Scott Fitzgerald, Walker's
most essential and visible ally. The following year, after no one
stepped forward to challenge Fitzgerald in the election itself,
she became his improbable opponent. Compas had never run
for office before. "What struck me was that Scott Fitzgerald
was using his power to shut people out of the process," she
told me.

I met Compas for lunch a few months before the election at
Cafe Carpe, a sunny restaurant and folk club in Fort Atkinson
that doubles as an informal community center. Compas, who

has dark blond hair and a raspy laugh, grew up on a small farm in southwestern Missouri. She majored in agricultural journalism in college, drifted to Montana for a spell, and then, in 2007, came to Fort Atkinson with her husband, a geography professor at a small state university nearby. "I had never paid attention to state politics until about a year ago," she said. "I started paying attention, and I got really upset at what I saw our senator doing."

For Compas, the pivotal moment came on the evening that Act 10 passed. She was walking from her house to the Main Street Bridge in Fort Atkinson to attend a late-afternoon rally for the teachers. "I was checking my phone on the way and looking at Twitter, and all of a sudden it just blew up," she said. "People were saying they're holding a meeting in the capitol tonight. They were saying get to the capitol *now*, but I couldn't get there, so I went to our little rally."

That was the evening of the heated argument between Fitzgerald and Peter Barca, the assembly minority leader, which was captured on WisconsinEye. "Barca's standing there yelling, 'This is a violation of the law!'" Compas said. "I just sat there, and I cried. I've never felt so powerless and so frustrated. Regardless of where you stood on this issue, the complete contempt that Fitzgerald was showing for his legislators was unacceptable. That night I think I tweeted: 'I will recall Scott Fitzgerald if I have to crawl on my hands and knees through the snow to every house in his district.'"

Despite Fitzgerald's prominent role in shepherding Walker's agenda through the senate, the Wisconsin Democratic Party chose not to pursue a recall campaign against him. Fitzgerald's district is solidly Republican, and he won his 2010 election with two-thirds of the vote. A secretive Republican gerrymandering of the state the following year, which was spearheaded by Fitzgerald, added more Republican voters to his district. It also drew out of the district his two most formidable potential rivals.

The gerrymandering plans were drawn up across the street from the capitol, at the law office of Michael Best & Friedrich, by Tad Ottman, an aide to Scott Fitzgerald, and Adam Foltz, an aide to Jeff Fitzgerald, the speaker of the assembly and Scott's brother. Working with a mapping expert they hired, the two aides created several different maps and performed a regression analysis—what happens if there is a six percent Democratic victory margin, for example—on each one. Republican leaders settled on the most partisan version. During the spring of 2011, nearly all of the state's seventy-nine Republican senators and representatives walked across the street to the law firm, signed a nondisclosure agreement, and were then shown a map of their new district. No Democrats and no member of the public saw the maps until they were unveiled in the state legislature in July 2011 and rushed through before the first wave of recall elections that August. Michael Best & Friedrich and another law firm were paid $400,000 in taxpayer money for their work on redistricting. "Republicans have been keeping our promises and getting the job done since day one," Scott Fitzgerald said in a joint statement with Jeff Fitzgerald when the new districts were unveiled. "Now we're fulfilling our constitutional requirement to properly reapportion the state's legislative and congressional districts."

Compas was sure that Democrats would target Fitzgerald for recall. But as the deadline for filing a recall petition approached, Compas hadn't heard anything. "I started asking:

'What about Fitzgerald?'" she remembered. "Nobody seemed to know anything, and then I began seeing in the newspaper that the Democrats were going to recall these three state senators who I never heard of. Low-hanging fruit, I guess you could say. The Democrats thought they'd be easy pickings, but I just thought: Fitzgerald is the obvious one. He's the one that needs to go—even more than Walker, in my opinion."

A petition to recall Fitzgerald would require collecting at least 16,000 signatures from voters in his district, which most political observers saw as a waste of resources. "My husband takes the kids to school on Friday, and that's my day to just be home and focus on my business," Compas said. "They all left, and the house got quiet." She decided to call the Government Accountability Board. "I asked, 'What does a person need to file recall papers? Do they need a team of attorneys and accountants and all that?'" Any citizen could file for a recall, she learned, and that afternoon Compas designed her petition and set up a website, a Facebook page, and a Twitter account. When her husband came home, he was startled to find the change in her. "He was actually a little upset," she said. "He was saying, 'I left for work and it was a normal Friday, and I come home and you're recalling the senate majority leader.'"

The overwhelming and immediate response told her she had a chance. "There was a group in Columbus, Wisconsin, that called themselves the Grass Roots Office," she said. "Republicans, Independents, and Democrats who had come together and set up in an old abandoned auto body shop. They called right away and asked if they can get a petition. I told them where it was online, and they printed them, copied them, and distributed them. Same thing in Horicon and Oconomowoc. All these little towns at the beginning. I couldn't be everywhere that Monday night, since it was so rushed. They just printed them out themselves and took them out, and then from there it grew to where I would drive around, and I would pick up signed petitions and cheerlead everybody."

Compas wound up submitting more than 18,000 valid signatures in a district Fitzgerald routinely won with more than 60 percent of the vote. At a small press conference after they had been submitted, a reporter asked if she would run. "I physically recoiled from the podium when the question was asked," she said. "I just stepped back and said absolutely not. That's not why I did this, that's not in my future. If you had told me a few months ago that I would be doing this I would have just laughed in your face." But her preferred candidate, Andy Jorgensen, a former radio announcer, dairy farmer, and GM worker who had been gerrymandered out of Fitzgerald's district in 2011, did not want to move. People began clamoring for Compas to run, and in late February she announced her candidacy. More than anything, she did not want Fitzgerald to walk away unchallenged.

EARLY ONE MORNING, a month after the New Glarus meeting, Chris Taylor tiptoed around her house in Madison preparing to resume her double life. It was not yet 5 a.m., and her youngest son, Ben, had had a sleepless night, so she moved extra quietly, gathering her things for the drive to Indianapolis to attend ALEC's biggest conference of the year. After she'd loaded her car, she went back inside to pack an emergency stash of Luna Bars. ("They serve so much red meat," she said.) The sky was shifting from black to a pale, thin blue. Taylor's pastoral East Side neighborhood was quiet except for an eruption of crickets. We piled into her car and began driving southeast on the interstate through the fog-covered Wisconsin prairie. I asked Taylor if she considered herself a spy. "No, I'm not," she said. "I'm totally open about it."

But as we drew closer to Indianapolis, Taylor grew more tense. "I'm not super anxious to hang out with my Republican colleagues," she said. "I try to steer clear of them because they out me." One strategy was trying to avoid ALEC's subcommittees. "They're smaller, and they make you introduce yourself," she said. "If I go to one, I won't give my party affiliation. I just say, 'I'm Chris Taylor from Wisconsin.'"

Taylor's efforts to go unnoticed have not always been successful. In 2015, she was nearly thrown out of an education task force meeting at ALEC's conference in San Diego, when a Wisconsin legislator told an ALEC staffer that she was "a lefty," not one of them. (ALEC's eight task forces, which cover different policy areas, are where model bills are introduced, amended, and voted on.) Baffled, the staffer initially said nothing. But before the meeting began, he angrily confronted Taylor and asked her to leave, arguing she wasn't a member of the task force. Taylor protested, pointing to several other legislators in the room who weren't members.

"I don't think he had the stomach to kick me out," she said. "I'm not disruptive. I just sit there and take notes. The hardest thing really is *not* engaging. It's just not natural for me." Taylor laughed. "Besides, ALEC is supposed to be nonpartisan: How can they kick me out?" The staffer finally relented.

A few miles into Indiana, Taylor chuckled at a sign that

said, "Hell is Real." We decided to stop for gas and a cup of coffee before we went our separate ways at the conference. Taylor told me she only realized the extent of ALEC's reach after the 2012 shooting of Trayvon Martin, an African American teenager, in Florida. Local prosecutors did not initially charge George Zimmerman, Martin's killer, citing the wide latitude for self-defense claims in the state's 2005 stand-your-ground law. An NRA lobbyist, Marion Hammer, helped draft that law, and it was introduced into the state legislature by Representative Dennis Baxley and Senator Durell Peaden, both ALEC members. A few months after it passed, Hammer presented it to a task force at ALEC's annual conference, which unanimously adopted it. The bill soon began appearing, sometimes in almost identical form, in state legislatures across the country. By the time of the shooting, twenty-six more states, including Wisconsin, had passed a version of it.

Outrage over Trayvon Martin's death prompted rare scrutiny of ALEC's influence and secretive process. A pressure campaign persuaded dozens of large corporations, including Coca-Cola, Kraft, and Walmart, to drop their ALEC memberships. In April 2012, ALEC shut down the Public Safety and Elections Task Force responsible for the bill. Two years later, Facebook, Google, Microsoft, and Yelp announced that they too would quit ALEC, this time over the organization's hostility to renewable energy and climate-change science.

Some observers believed ALEC's power was waning, but Taylor wasn't among them, and she continued to write dispatches detailing the group's initiatives. In 2014, Taylor drew attention to ALEC's role in pushing preemption laws in a widely cited article she wrote for the *Capital Times*, which quoted a Utah state senator, Howard Stephenson, at ALEC's annual conference. "We need to stomp out local control," Stephenson told a subcommittee of the education task force.

Taylor's drive to expose ALEC correlates with her party's helpless position in Wisconsin. Since Republicans passed their redistricting plan in 2011, the state assembly's Democrats have never held more than thirty-nine of ninety-nine seats, even in 2012, when they won 175,000 more aggregate votes than Republicans. "There was a three-prong attack on elections: gerrymandering, voter ID, and *Citizens United*," Taylor said. She was most upset about a recent law that gutted Wisconsin's once rigorous campaign-finance regulations. "It was probably the worst bill of the entire legislative session, but it got almost no scrutiny, because it was complicated.

"We don't have any power and we have few options to expose ALEC," she continued. "Honestly, it's a pain in the ass for me to go to the conference. I have to raise the money myself to go, and I'm totally shunned there. But I have to keep watching." Lisa Graves, codirector of Documented, an organization that tracks corporate influence on American democracy, calls her "the eyes and ears to the state—and the country—about the operations ALEC puts together."

When we arrived in Indianapolis, Taylor rushed into the hotel hosting the conference, an upscale Marriott downtown, and made a beeline for the check-in booth to get her ID badge and find a conference agenda. She pored over it, trying to parse the anodyne-sounding events ("A Balanced Discussion About Energy Policy in the Next Administration") to decide what to attend. She focused on energy and education, two of the most powerful ALEC task forces. She also planned to take in Kellyanne Conway's workshop on conservative policy for women ("All Issues Are Women's Issues") and ALEC's media training for state legislators.

Downstairs, the Heritage Foundation, Heartland Institute, National Right to Work Legal Defense Foundation, and other ALEC sponsors staffed trade-show booths piled with offerings like "Stranglehold: How Union Bosses Have Hijacked Our Government" and "Why Scientists Disagree About Global Warming." Despite ALEC's professed avoidance of social issues, there were several booths devoted to them. Groups like the Susan B. Anthony List offered literature on "Advancing Pro-Life Leadership to End Abortion in America," while the evangelical Family Research Council distributed an issue brief titled "'Sexual Orientation' and 'Gender Identity' Laws: A Threat to Free Markets and Freedom of Conscience and Religion."

There were plenty of regular lobbyists, like a genial repre-sentative for the National Fireworks Association I met at a cocktail hour who had come to persuade state legislators to ease restrictions on his product. But the conference's animat-ing spirits were ambitious libertarians like Nick Dranias, a research fellow and policy adviser at the Heartland Institute who led an "educational foundation" called Compact for Amer-ica. I heard Dranias present a dense, legalistic workshop mar-keting "Prosperity Zones," nearly government- and tax-free areas of at least one square mile, which he said he modeled on aspects of Disney World, Singapore, and Dubai. He said they would "bring back the American dream."

Throughout the conference, attendees could pick up a free

copy of the 2016 edition of *Rich States, Poor States*, ALEC's influential guide ranking economic competitiveness among states with a foreword by Scott Walker. The three authors, Arthur Laffer, one of the originators of supply-side econom- ics, Stephen Moore, the first president of the Club for Growth, and Jonathan Williams, ALEC's chief economist, gauge a state's economic outlook by weighing variables such as the compensation costs for an average worker or whether a state's minimum wage is higher than the federal floor of $7.25 an hour. The lower the wages, the higher a state's ranking. Lower corporate and personal income taxes also boost a state's rank- ing, just as higher ones diminish it. The authors' choice of criteria led to some bizarre results. Minnesota was ranked forty-fifth, though it had the country's fourteenth-highest median household income and a projected budget surplus of $1.4 billion. Wisconsin, ranked ninth, had the twenty-fifth- highest median income and faced a budget deficit of $700 million. Unemployment rates in the two states were virtually identical.

Taylor's media training was canceled without explana- tion. She focused instead on the education task force. In the past decade, ALEC has created dozens of model bills increas- ing school voucher eligibility. Its most sweeping, the "Educa- tion Savings Account Act," provides for universal vouchers, regardless of income or location. So far, a version of the bill has passed in six states; the most extreme was in Nevada. In 2016, the Nevada Supreme Court declared its funding mechanism unconstitutional, but a modified bill was sub- sequently introduced. "In the Nevada bill, the money goes to the parents, and they can spend it almost however they want," Taylor said. "That means you no longer have consistent funding for infrastructure, and the public schools won't be able to maintain their buildings: It's the death of public education."

A FEW DAYS AFTER we met, I watched Lori Compas speak before a large rally at the state capitol in Madison marking the one-year anniversary of the passage of Act 10. It was early in her campaign in the new election she had forced against Scott Fitzgerald. Organizers estimated that more than sixty thousand people attended. Standing halfway up the building's steps, I could see the surrounding streets filled with protesters and signs. The most ubiquitous was a clenched blue fist in the shape of the state map, the unofficial symbol of the movement that rose up to oppose Act 10. One of Compas's friends had written a speech for her, but the day before, she decided to start from scratch. She told the crowd that Fitzgerald's recall election had just been certified. Then she talked about how she had seen the first sandhill cranes of spring. "Every year their return tells me that even after the most difficult winters, new life is stirring," she said.

A few days later, Compas appeared at the public library in Fort Atkinson. She had held eight public meetings over a two-week period, and one of them, in Lake Mills, grew fairly contentious. "I'm not used to hatred being directed at me," she said. "There were ten people in that room who hated me, and they never met me." She was relieved to be back home, and with the exception of some polite but pointed questions from several College Republicans, the library event seemed almost sedate.

Afterward, Compas and a few of her supporters wandered over to Cafe Carpe. A community meeting was finishing up in the back, and one of the people leaving was Barbara Lorman, the district's former Republican state senator. In 1994, Lorman lost in a Republican primary to Scott Fitzgerald. "There's always partisanship," Lorman said, as Compas and her entourage gathered around her. "When I was first elected in 1980, I thought: It's them against us. These Democrats are the enemy, so I need to stay cool about them. Then you see them all going out for dinner together and drinking together and sitting in each other's office, and I thought, What's the deal here? It was quite collegial. You go to the floor, you have your issues, you have your rhetoric and your disagreements, but at the end of the day you leave it behind. Things are not like that now."

Lorman was surprised at the introduction of the collective bargaining measure. "It was like being blindsided," she said. "Walker's agenda, which was always there but nobody knew it, really came from somewhere else, like the Koch brothers, the national party, and ALEC. I don't think it was a local agenda, frankly." Before running for office, Lorman had owned a scrap-iron plant, and had fought an effort by the Teamsters to unionize her small group of drivers. "I might not be a union lover. There's a lot wrong with unions—a lot. But I do believe in a right to bargain collectively. In a lot of cases it's what you need, it's what works." Lorman said she felt that Walker should have accepted the unions' financial givebacks in exchange for keeping their bargaining rights. "He had everything he wanted," she said. "They were making the concessions that everybody was asking for. Pay more for your retirement, pay more for your benefits." Lorman told me she would be supporting Compas in the coming election.

When I visited Fitzgerald in his office that week, he told me he wasn't taking Compas's challenge lightly. He quickly raised more than $700,000 to defend his heavily Republican seat. That included funds from a $1,000-per-head fundraiser in Washington. Though he always led comfortably in the polls, a few weeks before the election he grew a bit flustered, telling the *Wisconsin State Journal* that he believed Compas's husband and the unions were behind her effort. "I don't for one minute believe she is the organizing force behind this whole thing," he said. In response, Compas posted an irreverent, sepia-toned video featuring herself as an obedient 1950s housewife asking her husband, "What's a senator?"

When District 13 cast its votes for state senate that June, Compas lost, but she had become the only Democrat to break 40 percent since Fitzgerald was first elected, in 1994. "You hear about money in politics, and you hear about how we just can't get good candidates," she said. "Well, you can't get good candidates if there is no way for them to win. People ask me if I would run again, and I say not in this district. The night that I lost the election, I called Scott Fitzgerald to concede. We had a brief but cordial conversation, and at the end of it, he said, 'Boy, Lori, you ran one heck of a campaign. I would hate to run against you in a fifty-fifty district.' I wanted to say, 'Well, you and your staffers have ensured that you will never run against anyone in a fifty-fifty district.' But I bit my tongue."

AT THE ALEC conference in Indianapolis, a phalanx of armed private security guards stood outside the Marriott watching over a couple of hundred teachers, postal workers, and UAW and Sierra Club members who held signs denouncing ALEC. Several conference-goers stared through the glass walls of the lobby bar at a protester holding an enormous papier-mâché effigy of Mike Pence, at the time the governor of Indiana, who had just been chosen by Donald Trump as his running mate and was the conference's marquee speaker.

Pence is a former ALEC member and a longtime friend of the organization. As governor, he wrote the foreword to the *19th Report Card on American Education*, the 2013 edition of ALEC's annual publication promoting school vouchers, and signed into law versions of several ALEC model bills including the repeal of prevailing wage, a Depression-era law that required public works projects to pay the going wage in a local area. When Pence arrived on the stage for his ALEC address, he was greeted by a rapturous crowd, some still leery of Trump's apostasies, like his campaign pledges to leave Social Security, Medicare, and Medicaid untouched. "I know who you are, I know the example you set," Pence reassured them. "I was not going to miss the chance to welcome the premier gathering of state legislators in the United States of America."

Pence thanked ALEC's leadership, singling out the national chair, state senator Leah Vukmir, from the "great state of Wisconsin." Taylor clapped politely, murmuring, "Yay, Wisconsin." Pence then launched into a tribute to federalism. "I want to speak to you about the centrality of the states today," he said. He described a 1982 visit Ronald Reagan made to the Indiana

General Assembly during a nationwide tour promoting federalism. "The federal government has taken too much tax money from the people, too much authority from the states, and too much liberty with the Constitution," Reagan told the legislators. At the time, Reagan was trying to transfer dozens of federal programs, including food stamps and Aid to Families with Dependent Children, to the states, and advocating a balanced-budget amendment. Pence praised Reagan's attempt to devolve power from the federal government to the states as visionary but premature. "It just wasn't something people were ready for," Pence said. "We are now."

IN EARLY MAY, a month before the recall election for governor, Marquette University, the state's top polling organization, released a poll that showed Tom Barrett with an ever-so-slight lead over Scott Walker: 47–46. A couple of weeks later, ads began filling the state's airwaves. They featured iconic images of Wisconsin life—farms, fishing piers—and a new poll-tested message attacking the process itself. "There's a right way, there's a wrong way, and I think this is the wrong way," a woman identified as a teacher said. "Recall isn't the Wisconsin way," a restaurant owner said in another ad. The ad closed with a man fishing. "I didn't vote for Scott Walker," he said. "But I'm definitely against this recall."

The ads ran until the June 5 election itself, and as the Center for Media and Democracy reported, all the funding for them—$400,000, which bought a lot of time in Wisconsin's small, cheap market—came from an out-of-state group linked to the Koch brothers. (It was a curious message, describing an

eighty-five-year-old process as not being the Wisconsin way;
Walker himself was first elected to county executive, in 2002,
after his predecessor resigned instead of facing a recall.) In the
final days of the campaign, the drama continued to build. Tim
Phillips, the president of Americans for Prosperity, staged a
rally in Madison the Friday before the recall vote. "The rest
of the country is watching you," he told a couple of dozen Tea
Party activists. "When I was a young man in the late 1980s,
the early 1990s, I remember that out of Wisconsin began the
very first state-based welfare reform. Remember that? That
was you!"

Phillips went on: "Welfare reform that swept this country.
We passed welfare reform in Virginia, my state, in 1995, and
we called it the Wisconsin plan." Phillips then extolled the
passage of Wisconsin's private-school voucher program, also
the first in the nation, imploring the small crowd to reclaim
the state's role as the nation's conservative laboratory. "Today,
every other governor in the country and every state legislator
in the country is watching Wisconsin," he said. "You are the
model for the country!"

On June 5, Walker beat Barrett, 53–46, almost the exact
margin of his previous victory less than two years earlier.
Walker raised $30 million to Barrett's $4 million and had the
support of his entire party and its funders. With the exception
of President Obama, who issued a single election-eve tweet
urging voters to support Barrett, no national Democrat lent
a hand. Most effective, perhaps, was the last-minute flood of
recall ads, whose message seemed to resonate. When polls
were taken in November 2011, as the recall process began, 58
percent of voters supported recalling Walker. But after the bar-

rage of ads, exit polls showed that 60 percent of voters thought recalls were appropriate only for cases of official misconduct.

In his election-night victory speech, Walker promised to put division behind the state. "Tomorrow we are no longer opponents," he said. "Tomorrow, we are one as Wisconsinites."

5

WORKER AGAINST WORKER

At the vast, hulking Kohler plant near Sheboygan, an hour north of Milwaukee, workers are greeted by a large copper medallion whose inscription reads: "He who toils here hath set his mark." The company was founded during the depression of 1873, by an Austrian immigrant named John Michael Kohler. Kohler's company started out making farm implements and ornaments like urns and cemetery crosses, but his breakthrough came a decade later, when he had the idea to heat enamel powder to 1,700 degrees and sprinkle it on a large cast-iron basin. He featured the item in his one-page catalogue with a caption that read: "Horse Trough/Hog Scalder—when furnished with four legs will serve as a bathtub." In the end, the demand for bathtubs turned out to be larger than for horse troughs and hog scalders—a demand that spurred fantastic growth for Kohler's company.

Kohler built a factory, and his son Walter built a picturesque town, Kohler Village, to go with it. The elegant planned community, designed by Frederick Law Olmsted, would later include a beautiful Tudor mansion with a resort, spa, and temporary lodging for European immigrant workers. (A decade later, Walter was elected governor of Wisconsin.) At its dedication in 1918, Walter declared: "A worker deserves not only wages, but roses as well."

By then the company's labor troubles had already erupted. On March 13, 1897, seventy-five molders walked off their jobs, protesting a 50 percent cut in wages. Labor relations were calm for a time; Walter Kohler tried to keep his workers happy by offering perks like a goose, or a gold watch after twenty-five years of service. But in 1933 accumulated grievances—declining wages and hours, an unfair system of layoffs that favored workers with houses mortgaged to the company, dangerous working conditions—led to the establishment of the company's first union, chartered by the American Federation of Labor. Kohler had recently completed his single term as governor and steadfastly opposed unions. In response to the formation of the AFL-affiliated local, he formed a company union, Kohler Workers Association. In the spring of 1934, he forced the AFL union's officers, who all worked at the company, to attend a meeting. Kohler had gathered his handpicked officials for his company union and put them on a platform. He pointed to the men. "Here is your union," he said.

Kohler refused to meet with the independent union, and tensions continued to mount until, on July 16, 1934, workers called a strike. Less than two weeks later, the company's armed guards escorted a coal car through the picket lines, and a riot ensued. Guards shot two strikers in the back, killing them and wounding forty-seven others, many of them also shot in the back. The strike lasted seven years, until the United States entered World War II. In 1954, workers at

Kohler had gone out on strike again, only returning to work eleven years later, when the strike finally ended. It was one of the most rancorous, and longest, strikes in American history.

The violence of the Kohler strike recalled an earlier Wisconsin labor battle, which built to a climax on May 5, 1886, when some 1,500 workers, most of them Polish immigrants, marched on the Rolling Mills iron plant. The Milwaukee Iron Company had built the plant and the neighborhood where its employees lived, and it demanded in return that they work as many as sixteen hours a day, six days a week. A citywide strike for an eight-hour day and better working conditions had shut down every large factory in Milwaukee except Rolling Mills, and as the marchers began climbing the hill toward this last holdout, members of the Wisconsin National Guard fired down on them. They killed seven people, including a thirteen-year-old boy. Jeremiah Rusk, the governor of Wisconsin, had given the order. "I seen my duty, and I done it," he later said. At the time, he thought he might become president, but in the end he never ran. The event, largely forgotten until 1986, when the Wisconsin Labor History Society began holding an annual commemoration, became known as the Bay View Massacre.

Many of the great labor battles that followed the Bay View Massacre—Pittsburgh's Homestead Strike of 1892; Colorado's Ludlow Massacre of 1914—also ended in violent defeat for the workers. Yet the defeats, in their very brutality, also forged a sense of solidarity that eventually produced great labor victories, including the eight-hour workday, enshrined into federal law during the Depression, and the passage of the 1935 Wagner Act, which guaranteed the right of workers—like those at Kohler—to strike, and remains labor's greatest means of leverage. From 1935 to 1947, union membership in the United States quadrupled, from 3.5 million workers to nearly 15 million workers, fueled by the pro-union policies of the New Deal and a labor shortage during World War II. In the mid-1950s, more than one out of every three American workers belonged to a union.

By 2017, the percentage of private-sector workers who belonged to a union had fallen to 6.5 percent. Union membership shrank for many reasons—some union bosses turned corrupt, manufacturers pursued cheaper labor overseas, automated systems replaced skilled workers in industry after industry. And some politicians saw a chance to show that they were not beholden to "special interests." But the passage of "right-to-work" laws, which began in Arkansas and Florida in 1944, has proved able to corrode labor's strength from the inside. Right-to-work laws eliminate the requirement for workers in a unionized workplace to pay dues, but not the union's obligation to provide services to non-dues-paying employees. The more workers "opt out," the thinner a union has to stretch its funds. Limited funds and fewer members diminish a union's capacity to negotiate for better wages and benefits, which in turn fuels the desire of more and more members to stop paying dues.

By 1964, twenty states were right-to-work. Over the next four decades only three more—Louisiana, Idaho, and Oklahoma—joined them. But in 2010, as Republicans swept statehouses across the country, conservative organizations such as ALEC and the Bradley Foundation intensified their efforts to pass right-to-work laws. They devoted special attention to transforming the industrial Midwest, the symbolic heart of the American labor movement. In 2012, Indiana became the first state to become right-to-work in more than a decade, and the following year, Michigan, the birthplace of the UAW, the most powerful trade union in American history and the union that stood by the striking Kohler workers for eleven years, followed.

Senate Majority Leader Fitzgerald began floating a right-to-work law for Wisconsin in 2010. "I just attended an American Legislative Exchange Council meeting," he told a reporter, who asked about making Wisconsin a right-to-work state. "And I was surprised about how much momentum there was in and around that discussion, nothing like I have ever seen before." But in Scott Walker's first term, the governor and his allies focused on the passage of Act 10. After Walker coasted to reelection in 2014, with Republicans retaining control of the state senate and assembly, Fitzgerald began speaking of it again. And in early December he announced he was intent on passing a right-to-work bill. "There's no way we avoid this issue," Fitzgerald told Charlie Sykes, the conservative talk-radio host. "We have to deal with this issue right now."

IN 1941, when the labor movement was still ascending, William Ruggles, a forty-year-old editorial writer for the *Dallas Morning News*, coined the slogan "right to work." Ruggles was alarmed by labor's growing strength, which in his view was intent on forcing all workers into unions. He proposed a constitutional amendment that would prohibit workers from having to pay dues to a union in order to hold a job in a "union shop." "If the country does not want it, let us say so," he wrote.

"If we do want it, adopt it and maintain forever the right to work of every American."

The day after the paper printed the editorial, a Houston political activist named Vance Muse called Ruggles to ask permission for his organization, the Christian American Association, to pursue the proposal. Ruggles agreed and suggested to Muse that he call it a "Right to Work Amendment." Muse, an avowed racist—he told a United States Senate committee in 1936, "I am a Southerner and for white supremacy"—held a special animus toward unions, which he believed fostered race-mixing. In *Southern Exposure,* a 1946 book about racism in the South, the muckraking journalist Stetson Kennedy quoted Muse's pitch on the need for right-to-work, in which he said: "White women and white men will be forced into organizations with black African apes, whom they will have to call 'brother' or lose their jobs."

But Muse was also an effective fundraiser—he received support from General Motors and the du Pont family, among others—and lobbyist. In 1944, the Christian American Association sponsored the amendment that made Arkansas one of the country's first right-to-work states. By 1947, ten more states, most of them in the South, had become right-to-work, embodying the growing national backlash against labor brought on by the Red Scare. That same year, over President Harry Truman's veto, Congress passed the Taft-Hartley Act, which undercut the Wagner Act by placing numerous restrictions on unions, among them a clause granting states the power to become right-to-work. Muse died in 1950, but his campaign had already been taken over by more mainstream proponents. In 1955, Fred Hartley, the former congressman from New Jersey who helped draft Taft-Hartley, founded the National Right to Work Committee. Three years later, Kansas legislators, with the enthusiastic support of the oil magnate Fred Koch, David and Charles Koch's father, adopted a right-to-work amendment in their state.

Though Walker had long supported right-to-work, he did not push the measure after he was elected governor in 2010. Even when he was attacking public unions for robbing the taxpayers of Wisconsin, Walker had consistently praised private-sector unions, particularly those in the construction trades, calling them "my partners in economic development." During his first term, many of those unions, including Local 8, had backed Walker's effort to rewrite the state's environmental law so that GTac's enormous iron-ore mine could be built in the Penokee Hills. The mining company promised to deliver hundreds of union jobs, creating a split in Walker's broad-based opposition.

Walker continued to publicly oppose right-to-work. "I have no interest in a right-to-work law in this state," he said in 2012. "We're not going to pursue that in the remainder of our term, and we're not going to pursue it in the future." As late as December 2014, he dismissed right-to-work as a "distraction." But Fitzgerald kept pressing the idea, and in February 2015, Walker agreed he would sign a right-to-work bill "if it came" to his desk.

Many Wisconsin business owners—and Walker supporters —who might be expected to cheer the demise of unions, and welcome cheaper labor costs, did not support the right-to-work bill. Contractors rely on the unions to certify and drug-test workers and keep their workers current on new technologies and job skills. Collectively, Wisconsin's trade unions contributed more than $30 million in 2014 to training programs.

Ironwork, for example, is a dangerous job. It has the fifth-highest fatality rate in the country, according to a *Bloomberg News* analysis of Bureau of Labor Statistics data. A 2011 University of Michigan study concluded that the fatality rate in construction trades was 40 percent higher in right-to-work states. Local 8 offers a four-year training program that requires more than 7,000 hours of combined classroom and on-the-job study. Even many right-to-work proponents single out the building trades' training programs, like Local 8's, as exemplary.

Bill Kennedy, the president of Rock Road Companies, a family-owned asphalt-paving operation with headquarters in Janesville, flew back early from a Florida business trip to testify against the right-to-work bill at the senate hearing for the bill. Kennedy also helps run the Wisconsin Contractor Coalition, an organization of business owners whose positions on labor issues counter those of Wisconsin Manufacturers & Commerce, the most powerful statewide business lobby, which has pushed hard for right-to-work. Within a few months of its founding in 2014, Kennedy's coalition attracted nearly 450 like-minded businesses that collectively employ some 120,000 people. Like many of the group's members, Kennedy voted for Walker and contributed to each of his campaigns.

"There's this misguided myth that unions and management don't get along," Kennedy told me the day after the hearing. Rock Road was founded in 1913 by Kennedy's grandfather. It was a hauling business until the Depression, when it began bidding on government-funded projects like railroad beds and town roads. At its summertime peak, Kennedy's company employs about 150 workers. His opposition to right-to-work is rooted in pragmatism. "It's a business bottom-line issue," he said. "Right-to-work is going to compromise my quality, my competitiveness. The unions are my partner. They're almost like a screening agency." Kennedy's greatest fear was that right-to-work would undermine the unions' contribution to training programs, and eventually the quality and skills of his employees. "This is a working system," he said. "I have never understood this right-to-work agenda."

Also testifying against the right-to-work effort was Terry McGowan, the president of Local 139, the statewide union of heavy-machinery operators. McGowan had endorsed Walker in 2010, because Walker had promised to increase highway funding and build more roads, and he supported Walker again in 2014. But speaking at a March 2015 assembly hearing, McGowan's voice cracked as he described the death, three days earlier, of Ryan Calkins, a thirty-three-year-old union operating engineer who got caught in a drilling rig while working on a highway interchange in Milwaukee. "Remember that name—Ryan Calkins—because he will just be a little blurb in the newspaper," McGowan told the legislators. Five hours after Calkins was killed, McGowan said, he received a call from a lawyer for Calkins's employer; it needed someone who knew how to operate the specialized drill to help remove the mutilated body. McGowan sent one of his union members, who had trained at Local 139's facility in central Wisconsin. "Now we're talking about possibly taking training and safety away from our industry?" McGowan asked in disbelief.

A few days later, I went to see McGowan at Local 139's

impressive new glass-and-steel union hall in wealthy suburban Waukesha County, a stronghold of support for Walker.
McGowan greeted me warmly, but I could see he was still
shaken by Calkins's death. "I gained a lot of respect for the guy
that I called, because he made it very obvious he didn't want to
do it," McGowan said. "But he said he was not going to allow a
fellow operating engineer to sit wrapped around that drill bit
in that weather and freeze solid. You could hear his family in
the background. I'm sure he was looking at his wife and kids
while I was talking to him."

In his testimony, McGowan described his members as
"beer-drinking, gun-toting, pickup-driving rednecks" and
reminded legislators that many of his workers are politically
conservative and usually vote Republican. Local 139's special
relationship to Republican politicians was made clear when
Fitzgerald floated the idea of exempting McGowan's union,
along with a few others.

"One side of the aisle likes the work we do, but not our organization, while the other side likes our organization, but not
what we do," McGowan told me. He had lobbied heavily on
behalf of the iron-ore mine. "I was surprised that the United
Steelworkers fought the mine so hard, when the mine would
have used their equipment. The mine became political, and
a lot of the unions that opposed it, they did it so that Walker
couldn't get a victory out of it. My thinking was: jobs."

Fidgeting behind his desk, McGowan rubbed his bald scalp
and half-smiled. "I sort of trusted the guy," he said, recalling
his 2010 endorsement of Walker. "I took some bullets at the
time from the other unions." When Walker's "divide and conquer" video was released in 2012, the *Milwaukee Journal Senti-*

nel asked McGowan about the governor's remarks. McGowan told the paper that the phrase "divide and conquer" troubled him. "It means turning worker against worker," he said.

RANDY BRYCE RESPONDED to Walker's push for a right-to-work bill characteristically: by organizing. Since Walker's election in 2010, he had worried about Wisconsin becoming a right-to-work state, and after the 2014 election, his fears intensified. As soon as Fitzgerald raised the idea on talk radio, Bryce began traveling to job sites across southeastern Wisconsin to warn his fellow union members about what he believed was coming. It was an old-fashioned organizing effort, talking to workers one on one, made more difficult by a bitterly cold Wisconsin winter. The men respected Bryce's passion, even if they didn't share it, and they would shinny down the skeletal building frames in subzero temperatures to take some of the flyers he'd prepared. Bryce would tell them what right-to-work meant, and that he might ask them to join him at the capitol one day soon.

In February, that day came. Bryce went to the state capitol in Madison to testify against the right-to-work bill Fitzgerald had just introduced. Bryce had finally picked up some work after months of unemployment. He was unloading truckloads of steel beams to build a warehouse near Kenosha, and he needed the job. His son, Ben, was eight years old, his debts were piling up, and a ten-hour shift paid more than $300. But the legislation, which Republicans were rushing through the state senate, angered him enough to sacrifice the hours.

Early that morning, Bryce drove his gray Mustang to the

capitol. Dozens of state troopers (who kept their bargaining rights) and capitol police officers (who lost theirs) were now patrolling the rotunda to prevent it from being occupied as it was during the fight over Act 10. The senate hearing room was already packed, so Bryce watched the hearing on monitors outside while he waited for his turn to speak. First came the expert witnesses. James Sherk, an economist at the conservative Heritage Foundation, said that unions operate as cartels: "They try to control the supply of labor in an industry so as to drive up its price, namely wages. But like all cartels, these gains come at the cost of greater losses to the rest of society." Greg Mourad, a spokesman for the National Right to Work Committee, which has received significant funding from the Koch brothers, compared the experience of being made to pay union dues to being kidnapped and extorted. Gordon Lafer, a political scientist at the University of Oregon, noted that, on the other hand, while right-to-work laws in other states had generated no identifiable economic gains, they did drive down wages for union and non-union workers alike.

Ordinary citizens got their chance to speak in the afternoon. Nearly all of them opposed the bill. A crane operator cited statistics showing that workers in right-to-work states are killed on the job more frequently. "Are you prepared to be accountable for the deaths that being a right-to-work state can create?" he asked. Anthony Anastasi, the president of Iron Workers Local 383, broke down in tears as he pleaded to the legislators, "Please think about the families that will be impacted by this."

At 6 p.m., Bryce's name finally appeared on the list of coming speakers. He paced the hallway outside the hearing room in anticipation. But twenty minutes later, Stephen Nass, the

Republican senator who is the chairman of the Labor and Government Reform Committee, announced that there was a "credible threat of disruption" and that the hearing would be adjourned so the committee could vote to move the bill forward. A labor organizer, it turned out, had told the *Milwaukee Journal Sentinel* that some people planned to stand up in protest at 7 p.m., when testimony was to be cut off. ("I went through Act 10—it was ugly," Nass said earlier in the hearing, referring to the difficulty some senators experienced reaching various parts of the capitol after the rotunda was occupied. "We had to go through a tunnel like rats. We don't want to go through that again.") About a hundred people were still in line to testify. A chant of "Let us speak" erupted. But Nass quickly took the committee members' votes—the bill passed—and was then escorted out, with his two Republican colleagues, by a phalanx of state troopers.

Bryce still wanted to speak. He had lost a day's wages, and the committee's two Democratic senators had remained to hear more testimony. State troopers were now blocking the door to the hearing room, though, so he decided to address a group of protesters in the hallway outside instead.

"My name is Randy Bryce," he began in a loud voice. "I've been a member of Iron Workers Local 8 since 1997. I've had the privilege in that time to work on many of Wisconsin's landmarks, private businesses, and numerous other parts of our infrastructure." As Bryce spoke, the protesters began to quiet. He described how he had wandered from job to job after he left the army, how Local 8's apprenticeship program had turned his life around. Finally, he presented the case against what he called "a blatant political attack" on his union. "All of our representatives are elected," he said. "All of the decisions that we make are voted on. The general membership is given monthly reports on how every dime is spent. Every dime spent is voted on. Unlike what is taking place this week, Iron Workers Local 8 is pure democracy. I am disappointed beyond words at not just what this bill contains, but how it is being passed."

The following day, the full senate took up the bill. Bryce, who had asked for another day off, took a seat in the gallery. Fitzgerald stood up and said that the bill established "true workplace freedom" for the first time. "Such freedom," he added, "has been available to most public-sector workers since the passage of Act 10 in 2011." Fitzgerald continued to praise the measure until Bryce rose up from his seat.

"This bill is turning Wisconsin into a banana republic," he shouted as the senators and media on the ground floor gazed upward. "We were not given the chance to speak our minds." Mary Lazich, the president of the senate, tried to quiet Bryce, but he continued talking until two Wisconsin state troopers approached him, placed their hands on his shoulders, and asked him to leave. Bryce did not resist, but as the troopers led him out, he kept on denouncing the bill, especially the way it was being sped through the legislature. The last words listeners could make out from the chamber, before his voice faded into the distance, were: "This bill is an attack on democracy."

HOURS AFTER THE state troopers pulled Bryce out of the gallery, the full senate passed the bill that would make Wisconsin the twenty-fifth right-to-work state. Two days later, Scott Walker went to Maryland to speak at the Conservative Political Action Conference, the annual showcase for conservative activists and Republican presidential hopefuls. At a question-and-answer session, one attendee asked Walker how he, as president, would confront the threat from radical Islamist groups like ISIS. Walker's answer was simple, and defined his worldview. "If I can take on 100,000 protesters," he said, "I can do the same across the world."

The right-to-work bill passed the assembly in early March, and Walker's signature came a few days later. He signed the bill at Badger Meter, a manufacturer of water-flow measurement devices. He sat at a desk on the manufacturing floor affixed with a placard that proclaimed "Freedom to Work." (Paradoxically, that freedom did not extend to the employees of Badger Meter, who were not allowed to be on the floor during the signing.) Four months later, Walker announced his candidacy for president. He was widely seen, along with Governor Jeb Bush and Senator Marco Rubio of Florida, as one of the frontrunners for the GOP nomination.

Walker's presidential run lasted less than two months, and it ended with a press conference announcing that he was dropping out to stop Trump, whose campaign was gathering momentum and frightening the GOP establishment. "Today, I believe that I am being called to lead by helping to clear the field in this race so that a positive conservative message can rise to the top," Walker said. (A poll had shown Walker with less than 1 percent support among the Republican electorate.) To the shock of his rivals and the media, Trump was proving unstoppable, and by the time of the Wisconsin primary, in April, the only remaining Republicans in the race were Senator Ted Cruz of Texas and Governor John Kasich of Ohio.

For the Never Trump forces of the GOP, the Wisconsin primary was their last chance to derail Trump's nomination. In late March, Wisconsin anti-Trump Republicans began coalescing around Cruz, his most significant rival. Walker endorsed Cruz a week before the primary, and the radio host Charlie Sykes relentlessly attacked Trump on his three-and-a-half-hour daily show. "You can't parachute in here from Manhattan and crap on everything we've been doing for the last twenty years," Sykes said a few days before the primary. The Never Trump supporters hoped for a Cruz victory in Wisconsin that would provide enough momentum to prevent Trump from winning an outright majority of the delegates, bringing the Republican convention to a second ballot, where another candidate besides Trump could win.

Trump responded by staging ten rallies in Wisconsin in the week before the primary, and using them to attack the state's Republican leadership—especially Walker and Paul Ryan. "He came up to my office about a year ago," Trump said of Walker at a town hall in Janesville. "I supported him, I gave him $50,000 or $100,000," he continued. "He certainly can't endorse me after what I did to him in the race, right?" Trump also appealed to the working class, or at least a segment of it. He went after Walker's record in Wisconsin: the state's high debt, the decline in labor-force participation, and the ballooning number of food-stamp recipients. "Middle class hit very, very hard due to loss of manufacturing jobs," Trump said. "Wisconsin has lost 15,000 net jobs to Mexico since NAFTA. . . . But you have a governor that has you convinced that [Wisconsin] doesn't have problems."

Amid the vitriol directed at immigrants and the common

violence at his rallies—a teenager in Janesville was pepper-sprayed after she punched someone who allegedly groped her—significant portions of Trump's speech defended the welfare state, an especially appealing message to the aging voters in the crowd. "I'm going to save Social Security, Ted Cruz is going to cut the hell out of Social Security," he said at a rally in Racine. "They're going to cut the hell out of Medicare. I'm going to save your Medicare."

It wasn't the first time right-wing populism made inroads with Wisconsin's white working class. In 1964, on a speaking trip to Madison, George Wallace, the segregationist Alabama governor, learned he needed only sixty Wisconsin residents to act as delegates to get on the state's ballot in a run for president. He quickly found them, filed his candidacy, and started his presidential campaign, focusing on Wisconsin and a few other states. Though he ran as a Democrat, Wallace's hastily conceived presidential bid was meant to rebuke Lyndon Johnson for his support of civil rights legislation, and to push conservative economic policies—especially cutting the federal government, taxes, and business regulations. By the end of March, Wallace's stops in Wisconsin had become more frequent, drawing enormous crowds—supporters and protesters alike. Bomb scares were common, and Wallace always traveled with armed guards.

In April 1964, Wallace's Wisconsin campaign crested with an appearance at American Serb Memorial Hall, a community center on Milwaukee's heavily Polish South Side. Milwaukee had been in the throes of a growing racial backlash for eight years, since a race-baiting whisper campaign suggested that Frank Zeidler, the city's last Socialist mayor and an unapologetic advocate for civil rights, had paid for bill-boards across the South encouraging African Americans to move to Milwaukee. The smears led to death threats against Zeidler and his family and contributed to his decision not to seek reelection in 1960. Milwaukee's next mayor, a machine politician named Henry Maier, stayed silent about Wallace's visit. Despite Wallace's fears about his reception in this urban ethnic enclave, hundreds of people waited outside the hall that night after the room had been filled to capacity.

As the event began, a riot nearly broke out when the organizer, a former Marine named Bronco Gruber, singled out two black civil rights advocates who, in protest of Wallace's appearance, had refused to stand during the national anthem. "Your countrymen or whatever you want to call them, they beat up old ladies, eighty-three years old, rape our women folk," Gruber raged at the seated activists. "They mug people. They won't work. They are on relief. How long can we tolerate this? Did I go to Guadalcanal to come back to something like this?" Several men stood up and glared threateningly at the protesters. "Send them back to Africa," someone shouted. But the two men managed to slip out of the hall without violence breaking out.

Before Wallace went onstage, a polka band played "Dixie," with the crowd singing along in Polish. Wallace played to the working-class crowd's fears. Johnson's civil rights laws "would destroy the union seniority system and impose racial quotas"; open housing bills would diminish the value of their homes. He was met by rapturous adulation. "If I ever had to leave Alabama, I'd want to live on the South Side of Milwaukee," he told a reporter.

A week later, he would shock political pundits, who didn't believe his racist style could appeal to voters outside the South, by winning 25 percent of the statewide vote and 31 percent in Milwaukee. His success paved the way for his next campaign, in 1968. An internal AFL-CIO poll before the 1968 election suggested that one in three union members supported him. Running that year as an independent, Wallace won 13 percent of the national vote. His success among Northern blue-collar voters, like those who came to hear him at Serb Memorial Hall, almost certainly cost the Democratic nominee, Hubert Humphrey, the presidency.

Yet the Milwaukee vote was more complex than the narrative of white working-class racial resentment that predominated. Wallace also received a great deal of support from voters in the affluent Republican counties surrounding Milwaukee. Moreover, the results showed the power of labor to push back against racist appeal. The AFL-CIO started a concerted campaign to highlight Wallace's hostile record to unions in Alabama, which likely shrank his vote totals in Milwaukee's blue-collar wards. A post-vote analysis comparing eight primarily working-class wards and eight wards with greater percentages of white-collar residents revealed higher vote totals for Wallace in the latter.

The trend seems to have continued to this day. Recent studies in Europe and the United States have shown that union membership exerts a significant impact on its members' political views and diminishes the appeal of far-right, authoritarian parties. As recently as 2008, labor played a pivotal role in electing a Democratic president. That year, the AFL-CIO dedicated $250 million, its largest election effort ever, to helping Barack Obama win. A significant portion of that money was devoted to educating white union members, who, exit polls showed, were much more likely to support Obama than whites who were not in a union.

ON THE DEMOCRATIC SIDE, Bernie Sanders was surging in Wisconsin as the state's 2016 presidential primary approached. Working-class voters had rallied to Sanders's campaign, saving it from an almost certain end by delivering Sanders an upset primary victory in Michigan. Polls had shown Sanders trailing Clinton there by as much as twenty points, but anger over NAFTA and growing support from African American voters propelled Sanders's unexpected win. Exit polls showed that Clinton narrowly lost Michigan's union households to Sanders. She also lost, by a larger margin, the Democratic voters who thought free-trade agreements caused job losses. Clinton's weakness in the industrial Midwest was exposed.

A week before the Wisconsin primary, the Sanders campaign invited Randy Bryce to speak at a rally at the Wisconsin State Fair, in West Allis. Sanders had drawn 8,000 people in Madison a few days earlier, and his grassroots politics were a natural fit for the state's progressive voters, many of whom were steeped in the La Follette tradition. A year and a half before the Iowa caucuses, he had drawn an astonishing 10,000 people for a rally in Madison. "Wisconsin is my second favorite state," Sanders once said.

But pundits and the Clinton campaign discounted the importance of crowds, and Clinton continued to run a traditional race, racking up endorsements from Democratic power brokers and trying to avoid gaffes. Clinton's campaign efforts in Wisconsin were limited to small, exclusive gatherings. On the day before Bryce spoke to thousands in West Allis, she hosted an invitation-only talk for 250 people at Gordon Commons, a dining hall and event center at the University of Wisconsin–Madison.

When a Sanders staffer called Bryce to ask if he would speak, Bryce didn't hesitate. He admired Sanders's unequivocal opposition to free-trade deals like NAFTA and the proposed Trans-Pacific Partnership, and how he had recently walked a picket line at an industrial food plant in Cedar Rapids, Iowa. Bryce also remembered the visit Sanders made to Wisconsin in 2011, a few months after the passage of Act 10, to speak at Fighting Bob Fest, an annual event celebrating progressive politics, where Sanders paid tribute to the grassroots resistance still battling Walker's attacks on public-employee unions. "There are a lot of reasons as to why the middle class is collapsing," Sanders said. "Certainly the anti-union efforts on the part of corporate America have been significant, because if we do not have workers—public and private—engaged in collective bargaining, fighting for a living wage, not only do those workers suffer, but every worker in America suffers as we engage in a race to the bottom."

Bryce came dressed in a gray suit jacket and black tie, though a few hours earlier he had been installing windows from a hanging platform thirty stories high for a new office tower in downtown Milwaukee. He stepped onto the podium and began by reminding the crowd of Sanders' show of support in 2011. "After Scott Walker dropped the bomb five years ago, Senator Sanders was the first to show up at Fighting Bob

Fest and help us dust off from our union-built bomb shelters,"
Bryce told the crowd, estimated at more than five thousand. He
cited the contract won by striking workers at the Kohler plant
in Sheboygan the previous winter. "Even in the state of Wisconsin, under a bomb that has been dropped on us, we can still
win if we stand united," he said. Bryce had joined the Kohler
workers on the picket line. He believed workers might finally
be grasping Walker's divide-and-conquer strategy, which had
cleaved the labor movement in Wisconsin. "I've had union
brothers come up to me and say, 'I'm sorry for voting for Scott
Walker, I apologize,'" Bryce told the crowd. "Coming from a
construction worker to apologize to another one—that meant
something to me.

"Too often we hear during a campaign about what someone
will do for us. I'm done hearing words. I'm *done*," Bryce said.
"We hear things like, 'I love collective bargaining,' we hear
things like, 'I have a comfortable pair of shoes that I'm going
to put on and wear wherever collective bargaining is under
attack.'" Bryce was referring to a comment made by Barack
Obama in a South Carolina speech during his 2008 presidential campaign: "If American workers are being denied their
right to organize and collectively bargain when I'm in the
White House, I'll put on a comfortable pair of shoes myself,"
Obama said. "I'll walk on that picket line with you as president of the United States of America." The remark became
notorious in the protests against Act 10, because Obama had
failed to show up; in his memoir, Scott Walker taunted his
opponents with Obama's absence. When Bryce traveled to
Washington for a union conference in 2011, he brought a pair

of sneakers and tied them to the White House gate, a reminder of Obama's abandoned promise to labor.

AS SHE GRAPPLED WITH the rising appeal of the Bernie Sanders campaign, Hillary Clinton was in no position to galvanize rank-and-file union member support. Her own troubles with labor were decades old, having started before she arrived in Washington. From 1986 to 1992, as a corporate lawyer in Arkansas, she served on the board of Walmart. By then, Sam Walton, the company's founder, was notorious for his anti-union fervor; an attorney named John Tate, who was also on the board and drove Walmart's labor strategy for decades, told a meeting of Walmart managers in 2004 that "labor unions are nothing but blood-sucking parasites living off the productive labor of people who work for a living." During Clinton's first presidential run, a former Walmart board member told ABC News that he could not recall her ever defending unions during more than twenty private board meetings. "She was not a dissenter," Donald Soderquist, the vice chairman of the board during Clinton's tenure, told the *Los Angeles Times* in 2007. "She was a part of those decisions."

"I'm always proud of Walmart and what we do and the way we do it better than anybody else," Clinton said at a 1990 shareholders' meeting in Fayetteville, Arkansas, when Bill Clinton was governor. But over the years, as Walmart's reputation was sullied by allegations of unsafe working conditions, overtime-wage theft, and sex discrimination, Clinton distanced herself from the company. Still, the Walton family's fondness for her endured; Alice Walton, Sam Walton's daughter, donated more than $350,000 to the Hillary Victory Fund in 2015.

It was Clinton's past support for free-trade agreements, though, that most antagonized labor. In 1996, she said that the two-year-old North American Free Trade Agreement was "proving its worth," a position she reaffirmed years later as a senator. In 2000, while running for her Senate seat, Clinton supported China's entry into the World Trade Organization and granting the country permanent normal trade relations. More recently, as secretary of state, Clinton praised the twelve-country Trans-Pacific Partnership dozens of times—at one point she called it the "gold standard" of free-trade deals—and lobbied foreign governments for its adoption. But in October 2015, as a presidential candidate, Clinton announced that she opposed the agreement.

During her 2008 presidential campaign, Clinton also publicly opposed free-trade agreements with Panama, South Korea, and Colombia, the last of which was also opposed by human rights groups as well as organized labor in Colombia and the United States. "I will do everything I can to urge the Congress to reject the Colombia Free Trade Agreement," she said at a gathering of the Communications Workers of America in Washington. But emails released from Clinton's private server show that as secretary of state she lobbied Congress to support the agreement with Colombia, which passed in 2011. Describing her effort to sway Representative Sander Levin, a Michigan Democrat, Clinton wrote to a State Department official: "I told him that at the rate we were going, Columbian [sic] workers were going to end up [with] the same or better rights than workers in Wisconsin and Indiana and, maybe even,

Michigan." According to Escuela Nacional Sindical, a Colombian labor rights group, as of March 2018, 143 union activists have been assassinated since the agreement passed.

Robert Scott, a senior economist at the Economic Policy Institute, estimates that NAFTA was responsible for the net loss of roughly 700,000 American jobs to Mexico in its first fifteen years, while China's admittance to the WTO cost the United States more than three million jobs. Roughly three-quarters of those losses were in the more highly unionized manufacturing sector, contributing to the steep decline in private-sector union membership, which went from 15.7 percent in 1993, when NAFTA was passed, to a nadir of 6.4 percent in 2016, the lowest figure in a century.

Since 1960, no Democrat has won the general election without winning the Wisconsin primary. After Clinton's Michigan loss, another Midwestern defeat by Sanders would foreshadow trouble against Donald Trump, whose opposition to free trade also helped propel him to victory in Michigan. Exit polls there showed that a majority of Republican voters also believed that free trade takes away American jobs. Trump decisively won that group. "You know, Michigan has been stripped," Trump told CNN's Anderson Cooper the day after his victory. "You look at those empty factories all over the place. And nobody hits that message better than me."

At a Democratic primary debate in Milwaukee, Clinton told the audience, "We've got to stand up for unions." The line generated passionate applause, but many of Wisconsin's labor activists remained skeptical. "A lot of our job problems stem from NAFTA, and the TPP will kill us," Gerry Miller, a United Steelworkers welder then working at a Caterpillar plant in South Milwaukee, told me. "We can't compete with people being paid two dollars a day in Vietnam. The thing that we're most upset about is the pandering. Democrats like Clinton speak labor out of one side of their mouth, but the corporate interests pull the strings." (Scott, of the Economic Policy Institute, estimates that adoption of the TPP would result in the net loss of roughly 40,000 jobs in Wisconsin, 215,000 in Michigan, and 113,000 in Ohio.)

While Clinton received the endorsement of many of the large national unions, many union locals chose to back Sanders. David Poklinkoski, the president of IBEW Local 2304, said his local had never endorsed anyone for any office before, but had passed a unanimous resolution endorsing Sanders. Poklinkoski praised the senator's consistent opposition to free-trade agreements. After the Milwaukee debate, he told me that two of his members who watched it came away as Sanders supporters. But Poklinkoski was alarmed to hear that the men's second choice was Trump. Nine months before the general election, Poklinkoski told me Clinton was vulnerable in Wisconsin.

"I'm worried about Trump versus Hillary," Poklinkoski said. He noted that at home, Walker had successfully portrayed himself as an anti-tax, blue-collar politician, an image that helped him divide Wisconsin's workers during the state's labor battles. "If you have a right-wing populist, you can beat a corporate Democrat," Poklinkoski said. "Scott Walker did it three times here."

TWO WEEKS AFTER Walker signed the right-to-work bill, Local 8 held its monthly meeting in its union hall just outside Milwaukee. On the way there, I drove past Miller Park, the Milwaukee Brewers' stadium, which Bryce worked on in 2000, during the final phase of its construction. It was the project he was most proud of. From the interstate, I could see the elaborate arched ironwork crowning the stadium's top. It reminded me of a photograph I had glimpsed on the wall of Bryce's home showing him and two other ironworkers decking the top of the stadium. They looked tiny in the far distance, but you could tell how strong the wind was from the way a tarp was blowing.

Bryce's grandfather, Eugene, had taken the photo. He used to drive by the stadium several times a week, because he loved watching Bryce work. It was difficult to see Bryce and his coworkers, 350 feet in the air and bracing against the wind, as members of a cartel, as James Sherk, the Heritage Foundation economist, had described unions in his senate testimony. Miller Park had claimed the lives of three Local 8 ironworkers, who fell 300 feet to their deaths when a giant crane collapsed into the stadium on a fiercely windy day.

Bryce arrived at the Local 8 meeting straight from work, wearing mud-caked overalls. He walked into the office to pay his $53 in monthly dues and then chatted with a few other ironworkers before wandering into the meeting hall. After the men recited the Pledge of Allegiance and the recording secretary read the minutes from the previous month's meeting, the executive board began a series of briefings: the prospects for building a new arena for the Milwaukee Bucks, the restructuring of the local's dental plans, what happened at the annual conference of the international union in Las Vegas.

Last on the agenda was Bryce's political report. He stood

up and started talking. He told the union workers about being locked out of the senate hearing. He told them about the next day, when he went back to protest and was thrown out of the senate debate for shouting, "This bill is turning Wisconsin into a banana republic." He talked about his organizing trips in anticipation of right-to-work and the dispiritingly small crowds at the rallies. He implored Local 8's members to become more active and not to think of themselves as elite tradesmen whose concerns were distinct from those of other workers and other movements. "Unions are not separate from the community," he said. "We build the community. Yet you're seen as the enemy, the reason people are broke. We have to stop this union-versus-non-union mentality."

After the meeting, Bryce headed out to the parking lot. There had been some defeats, he acknowledged, but he still saw the attacks on unions as an opportunity to build solidarity. "At last month's meeting, I talked about how the only way to fight back is to stage a massive general strike," he said. "It doesn't need to be that, but we do need to build ourselves up to a strength where they fear that. Now they're not afraid of anything, because we haven't done anything to fight back."

Bryce blamed the timidity of both union leaders and the rank-and-file, as much as the Republicans, for allowing Act 10 and right-to-work to become law. "People think that unions are useless today, that we're dinosaurs," he said. "Well, how did that happen? We let it happen. The labor movement has become lazy, because it's something that's been handed to us." He leaned against his Mustang and stared out into the industrial landscape surrounding the parking lot.

"A lot of guys in our local didn't see Act 10 as being important for ironworkers," Bryce said, because it targeted public employees. "I would ask them, how can you say there are good unions and bad unions? It's an *idea* that they're trying to kill— it's not the union itself. This is the strategy they're using to do it. They're splitting everything up. They're going after them first, then it's going to be somebody else. Then they're going to get to us too."

SANDERS CRUSHED CLINTON by thirteen points in the Wisconsin primary, and like La Follette in 1910, he won every county except one. Dale Schultz, the Republican state senator from western Wisconsin, told me his message of strengthening the welfare state and railing against economic elites resonated with his rural voters. "Whether you agree with the guy or no—and there are substantial things that I didn't agree with—you couldn't deny that he was authentic, that he hadn't said the same things for years," Schultz said. "Bernie Sanders was putting people on fire with ideas. All the Democrats were on fire out by us. I have never seen anything like that." That energy dissipated three and a half months later, when Clinton won the Democratic nomination. "Once he was out and it was just Hillary and Donald Trump," Schultz told me, "the anger shifted over and got behind Trump because they didn't care. They just wanted to crush the establishment."

After her primary loss in April, Hillary Clinton did not return to Wisconsin until November 2017, when she came for an appearance at the Riverside Theater in Milwaukee to promote her new book, *What Happened*. "We now know that Russian agents used Facebook, Twitter, Google, YouTube, even Pinterest to place targeted attack ads and negative stories intended not only to hurt me, but to fan the flames of division within our society," she told the crowd.

But she didn't tell them why she was the first presidential candidate of either party to skip Wisconsin since Richard Nixon, in 1972, or how she found time for a last-minute campaign stop in Arizona, which had gone for a Democrat just once in the past twelve presidential elections. She didn't explain why her campaign did not run ads in Wisconsin until a week before the election. Or why, during the final weeks of the campaign, she spent more on advertising in Omaha, for its single Electoral College vote, than in Wisconsin and Michigan combined. Nor did she tell them why she believed sending surrogates like Chelsea Clinton and New Jersey Senator Cory Booker to Wisconsin would inspire the state's beleaguered progressives to vote for her. Her negligence of Wisconsin almost certainly contributed to her loss, which was by only 22,000 votes, and along with narrow defeats in Michigan and Pennsylvania cost her the presidency.

According to Chris Taylor, even Clinton's vaunted data-gathering operation turned out to be deficient. "The Hillary campaign's lists sucked," Taylor, who canvassed for Clinton and supported her in the primary, told me. "I used my own lists in my district, because I was walking by doors of people that I *knew* were Democrats, but they were not on her lists."

Although Trump lost the Wisconsin primary by as large a margin as Clinton, he went on to campaign heavily in the state for the general election, staging five large rallies. Many pundits wondered what he was doing there, since Wisconsin was supposed to be a "blue wall," but he saw an opening, twinning his message of racial resentment with a defense of Social Security and Medicare that resonated with many older, white, working-class voters. That was clear in Kenosha County, the former home of the American Motors Corporation and many other manufacturing plants. Trump won the county narrowly, while four years earlier Obama prevailed there by twelve points.

Anti-union laws like Act 10 and the right-to-work bill may have played the biggest role in Trump's victory. Wisconsin's union density has declined by nearly 40 percent since the passage of Act 10, a decline accelerated by the right-to-work law. Now Wisconsin, once a cradle of the labor movement, has just 8 percent of its workforce unionized. Unions have historically been a central pillar of civil society, and in Wisconsin they provided the essential financial support for the Democratic Party, as well as supplying the ground troops and organization muscle to generate turnout on Election Day. The decline of union membership in America correlates almost perfectly with the exponential rise of income inequality. More than that, the diminishment of Wisconsin's unions erased a context for workers to share ideas about policy—and to organize; they were the only real counterweight to the right's infrastructure. That was clear by the massive protests against Act 10.

Since Trump's victory, Missouri, West Virginia, and Kentucky have become right-to-work, bringing the total to twenty-eight states, as conservatives continue to aggressively convert even more of them. And for good reason. A 2018 study published by the National Bureau of Economic Research suggests that right-to-work laws decrease the Democratic presidential vote share by 3.5 percent, a decline that far exceeds the amount Clinton lost by in both Michigan and Wisconsin. The authors noted that right-to-work laws also affect Senate, House, governor, and state legislative races. The study underscored the importance of the anti-union strategy that began in Wisconsin with Act 10, which functioned as a right-to-work law for public-sector employees, going so far as to bar them from even choosing to have the union automatically collect dues. (They could, however, elect to have automatic donations for organizations like the United Way.) When the attacks on unions began in Wisconsin, many of the protesters noted that the first step the Nazi Party took to cement its hold on power was banning independent trade unions. The analogy seemed like gross hyperbole at the time, but with the rise of white nationalism since Trump's election, the parallel has become more disturbing.

After the 2016 election, an underlying goal of attacking Wisconsin's union movement—transforming the electorate—was articulated by Grover Norquist, the conservative anti-tax activist. "Donald Trump's unexpected victory in 2016 did not lay the groundwork for Republican political dominance," Norquist wrote. "But the March 2011 signing of Act 10, a dramatic reform of public-sector labor laws, by Wisconsin's Scott Walker certainly did. To understate it: If Act 10 is enacted in a dozen more states, the modern Democratic Party will cease to be a competitive power in American politics. It's that big a deal."

NOT LONG AFTER Trump's victory, I went to a basement conference room in Emil Mazey Hall, in Sheboygan, to meet with three retired Kohler workers—Charles Conrardy, Kenneth Holzer, and Larry Meyer, all in their late eighties. The men had gone out on strike in 1954 and returned to work eleven years later, when the strike finally ended. They recalled it vividly, especially the solidarity among the strikers. In the early 1950s, the Kohler workers had succeeded in bringing the UAW in to represent them, but Herbert Kohler Sr., then the company president, made it clear he would negotiate with only the company union. "It was a union, but not a union because we had our contract proposals, they had theirs, and we ended up with theirs," Conrardy said. "You talked, but you got nothing. That was the way he wanted it run. He didn't believe in unions."

The Kohler family was ideologically committed to defeating the union, even though their refusal to negotiate was devastating their profits. The company's uncompromising stance made them heroes to some activists and groups on the far right, including the John Birch Society. The most important grievance was the working conditions. When the workers would shake the sand off their molds, tiny particles of silicon could enter their lungs, scarring them and eventually impairing their ability to breathe. Many employees, particularly those working with porcelain, developed this condition, known as silicosis, and had to be sent to Rocky Knoll, a tuberculosis sanitarium in nearby Plymouth. The workers called it "Kohler disease." Holzer's father had been a patient at Rocky Knoll. "My father-in-law died out there," Meyer said. "He had six kids. I found papers rummaging around my wife's basement that showed Kohler was giving six kids and a widow eight dollars a month."

In 1954, the men met at the Sheboygan Armory and voted to strike. "The first day of the strike, I remember I was at the front gate, and all the fellows that wanted to break the union wanted to come in," Holzer said. "They were across the street and there was at least a hundred, something like that. But they never got through. We were fifteen deep. There were over two thousand people on that picket line." The men on the line were met with solidarity from workers around the country— Chicago plumbers, New York hotel employees—who refused to install Kohler products. Conrardy estimates that production at the plant fell to less than half its former capacity.

The strike split the community in two. "It was family against family, because of the scabs," Conrardy said. "My dad had to go in. He came to me with tears in his eyes. 'Gotta go in.' I said: 'You gotta go, I guess that's the way it is. You're my father, what am I going to do?'" Conrardy said there were still brothers who won't speak to each other, because one of them crossed the picket line. Sometimes the tension turned violent. "Down at the harbor, they would try and bring in new ships with pig iron and clay," Cal Potter, who had joined us because his father had been a striker, said. "We would show up and try to prevent the cranes from getting to the dock. I remember one time I was down there with my dad and a scab tried to drive his car through there. Somebody spotted this guy, and they tipped the car over." During the strike years, most of the workers found other jobs—at lumber companies, Milwaukee breweries—but continued to walk the picket line in shifts. The Kohler company lost a series of court cases and eventually, after the US Supreme Court refused to hear its last appeal, was forced to reinstate the striking workers and pay them $3 million in back wages.

"After the strike, we had as many as nine UAW locals in this community," Potter, a Democrat who represented Sheboygan for twenty-three years in the state legislature, said. Sheboygan had been very Republican, just like much of the region, "but this strike changed that. People saw where their bread was buttered. They became Democrats, and it helped me when I eventually got in."

Today, the area is Republican again and growing more so. In 2008, Obama lost Sheboygan County to John McCain by a few hundred votes, while Trump defeated Clinton by 10,000. "What we did just doesn't pass on from one generation to the next; they don't understand it," Conrardy said. "It doesn't seem like you can teach it anymore. I don't think you can have a class in school about unions, whether that would make a difference. Here were people who lost jobs because of NAFTA and other free-trade deals. Their jobs moved to China—everything you pick up is made in China, because it's cheap labor. They'd have to go through the same thing we did in order to really understand what's going on. That's why I keep saying it hasn't hit hard enough yet, that these people that think they don't need a union, they gotta lose everything again. Go through the same thing we did."

Near the end of the meeting, Tim Tayloe, Local 833's current president, came in to say hello to the old-timers. Tayloe led the last Kohler strike, in 2015, which lasted five weeks. His union fought the introduction of a two-tiered system for wages and benefits that amounted to pay cuts of up to 40 percent for newer employees, resulting in positions starting at as little as eleven dollars an hour. Tayloe won modest increases in wages, but the two-tiered system came with them, conceding the core demand of the union. Three and a half weeks into the strike, he met with Dave Kohler, the current president of the company, in a Town & Country golf course parking lot. Tayloe told Kohler they needed to get back to the negotiating table. The company was already talking about bringing in replacement workers, and Tayloe worried that he couldn't hold the strikers' solidarity beyond Christmas.

When I asked how his workers voted, Tayloe told me he had sensed that Clinton would lose. "You could tell the swing in this factory," he said. Tayloe had tried to push his members to get out the vote as they had in 2008, for Obama. "That was motivated," he said. "I think I put up 120 four-by-eight signs that we painted ourselves. This election, there weren't any four-by-eights anywhere. We didn't have any to put up. Even the yard signs were tough to get." Some of the people he cajoled into helping him do campaign literature drops for Clinton he knew would be voting for Trump. "When you look at the future, and you look at the Democratic Party, what do they have? They better get their heads out of their ass, 'cause they are going to get eaten up."

IN APRIL 2017, I met Randy Bryce outside the Hilton Hotel on Connecticut Avenue in Washington, DC. Trump was due to give a speech to the National Conference of the Building and Construction Trades, the same organization of building trades unions that President Reagan had addressed on March 30, 1981, the day he was shot by John Hinckley. Reagan had begun by boasting of his lifetime membership in the AFL-CIO, negotiating contracts for the Screen Actors Guild, the union he led for seven years, and his admiration for the AFL's founder, Samuel Gompers. Then he moved on to promoting his agenda: tax cuts, deregulation, and cutting government spending. He described a letter he received from an unemployed factory worker in Illinois, who urged Reagan to push ahead with his proposed budget cuts despite the harm it might do to people like him. "He wrote to say that if spending cuts in government affect his benefits, it'll be hard for his family, but they'll make it," Reagan told the crowd. Reagan owed his 1980 presidential victory to the shifting allegiances of union members, especially in the industrial Midwest. He won 45 percent of union households, only three points less than Jimmy Carter. The election had spawned the term "Reagan Democrat"—perhaps the only genuine swing group in modern America, and one that helped propel Trump to the presidency.

Trump had done nearly as well as Reagan with union households—Hillary Clinton won only 8 percent more union households than Trump, compared with Barack Obama's 18 percent margin over Mitt Romney. And with the nationwide propagation of anti-union laws spurred in part by Act 10 and right-to-work laws in Michigan, Indiana, and Wisconsin, there were far fewer union households in key battleground states.

Press passes to Trump's speech at the Hilton were reserved for the White House press corps, but a vendor Bryce knew lent me his ID tag. Inside, a collection of bricklayers, ironworkers, electricians, laborers, and other assorted construction workers had gathered from across the country, and would end their visit with a day of congressional lobbying. The room held a smattering of women and a slightly larger number of African Americans and Latinos, especially among the laborers' and painters' unions. In January, Trump had a meeting about infrastructure with Sean McGarvey, the head of the Building Trades Unions, in the White House, and McGarvey urged conference-goers to be civil and polite. The elected officials who spoke before Trump, almost all of them Democrats, offered mea culpas for their abandonment of the working class. A few East Coast Republicans—Staten Island's congressman, Dan Donovan; Long Island's Peter King—pledged loyalty to organized labor, invoking their patriotic efforts on 9/11. There were warnings, too. Without mentioning any names, the Louisiana Democratic congressman Cedric Richmond implored the crowd to ask the courting politicians, "Whose side are you on?"

Trump entered the room to "Hail to the Chief," and was met by a mixture of boos and cheers. From the audience, Bryce stood up, held his phone toward the podium, and paused—there was a big commotion. A half-dozen protesters had gathered in the middle of the huge hall and unveiled white paper signs that said "#RESIST." They were escorted out quickly by the Secret Service, and Trump's speech began. "You're very talented people," he said. "It's time we give you the level playing field you deserve." Bryce began to inch past me, and under his breath, to himself, said, "Suckers." He weaved his way through the aisle toward the exit.

"One of my first acts as president was to stop one of the great sellouts of the American worker," Trump continued. "I immediately withdrew the United States from the disaster—this would have been a disaster—this would have been another NAFTA, which, by the way, is a disaster. I took you out of the Trans-Pacific Partnership." The crowd applauded loudly. Trump said he would approve the Keystone XL pipeline, which was met with bigger applause. He said he would "use American steel" and then said it would be "American steel made in America," which received a standing ovation. Then he said: "And from now on, it's going to be America First." Huge applause. Then, as had become his habit at any public appearance, he crowed about his election results. "But wasn't that an exciting one?" Trump said. "Places that nobody entered—Donald Trump has won the state of Michigan. They go, what? Donald Trump has won the state of Wisconsin." Trump did not say the word "union" once in his entire speech.

I exited onto Connecticut Avenue and wandered over to a coffee shop. The phrase "America First," and the response it received, lingered. The America First Committee of the 1940s advocated for staying out of World War II and included prominent Nazi sympathizers like Charles Lindbergh. Just then I saw Bryce walking past the window. "It felt good to walk out," he told me. "I wanted to make sure I walked through and not just out the back door." After he left, he said he had run into a Democratic attorney general, who told him how Trump had used undocumented Polish workers when building Trump Tower. One New York bricklayer had walked out of the hall and said, "That was nothing but bullshit, that's all it was: bullshit." Bryce laughed recounting it.

That evening, Bryce told me that his mother's multiple sclerosis was worsening, and his father, who suffers from Alzheimer's disease, was in hospice, because he had stopped eating. Bryce detailed the anger he felt toward his union for passing him over for an organizing job he badly wanted, and for reprimanding him for speaking at the Sanders rally before the Wisconsin primary—the international had backed Clinton. More enraging to Bryce was the way a new assistant who worked for the union had scolded him. "I don't know about you, but I never take off my ironworker's hat," she said. Bryce went on: "I've been doing this job for twenty years, and she's giving *me* book? I just wanted to support a guy who walked the picket line."

As we sat outside, Trump's motorcade drove by, reminding Bryce of what he had just walked out of: Trump successfully dividing the labor movement. "I can't believe that guys actually think he's going to do something for us," he said. "Even if he would, just the cost of all the people he's going after. Even if I had a job working on infrastructure, if I was driving home from work, going through my neighborhood and knowing there are people afraid to go outside because the same person that helped me get a job wants to break up their family and send them across the border. That's not worth it." It was all too familiar to Bryce. "We're the in-kids," Bryce said. "He's trying to get our group, but these other people," he said, gesturing with a sweep of his hand: "They're not worthy."

But Bryce wasn't giving up. He told me he was thinking of running for office again, despite losing badly in previous bids for the state assembly and state senate. His heavily gerrymandered district is almost impossible for a Democrat to win, but Senator Bob Wirch had asked him to run for the senate seat as a kind of sacrificial lamb, to have someone in place in case of a Republican scandal or a Democratic wave. "You have ninety days to get all your signatures," Bryce said. "I'm not worried about that part, it's just what I'm going to run for."

As improbable as it seemed for a construction worker a couple of paychecks away from homelessness, Bryce was mulling over a challenge to his own congressman, one of the most powerful men in the country and Trump's most essential ally. "I want to run against Paul Ryan," Bryce told me. "People have been asking me to run against Ryan, people who could do a lot to help from within the district. It seems so insurmountable with all of the huge money he has. A state senate race with decent maps would be a lot safer, but if Trump keeps being Trump, it's time to go after Ryan."

6

THE SEVENTH FIRE

Scott Walker has ignored Earth Day and its founder, Gaylord Nelson, every year he has been governor, with the exception of 2012, when Walker issued a proclamation announcing the restoration of a small patch of shoreline in front of the governor's mansion, in Madison. During a 2014 reception hosted by Terry Kohler, a wealthy conservative donor, Walker chatted with Tia Nelson, Gaylord's daughter, managing to slight her father's legacy while maintaining impeccable manners. "Governor Walker couldn't bring himself to say anything nice about my father," Tia told me. "But he went to the effort of telling me the story of someone that he liked who spoke well of my father, which I thought was very clever." Walker spent the following year's Earth Day at a groundbreaking ceremony in Appleton for the new corporate headquarters of Wisconsin's largest electrical supply distributor. That same week, fifty-seven employees of the state's Department of Natural Resources, including twenty-seven members of its scientific staff, received notices they faced layoffs owing to Walker's budget cuts.

For Donald Trump, offering words of praise for Nelson's achievement has been easier. "We celebrate our beautiful forests, lakes and land," Trump tweeted on Earth Day in 2017, his first as president. "We stand committed to preserving the natural beauty of our nation." That same morning, Mike Wiggins and Joe Rose, a Bad River tribal elder, met me at a restaurant near Ashland, on the coast of Lake Superior. Rose arrived ahead of Wiggins. Tall, burly, and eighty-one years old, he wore a flannel shirt and extended a large, weathered hand. Rose is an emeritus professor at Northland College, in Ashland, where he directed the Native American studies program and taught courses in ethnobiology, tribal history, and traditional craft making, which included fabricating Ojibwe artifacts such as a ceremonial lodge, birchbark canoe, and black ash basket.

Like many other Bad River children of his generation, Rose attended St. Mary's, a Catholic mission and boarding school in Odanah, the reservation's administrative center. Rose's mother, Dolly, who sent Joe to the school as a day student, was also a St. Mary's graduate. "She had tried to go to the public schools in Ashland, but there was no bus transportation between the reservation and Ashland then," Rose said. "She tried riding the train, but she was late for school every day. They raised hell with her for being late. Finally, she and her cousin signed away to go to boarding school."

St. Mary's was founded in 1883, part of a wave of Native American boarding schools whose assimilationist goals were enforced with corporal punishment and other cruel means. In an 1892 speech at George Mason University, Richard Henry Pratt, an army officer and Civil War veteran who founded one of the most influential of these, the Carlisle Indian Industrial School, outlined his vision for Native American education. "A great general has said that the only good Indian is a dead one," Pratt told the audience. "In a sense, I agree with the sentiment, but only in this: that all the Indian there is in the race should be dead. Kill the Indian in him, and save the man."

St. Mary's exerted a great influence on the tribe. By the time Rose attended, it had become less repressive. "We did do pow-wows and dances," Rose said. "They saw that as social instead of spiritual." But the school discouraged Native languages, ceremonies, and religion. Rose is still scarred from the school's suppression of his Native identity.

"They used to tell us only humans had an immortal soul," Rose said. "Nothing else in the natural world had a spirit. My mother would take my brother and me out to these ceremonies back in the woods. We'd learn from the elders that everything in the creation had a spirit. That was one of the first conflicts as a grade-school kid that I had trouble understanding." The wolf, whom the elders taught Rose was a blood brother to the Ojibwe, was soulless in Catholic theology. Rose sees a reason for that. "The wolf is always vilified in the Western tradition," Rose said. "In European literature, you can go all the way back to children's fairy tales—'Little Red Riding Hood,' 'Three Little Pigs.' Then you get into some of the adult tales, like the werewolves of Transylvania. The wolf is one of the most powerful symbols of wilderness, and that's what they want to exploit as a resource. They can do that in good biblical conscience."

Rose recalls his youth with great fondness, partly because he lived with his traditionalist grandparents. "I grew up in the time of kerosene lamps, outhouses, and wood heat," Rose said. The water from the reservation's shallow wells was clean enough to drink then, as was water from Lake Superior itself. Most important to Rose was spending time outside with his grandfather, Dan Jackson Sr., a master hunter who taught Rose how to set traps for wild game, gather medicinal plants, and harvest wild rice.

Rose's grandfather didn't become a US citizen until 1924, when the Indian Citizenship Act was passed. Jackson was forty years old. "They were politically impotent to fight against all of this corruption that was happening," Rose said of his grandfather's generation. That made an impression on Rose, who would become one of Mike Wiggins's mentors in the fight against the mine. Rose's age, stentorian voice, and scientific and traditional knowledge made him a persuasive opponent of the mine.

When Wiggins arrived, we headed with our coffees to the empty second floor, which overlooked a fog-drenched Lake Superior.

Wiggins and Rose believe the battle to retain Wisconsin's natural heritage is being waged on two planes: a temporal one of power politics and scientific argument, and a metaphysical one, where events, like the passage of GTac's mining bill, can be interpreted as part of Ojibwe mythology. During the mining fight, Rose sometimes drew an analogy between an Ojibwe monster called a *windigo* and GTac, a comparison Wiggins has occasionally echoed in public speeches. *Windigos* are giant, cannibalistic beasts, the ghosts of lost hunters forced by hunger to eat human flesh. "*Windigos* are the spirit of greed and excess," Rose said. Wiggins added: "The more they eat the hungrier they get."

Wiggins and Rose ran through a litany of the environmental changes Walker has supported. One was promoting the spread of frac sand mining, which has gone from just a few sites to more than a hundred, removing many of the hilltops of western Wisconsin in the process. A 2013 study by Crispin Pierce, a professor of environmental public health at the University of Wisconsin–Eau Claire, showed that areas surrounding active frac sand mining sites contained levels of tiny particulates, some of it carcinogenic silica, far exceeding the EPA's safe threshold. Another worry is a proposed 26,000-pig factory farm an Iowa company is trying to build near the shore of Lake Superior. The farm would generate millions of gallons of untreated liquid manure runoff, threatening two pristine watersheds that feed Lake Superior, which holds 10 percent of the world's fresh surface water. Just as distressing to Rose and Wiggins had been the reintroduction, for the first time in a half century, of a wolf hunt in Wisconsin. For decades, the wolf was listed as a state endangered species until a Department of Natural Resources management program fostered a rebound. Walker's hunt allowed for a target wolf population significantly below what most wildlife biologists say is necessary to sustain the animal's long-term stability. Wiggins and Rose are well versed in the scientific cases against these policies—Rose has a degree in biology—but they also see the dangers allegorically. "In prophecy, they tell us we're living in the age of the seven fires," Rose said. He began telling the Ojibwe version of creation.

"The world was created by the Great Spirit, according to the greatest vision of all time," he said. "First the physical world, then the plant world, the animal world, and last of all the human world. Let's skip part of that—it takes a long time to tell that. Let's go to the human world, where the Great Spirit came down to the earth and took particles and dust from mother earth, placed it in the sacred shell, the one we call the *megis*, and breathed life into it. The Great Spirit then lowered Anishinaabe from the sky world down to meet his mother." Rose took my pen and spelled "Anishinaabe," which means "original people" in Ojibwe, in my notebook. "His mother was Mother Earth, and so the first steps that he took on Mother Earth"—Rose abruptly put his coffee down, stood up, and briefly demonstrated that dance—"were *those* dances. When we bring the shakers and percussion instruments into our ceremonial lodges, we commemorate the sound that was heard out of the darkness of the void even before the creation." Rose paused as the waitress refilled our coffees. "Oh, thank you, Melinda," he said.

"The Great Spirit looked out into the darkness of the void," Rose continued. "The only thing that filled the emptiness of the void was a sound. The Great Spirit decided to send thought waves out all over the darkness of the void, all over the universe. In doing so, the Great Spirit expended a great deal of energy. After sending those thought waves out all over the universe, the Great Spirit lapsed into a deep sleep. While in that deep sleep, he was to experience the greatest vision that the universe has ever known. In that vision, the Great Spirit saw, the four orders of creation. He also felt all of these human emotions that went along with it. When the Great Spirit woke up, he decided to create everything that had been experienced in the vision. At the onset of the creation, everything was pure energy. Or we might say: pure spirit. For everything to take on a materialistic form, a corporeal form, the Great Spirit remembered that sound that had been heard even before the creation."

Rose tapped a loud beat on the table. "And the sound had a rhythm," he said, smiling. "The Great Spirit created all of these natural rhythms: we have day and night; at this latitude, we have four seasons; the tide flows and the heart beats." He tapped a single beat. (The word for "heartbeat" and "drum"—*deweyigan*—is the same, he noted.) "When we use these shakers, these percussion instruments, we are commemorating that sound that was heard even before the creation. Then the Great Spirit lowers Anishinaabe down to meet his mother and asks Anishinaabe—original man—to go out and to walk the earth—*bimosewin aki*—and name all things in the garden that was created.

"Anishinaabe expressed a loneliness, he didn't have a companion, so the Great Spirit sent *ma'iingan*, that's a wolf, to be his companion. And they walked the earth together. They were companions and in time became blood brothers. And the Great Spirit spoke to them again, so both *ma'iingan*—the wolf—and Anishinaabe—original man—stood in the presence of the Great Spirit. The Great Spirit spoke to them. 'In many ways, the two of you are alike. When you take a mate, it will be for life, your social order will be very complex.' And so Anishinaabe was given the totemic system, the clan system; *ma'iingan*, the wolf, was given the wolf pack. 'Both of you will make a living by the chase. Both of you will be excellent hunters.' And there were prophecies then. The Great Spirit spoke to them: 'From this day forward, I am going to put you on separate paths.' And this leads up to our prophecy.

"I talked about these different ages. We've recently entered into the age of the seventh fire, maybe just prior to when the Berlin Wall came down." Rose laughed. "I don't know *exactly* when it happened. But the Great Spirit spoke of a fork in the road. And right now, all humankind is standing at that fork in the road. And we'll be confronted with a choice. One fork in the road was said to be a hard surface. Today we see that as the fast lane, as that highway that pollutes and upsets the natural balance. The other lane is the more natural path. And it depends on which choice that humankind makes as to what will happen when the next new age is ushered in.

"This is where the wolf comes in. Whenever human beings encroach on a wolf's territory, the wolf retreats into what we know as the wilderness today. The wolf is a very powerful symbol of what little wilderness we have left. The Great Spirit said the time might come when you, *ma'iingan*, the wolf, you may no longer have a place to retreat. If that happens, you'll soon pass out of existence: You'll become extinct. And *you*, Anishinaabe, if your brother passes out of existence, you'll soon follow. You'll die of a great loneliness of spirit. And *you*, Anishinaabe, if you pass out of existence, all other humans will soon follow. The fate of *ma'iingan*, the wolf, as well as the fate of Anishinaabe and the human race, will be the same."

CROSSING UNDER THE Namekagon, the free-flowing river in northern Wisconsin that Gaylord Nelson vowed to defend before he died, is Line 61, a pipeline carrying tar-sands crude. Like GTac's mining bill, it is another emblem heralding the end of local control over Wisconsin environmental law. The pipeline, which cuts a diagonal swath across the length of the state, is owned by Enbridge, a $40-billion Canadian company that has been responsible for several hundred spills in the past decade. One of them—in 2010 near Marshall, Michigan— was the largest and most expensive inland oil spill in American history.

Line 61 is part of Enbridge's vast Lakehead System, a pipeline network running through Wisconsin, Minnesota, and Michigan that carries 13 percent of all US petroleum imports. The fight over the more well-known Keystone XL involved millions of dollars in advertising, dozens of activists arrested outside the White House, the rejection of the pipeline by President Obama, and the rescinding of that action by President Trump. Enbridge's plans, however, received little national attention. "Enbridge was very clever," Anthony Swift, a staff attorney for the National Resources Defense Council deeply involved in the Keystone fight, told me. "Keystone is one pipeline; what Enbridge did is break up its pipeline into half a dozen pieces." Unlike Keystone, Line 61 does not cross a border, so it did not require a presidential permit.

Over the opposition of a group of Wisconsin environmentalists, Enbridge mustered an increase of Line 61's capacity, making it a third larger than the projected capacity of Keystone. Before the expansion, Line 61, which was built in 2007, moved 400,000 barrels of tar sands and lighter conventional crude oil a day from Superior, in the state's far northern corner, to refineries in metropolitan Chicago or, through a network of connecting pipelines, to the Gulf Coast. In 2014, Enbridge sought to increase that, in stages, to 1.2 million barrels per day. Nonetheless, Wisconsin's DNR mandated just a single public hearing—for an air-quality permit related to storage tanks that would be built in Superior. The DNR maintained that a 2006 environmental assessment addressed all relevant safety concerns.

That 2006 DNR analysis took place four years before Enbridge's largest spill, in July 2010, which flooded Michigan's Kalamazoo River, near Marshall, with more than 840,000 gallons of tar-sands crude and cost the company $1.2 billion to clean up. The cost exceeded the cap on Enbridge's liability insurance by nearly $600 million. (The company paid the difference.) The Marshall spill demonstrated how much more destructive spills of tar sands crude are compared with spills of lighter crude. To move through a pipeline, tar-sands oil needs to be mixed with chemical solvents. When the spilled mixture was exposed to air, the chemical components, including carcinogenic benzene, separated and released toxic gases, which forced many people to evacuate their homes. Meanwhile, the heavier tar sands sank, which required a destructive dredging of the Kalamazoo River.

Although Enbridge completed the cleanup effort, the Environmental Protection Agency asserts that oil remains in the Kalamazoo River. In a scathing 2012 assessment of Enbridge's response, the National Transportation Safety Board likened the company's employees to "Keystone Kops," detailing their unconscionable lapses in the spill's aftermath. Since the Marshall spill, the company has built a new command center in Edmonton and invested $4 billion in maintenance, emergency response, and other safety improvements. Despite all this, 4,000 gallons of tar-sands crude spilled in January 2014 from the Alberta Clipper, the pipeline feeding Line 61.

The lack of oversight is unsurprising, given Governor

Walker's industry-friendly vision for the DNR. In December 2010, when Walker announced his first nominee to lead the agency, he said he wanted someone with a "Chamber of Commerce mentality." Walker's choice, Cathy Stepp, fit the bill. A former state senator who quit politics to run her family's construction business, Stepp was already a fierce critic of the agency she had been chosen to lead. In 2009, on a conservative blog, she railed against the DNR, calling its biologists "unelected bureaucrats" who "tend to be anti-development, anti-transportation, and pro-garter snakes." In 2015, she recounted in a speech how a DNR employee told her that the agency's "customers" were "clean air and clean water." Stepp countered: "Well, the last time I checked, they don't pay taxes and they don't sign our paychecks." Besides scrubbing references to climate change from the agency's website, she oversaw a dramatic decline in fines for pollution violations and issued no objection to Walker slashing more than half of the agency's scientists. (In 2017, Stepp left Wisconsin to take a job with the Trump administration as an administrator for the EPA.)

Line 61's opponents focused on Enbridge's need for new pump stations, which required a conditional-use permit from many of the counties in which they are built. Enbridge quickly secured these permits from each county except Dane, the state's second most populous. At an April 2015 meeting of Dane County's five-member Zoning and Land Regulation Committee, the committee voted to require Enbridge to carry a more comprehensive—and expensive—kind of liability insurance than it had during the Marshall spill. While county governments cannot override federal or state law, there is some precedent for attaching financial requirements to permits. Opponents believed that if Enbridge was forced to buy insurance to cover a Marshall-size spill, the price of expansion could become too onerous.

Several months before that vote, however, three lawyers representing Enbridge had met privately with a few county officials, including Patrick Miles, the chairman of Dane County's zoning committee, and presented a white paper outlining the company's position: The county, it said, did not have the legal right to attach insurance requirements to its permit. Miles told me the implication was clear: The company would sue if need be. Despite the pressure, Miles and the rest of the committee voted, 5–0, to mandate the insurance requirements. "My hands are tied, but I'm doing what I can to raise public awareness," Miles told me. "If that means we go to court and lose, then that's we do."

Instead, Enbridge and its supporters appear to have employed a more reliable tactic: legislating their prerogatives. In July 2015, an anonymous state legislator inserted a last-minute clause into the state budget prohibiting any town or county from imposing insurance requirements "on an operator of an interstate hazardous liquid pipeline." The action nullified Dane County's zoning committee. Though Enbridge denied it was involved with drafting the measure, and the legislator who authored it remains unknown, another last-minute budget addition benefiting the company is suggestive. Drafting documents obtained through an open-records request by Wisconsin Public Radio revealed that Enbridge's lawyers supplied the precise language for a clause to grant the company the right to seize private property, if necessary, so an adjacent pipeline can be built alongside Line 61 to deliver even more tar-sands crude.

REPUBLICAN LEGISLATORS HAD little to fear electorally, even after companies like Enbridge and GTac were exposed drafting legislation that benefited the firms at the public's expense. Their hold on power was supported by a robust conservative infrastructure that could help shape public opinion, enormous amounts of dark money to buttress their campaigns, and a weak opposition party. Another tool they would have was Wisconsin's restrictive voter-ID law, which was passed in 2011 and, after surviving many court challenges, put into effect for the 2016 election. The extent of the law's impact is still being measured, but its intent was made clear by Todd Allbaugh, a former aide to Republican state senator Dale Schultz, in testimony he delivered at a 2016 trial brought by plaintiffs arguing the law violated the federal Voting Rights Act. Allbaugh described a closed-door Republican caucus meeting he attended, observing that Republican senators were "giddy" about the law's ability to cement their power. One of them, he said, Mary Lazich, argued on behalf of the bill because it would diminish voter turnout in Democratic strongholds. Another senator, Leah Vukmir, the former ALEC national state chairwoman, was "frothing at the mouth," he said, over the voter-ID law's potential to maintain Republican political domination.

While the law did not go into effect immediately because it was challenged in court, the extreme Republican gerrymandering hatched in secret at the office of Michael Best & Friedrich had a far more immediate and deleterious impact on Wisconsin's democracy. Walker signed the bill privately on August 9, 2011, the day of the first wave of recall elections. The gerrymandering would soon play a decisive role in the state's politics: In November 2012, Republicans entered the election with 58 state assembly seats, received a total of 175,000 fewer votes for their state assembly candidates, and still gained two seats, giving them a 60–39 majority.

One Democrat who managed to hang on was Fred Kessler, a seventy-eight-year-old assemblyman and former Milwaukee circuit judge. But it wasn't easy for him. "They literally moved a ward of about 2,500 people out of my district out of the 57,000 people that belonged in it," Kessler, who has a Dutch beard, oval glasses, and an easygoing laugh, told me over coffee on Milwaukee's East Side. The boundaries for Kessler's new district included portions of Waukesha County and Milwaukee's wealthiest suburbs, two of the most Republican areas of the state. "I said, my God, why would they do this?" Kessler told me. "Why would they target me?" The assault on Kessler also involved a more personal, symbolic insult: "They took my house out of my district," he said. A few years earlier, Kessler and his wife, Joan, an appellate-court judge, had fulfilled a long-held dream to build their own house, which was solidly within Kessler's district until Republicans carved out a portion of his subdivision. Winning in his new district would be impossible, but Kessler realized that he was only a few blocks from the edge of another district, which contained eighty percent of his old constituents. He decided to move. "My wife was not happy," he said. "But I said I'm not going to let those SOBs get away with that."

After the Republican gerrymandering plan was unveiled

in July 2011, Kessler gave a floor speech denouncing it. "In a landslide, we could win fifty seats," Kessler predicted for the Democrats in his speech. "In a normal year, we're going to get forty." Kessler knew the intricacies of redistricting better than anyone else in the legislature, and probably the entire state. He began working on the issue in 1964, when the Wisconsin Supreme Court ordered reapportionment of legislative districts, because rural areas had been overrepresented. Later that year, the Supreme Court issued its decision in *Reynolds v. Sims*, which ruled that every state legislative district must be as equal in population as possible. *Reynolds v. Sims* also mandated that states across the country periodically update the reapportionment of their districts. Kessler was then serving his second term in the assembly and was chairman of its elections committee. In 1972, he was the principal Democrat on the governor's Reapportionment Commission, established for that year's redistricting. Kessler went on to work as a judge until the late 1980s, when he began working as a labor arbitrator and a redistricting consultant.

Nevada's Democrats hired Kessler in 1991, when the party briefly held control of all branches of state government. "I'm going to draw a partisan map, but it's not going to be really excessively partisan," Kessler told me, explaining his philosophy. "And when I'm done with the partisan stuff that I think is reasonable, then what I will do is I will go around to the Republicans and I will say, 'Did I screw you by accident? Did I take your base of support out of your district? Did I put your primary opponent in your district? Can I make some corrections that would make you at least feel this was a little bit more fair?' And I always did that." In Nevada, Kessler's success can be judged by the fact that only four Republicans voted against his map. "You're never going to raise a court case, if the majority of the Republicans voted for it," he said. "I understood that, and I thought anybody who is smart doing redistricting would do that. Why do you want to anger your opponents so badly that they're going to go into court?"

Wisconsin's law, in contrast, was immediately challenged in federal court and by lawsuits against the state over diluting Latino voter power and disenfranchising 300,000 voters who were suddenly moved out of their districts, depriving them of their right to vote in the 2012 state senate elections. Kessler soon began thinking of bringing his own case against Wisconsin's redistricting. He knew that Justice Anthony Kennedy had expressed reservations about partisan gerrymandering in a 2004 case.

In 2013, Kessler began recruiting like-minded, equally prominent opponents from Wisconsin's legal community, including his old friend from college, a University of Wisconsin law professor named Bill Whitford. No partisan gerrymandering case in the past three decades had ever gone beyond a motion to dismiss, but Kessler believed Wisconsin's law went far beyond normal partisan gerrymandering. In 2014, Kessler came across an article by Nicholas Stephanopoulos, a University of Chicago law professor, and Eric McGhee, a research fellow at a California think tank, that created a new metric they called the "efficiency gap" to determine the amount of wasted votes in a given year, and by extension the degree of partisanship. If the number of wasted votes was extremely high in one party's districts, it meant those voters were being packed in to dilute their strength. After analyzing every district in the

United States, Stephanopoulos determined that Wisconsin's state assembly was among the most gerrymandered of the last four decades in the country.

Bill Whitford became the named plaintiff in the case, which was filed in federal court in the western Wisconsin district in July 2015. Two weeks after Trump's victory, the three-judge federal panel ruled that the maps enacted by Wisconsin's Republican-controlled legislature in 2011 were an unconstitutional partisan gerrymander that violated both the Equal Protection Clause of the Fourteenth Amendment and the First Amendment's protection of freedom of association. The ruling was the first time in over three decades that a federal court invalidated a redistricting plan for partisan bias, and it was almost immediately appealed to the Supreme Court, which heard oral arguments in the case in October 2017. Justice Kennedy asked Wisconsin's solicitor general the first question. "Suppose the Court . . . decided that this is a First Amendment issue?" His query seemed to suggest that he might find favor with the Democrats' argument that gerrymandering violates the First Amendment's right to freedom of association.

While the effect of gerrymandering on the 2012 Wisconsin election was most obvious and defining, it lingered in subtler ways in the two subsequent elections, in which Democrats lost even more seats. "In 2014, we didn't have enough candidates," Kessler said. "It was very hard to get candidates once you got clobbered in a landslide year. The same in 2016: We just had a hard time getting candidates. You look at the result, and you see that the last time we had a candidate who was well financed, they got clobbered. It's demoralizing. And then you have Democrats like myself in these seventy-plus-percent districts."

As we were leaving, Kessler told me about the documents in the case from Michael Best & Friedrich. After a lengthy battle with both senate Democrats and the federal courts, Republicans, who argued the documents were protected by attorney-client privilege, were forced to turn them over. One of the computers that were also supposed to be turned over had likely been tampered with, and a hard drive of a second computer had been wiped clean. In 2016, however, the plaintiffs in *Gill v. Whitford* were able to hire a former Secret Service computer forensics analyst, who retrieved the contents of a hard drive on a third computer. One document was a note between Tad Ottman, Scott Fitzgerald's aide, and Adam Foltz, Jeff Fitzgerald's aide, discussing Kessler's opposition to the bill. "The day after I made my speech on the floor, when I said that the Democrats will not win more than forty seats under this map, they sent an email," Kessler told me. "It said: 'Kessler was wrong, they'll only win thirty-nine.'"

THE CONSERVATIVE EFFORT to influence Wisconsin politics goes much deeper than the governorship and state legislature. In March 2014, for example, Americans for Prosperity, began a campaign to sway the outcome of elections for the Iron County board of supervisors; its members are volunteers, and their candidacies normally go unchallenged. The home of GTac's mine site, Iron County has a population of less than 6,000 people. Winning county board candidates typically receive between 100 and 150 votes.

Despite the passage of GTac's bill, the county board has some regulatory authority, a fact that rankled AFP. The organization sent out two rounds of mailers, one of which featured a picture of a bearded, apparently homeless man holding a cardboard sign that read: "Please Help Need a Job." The flyer noted that Iron County was being targeted by "wealthy environmental groups from outside of Wisconsin" who don't care if "our families go on welfare." At the bottom were the names and home phone numbers of seven "radical environmentalists" whom AFP claimed opposed GTac's mine. One of those names was Karl Krall, a member of Operating Engineers Local 139 and a strong supporter of the mine. Krall had even been one of the union members Governor Walker used as a prop during a 2013 speech when he was trying to sell the bill by promising that the company would use union labor.

But AFP's interference in the Iron County board races backfired; four of the nine candidates it supported lost, including three incumbents, a rarity in such races. Ultimately, in fact, even after GTac's reshaping of state legislation and its multiyear battle against environmentalists and activists, the mining company pulled out of Iron County, withdrawing its plan for the controversial open-pit mine in February 2015.

Still, similar efforts by AFP to penetrate Wisconsin's political substrata followed. Around the same time, AFP tried to sway the outcome of elections for the Kenosha School Board. But the pettiest and most revealing campaign was directed at Gaylord Nelson's daughter, Tia, who headed an obscure state agency called the Board of Commissioners of Public Lands— until a conservative effort to oust her pushed Nelson to resign in 2015.

BCPL, as it is known, is one of the state's smallest and oldest agencies. It was authorized by the state's constitution in 1848, when Wisconsin was admitted to the Union. The agency manages close to 80,000 acres of land, most of it in the northern part of the state—the remnant of a larger gift from the federal government, a common practice for new states in the nineteenth century, when the federal government had little money but a great deal of land. Wisconsin sold most of this donated land, but the state had been unable to sell these acres, so they were managed, with the profits from forestry used to benefit public school libraries.

In November 2014, a Tea Party Republican named Matt Adamczyk was elected state treasurer. Adamczyk's platform consisted of a promise to abolish the treasurer position, which is largely powerless but, along with the secretary of state and attorney general, is one of three commissioners overseeing BPCL. Before he was even sworn in, Adamczyk requested from Nelson years of cellphone, email, and leave records. He soon discovered that her office subscribed to five newspapers— three from Wisconsin as well as the *Wall Street Journal* and the *New York Times*. "He went through them and all of our expenditures," Tia Nelson told me when I visited her in her modest ranch home in a Madison suburb, a few blocks from the governor's mansion. "That's where he found the expenditure for the *New York Times*, which he objected to."

Nelson wrote Adamczyk an email noting all the papers the agency subscribed to, and asking if he objected only to her subscription of the *New York Times*. "If he said, 'I don't think you should use state resources to buy any out-of-state newspaper,' I wouldn't have agreed with it, but at least it would have had a line of reasoning," she told me. "But he wrote back 'yes.'"

Adamczyk was equally concerned that Nelson's name

appeared on BPCL's letterhead just below the names of the commissioners. According to the minutes of a board meeting on January 2, 2015, "Commissioner Adamczyk said he felt 'passionately that the name Tia Nelson should not be listed.' He again stated his concern about her name being listed directly below the commissioners' names. MOTION: Commissioner Adamczyk moved that the executive secretary's name be removed from the letterhead. A second to the motion was not made."

The opposition got more substantive when Adamczyk learned that Nelson had served on a climate-change citizen task force in 2007 convened by the former governor Jim Doyle. Adamczyk alleged that Nelson had engaged in active "time theft" against the citizens of Wisconsin for serving on the climate-change task force during work hours. He called a vote of the three commissioners to have Nelson fired.

The effort failed when the Republican attorney general, Brad Schimel, sided with the longtime Democratic secretary of state, Doug La Follette, a distant relative of Bob La Follette. (In July 2015, Doug La Follette was himself a victim of Republican vindictiveness when legislators moved his expansive tenth-floor office overlooking the state capitol to a small, windowless room in the building's basement.) It did not matter that the climate-change task force had included a representative of every major utility, a conservative Republican farmer, and a Republican legislator, as well as a Democratic legislator. Nor that the vast majority of the task force's recommendations were unanimously supported by industry, environmentalists, and legislators. "It never occurred to me that someone serving in state government would not accept a gubernatorial request to serve on a citizen task force aimed at making Wisconsin more energy independent," Nelson said.

At a meeting to address the issue, Adamczyk and his fellow Republican Schimel briefly put Nelson under a gag order, preventing her and her staff from even speaking the words "climate change" during work hours. In an interview with the *New York Times*, Adamczyk said it would be permissible to briefly talk about climate "by the water cooler," in the same manner as a Wisconsin Badgers basketball game. A public backlash caused Schimel to partially reverse himself, allowing the words to be spoken but forbidding on-the-job advocacy related to climate change.

In July 2015, Nelson, exhausted from the conflict, resigned. "I do think the challenge that climate change poses to society must be discussed," she said in a press conference. The issue has resonance for Nelson, not only because of her father but because of her own career: She moved back to Wisconsin from Washington, DC, after seventeen years of climate-change advocacy for the Nature Conservancy. "I had traveled the world," she told me. "I'd gone to most of the UN climate meetings, I was in Rio in 1992 when George Bush signed the Convention on Climate Change, and I was in Kyoto in 1997 when the Kyoto Protocol was passed. Truth be told, I had left climate-change work because I was weary and heartsick at the lack of progress."

In addition to his gag order, Adamczyk had instructed Nelson to remove any reference to "climate change" from BPCL's website. That step was a precursor to the vanishing, in December 2016, of the issue from the website of the Wisconsin DNR. For several years before that deletion, the DNR had been gradually watering down climate-change references on its website, but it continued to host a page dedicated to the effects of global warming on the Great Lakes. "Earth's climate is changing," the page used to read. "Human activities that increase heat-trapping ('greenhouse') gases are the main cause. Earth's average temperature has increased 1.4° F since 1850, and the eight warmest years on record have occurred since 1998."

Now the same page states: "As it has done throughout the centuries, the earth is going through a change. The reasons for this change at this particular time in the earth's long history are being debated and researched by academic entities outside the Wisconsin Department of Natural Resources." As Tia Nelson noted to me, climate-change language has now been scrubbed from every Wisconsin state agency website except one: the Division of Emergency Management.

THE BRADLEY FOUNDATION has poured millions of dollars into all three of Wisconsin's conservative think tanks; in 2009, a third of the budget of Wisconsin's MacIver Institute was given by the foundation. While Scott Walker has denied that the think tanks had anything to do with Act 10, a post written by Brian Fraley, the MacIver Institute's communications director, on the organization's website three weeks after Walker won, and before he had signaled any attack on collective bargaining, suggests otherwise. "The next 60 days should bring a sea change to Wisconsin's anti-job creation, anti-innovation labor laws," Fraley wrote. "Two simple but fundamental steps to kick start the Wisconsin economy and get our state budget mess resolved would be to repeal collective bargaining for public employees and to make Wisconsin a right-to-work state."

In September 2017, I arrived at the Lion House and followed a Bradley Foundation secretary into the elegant, austere library for a meeting with Rick Graber, the group's current president. For decades, Graber, an Ohio native, worked as a corporate attorney in Milwaukee before serving as Wisconsin's Republican Party state chair and then, during the George W. Bush administration, as ambassador to the Czech Republic. The library's shelves were lined with conservative classics: Whittaker Chambers's *Witness*; a bound set of Cato's *Letters*, donated as a gift to the Bradley Foundation by the like-minded, libertarian Cato Institute. I also noticed a few books critical of the mission, including Jane Mayer's *Dark Money* and Jason Stahl's *Right Moves*. Framed pictures of medal-wearing recipients of the foundation's $250,000 Bradley Prize hung alongside a painting of the Milwaukee Brewers' stadium; an array of Germanic beer steins lined the tops of the bookshelves. After a few minutes, Graber, a trim, white-haired sixty-one-year-old dressed in a navy-blue suit, entered and took a seat at a large table near an ornate bar cart.

Graber was named to head the Bradley Foundation in the summer of 2016. He told me he was "shocked" by Trump's victory that fall. "I spent much of the election cycle in Washington, DC," he said. "I was not here on the ground until late in the process." I asked if he thought there was a connection between the result and the Bradley Foundation's work. "I think it's very difficult to tie election results to that kind of infrastructure directly, but the fact of the matter is Wisconsin is a different state politically," he said. "Certainly, it's different than when

I was Republican Party chairman. Bradley has played a role in building the conservative infrastructure in the state that didn't exist fifteen, twenty years ago. There are now public-interest law firms, think tanks promoting a lot of the ideas you see playing out: free markets, limited government, federalism." (Those three priorities also happen to be the exact motto of ALEC, a group the Bradley Foundation has funded since the mid-1980s.) Graber told me the foundation's main goal is to fulfill Harry and Lynde Bradley's vision. "We sit around this table all the time and say, 'What would Lynde and Harry Bradley do?'"

Just before the 2016 election, hackers from a group called Anonymous Poland breached the Bradley Foundation's server and briefly posted tens of thousands of the organization's documents online. Daniel Bice, an investigative reporter at the *Milwaukee Journal Sentinel*, confirmed the documents' authenticity and published a three-part series based on them. One document included a consultant's assessment of the states most ripe for political transformation. Colorado topped that list, and the Bradley Foundation gave $575,000 to five organizations in the state in 2016. Another document, a staff recommendation to approve an application for a three-year, $1.5-million grant that Bradley would give to the Freedom Foundation, an anti-union think tank based in Olympia, Washington, revealed the patience and long view of the Bradley Foundation's strategy. The Freedom Foundation is focused on diminishing the strength of unions in the same way Walker succeeded in doing in Wisconsin. "The Pacific Coast as a region is more unionized than the Midwest, where so much employee-rights progress has been made recently," the recommendation read. "While this might be an argument to philanthropically invest else-where, or in another issue area, staff believes it to be a reason to go there." The grant would "educate union workers them-selves about their rights—which, if and when exercised would defund Big Labor."

"States truly are the laboratory where things change," Gra-ber said. "Look at this state: School choice and welfare reform started here. They didn't start at the federal level." Graber believes the same transformation is possible elsewhere. (One of the other Bradley documents Bice analyzed ranked states on their conservative infrastructure: "think tank(s)," "receptive policymakers," "opposition research," and "investigative jour-nalism"; Wisconsin was tied for the highest score.) "You go to places where you can move the needle and make a difference," he said. I asked if he believed he could export the foundation's success in Wisconsin to other states, places that might be viewed as impregnable "blue walls," just as Wisconsin was not long ago. "Sure," Graber replied, without hesitation. "That's where it goes. Wisconsin is a laboratory for the rest of the country."

"SO WHY DO WE CONTINUE?" Peter Anderson, a founder of the Madison chapter of 350.org, Bill McKibben's climate-change organization, wondered aloud. He was driving his gray Prius to Medina, the site of Enbridge's new Dane County pump sta-tion and a painful reminder to Anderson of his defeat by the company and its allies in the Wisconsin legislature. Anderson, a voluble New York transplant who speaks in a gravelly Bronx accent, admitted to a growing sense of fatalism about staving off climate-change disaster. "If people changed their mind-set about what gives them satisfaction from *things* to family, it's eminently doable," he said. "But that's a huge hurdle. So why do I continue? I'm seventy years old. I have all these friends and they go to Europe or Asia three or four times a year. In between that they're fixing up their kitchen for fifty, sixty, seventy thousand dollars. That's how they consume their days." He paused and stared at the passing farmland. "I have maybe ten good years left. I have four kids and two grandkids: How can you *not* try, you know?"

Anderson designed the strategy to try and force Enbridge to buy additional insurance to cover a potential spill. "It's the marketplace's truth meter of where risk lies," Anderson said. If underwriters believe a project is safe, premiums will be low, but if the risk is high, expensive premiums might compel a company to abandon the project. Anderson learned that lesson during the 1970s, when he and other activists took on the nuclear-power industry. "There's no stake in the heart of nuclear power that killed it," he said. "It was the fact that the economic conditions could no longer attract capital to sustain it. It becomes riskier over time, compared to what it was, and more uncomfortable for the existing investors. They start saying, 'I'm not going to do this,' and the cost of capital goes up, and more and more wheels fall off the cart. The lesson from the nuclear fight is victory often comes from a battle of attrition."

Despite his urban upbringing, Anderson's environmentalism took hold as a teenager. "I remember the 1965 blackout," he said. "A window in our apartment faced south, and we saw Manhattan starting to go black, black, black, black, black. It was a mind-blowing event that showed the precariousness of these technological marvels." Another turning point came during college, at Cornell, when a young sociology professor abruptly told Anderson and his classmates that he was retiring the following year, selling all of his possessions except a record player, and heading to the Grand Canyon to become a nature poet. Instead of sociology readings, the professor assigned environmental writers like Loren Eiseley and Joseph Wood Krutch, a mid-twentieth-century critic whose skepticism about the value of technological progress resonated with Anderson. "The most important part of our lives—our sensations, emotions, desires, and aspirations," Krutch once wrote, "takes place in a universe of illusions which science can attenuate or destroy, but which it is powerless to enrich."

In 1970, Anderson moved to Wisconsin to work on the congressional campaign of Doug La Follette, an ardent environmentalist. After La Follette narrowly lost the Democratic primary, Anderson went to graduate school in Ohio, but he dropped out after a week and returned to Wisconsin. With La Follette, he cofounded Wisconsin's Environmental Decade, paying himself a salary of twenty dollars a week. Too broke to afford rent, he slept on the floor of a committee room in the state capitol. By 1980, he was earning $20,000 a year and living in a rooming house, but with the organization's relative prosperity came problems. "When you get money, you have salaries—and a lot of tensions," Anderson said. He started managing the group's canvassing operations, which became increasingly difficult to sustain. "We had 120 people on staff and four offices," he said. "I would wake up in the middle of the night on Tuesday and Wednesday and think: How the fuck am I going to be able to make payroll on Friday?" By 1989, it became too difficult to recruit canvassers. "Under Reagan, activism was no longer cool," he said. He quit and started working in the recycling industry. But in 1997, an extreme El Niño temporarily warmed the planet by 1 degree Fahrenheit and led to worldwide droughts, flooding, and a widespread recognition of the potentially calamitous effects of climate change. Anderson decided to return to grassroots organizing and has been dedicated to climate-change advocacy ever since.

From the rustic state highway we pulled off of, the new Medina pump station was barely visible. But planted behind the old pump station, which was not demolished, sits the new, undistinguished beige building. Orange posts dotting the grassy landscape read "Warning: Petroleum Pipeline." The posts appear across the entire state, marking Line 61's underground route. During construction of the new station, Enbridge fenced off the area and hired sheriff's deputies in anticipation of protests, but there were none. Anderson jogged eagerly up to the top of a hill, ignoring "no trespassing" signs, to get a better view of the new station. A worker mowing the grass stopped momentarily to stare at us before returning to the lawn. "The company would love to sue us for trespassing," Anderson said. "But these guys work for the local power company and don't give a shit."

On the hill, Anderson explained how he hadn't given up, even though the new fuel station was built and Enbridge might be pumping as much as 1.2 million barrels a day of tar-sands crude. Despite this, he had persuaded several nearby landowners to file a lawsuit on behalf of Dane County, contending that the provision inserted into the budget was not retroactive, so the county's stipulation mandating insurance prior to the budget passing was in effect. In July 2016, a circuit judge ruled

against the landowners, but the plaintiffs appealed that decision. Anderson returned to the slow, attritional success of the
campaign against nuclear power. "We want to win," he said.
"But if we lose, we win.

"Democracy measures intensity, not numbers," Anderson
continued. He described his arrest with Bill McKibben and
others protesting the Keystone pipeline at the White House,
in 2011. The Tea Party was new then, and ascendant, and had
helped block the Obama administration's modest cap-and-
trade bill from even being brought up for a vote in the Senate.
Anderson did not want the resistance to Keystone to be as pas-
sive. "Bill McKibben had a plan that fifty people are going to
be there every day, getting arrested, for the last two weeks of
August," Anderson said. "But somebody in the Obama White
House wanted to scare us off. So we got thrown in jail, in a
cell block underneath Judiciary Square, which has terrible
conditions." Anderson was held there for three days with fifty
others. "We were in the holding pen for five hours, packed
like sardines. All there was was one little toilet in one corner,
and when you're older . . ." He paused. "It was not fun. They
don't have any mattresses, it's just a steel plate, and I have a
bad back. When I woke up the next morning, I had lost sensation in my right toe. I still don't have sensation there, but you
say to yourself: 'I can hang in there for three days.' The reality
is that the fossil-fuel industry is so strong, the idea that we're
going to win by letters to editors and picketing—it's not going
to happen."

We walked back to the car and got in. "Besides," he said,
before starting the drive, "I could not *not* be there."

———

BEFORE I LEFT ASHLAND, Rose returned to the prophecy of the seventh fire. "Anishinaabe had been given a very special gift," he said. "We use the word *mashkiki* for that gift. Loosely interpreted, it means 'medicine.' But *mashkiki* also encompasses the knowledge and wisdom of how to live in harmony with the four orders of creation: the physical, plant, animal, and human worlds. That's at the very foundation of our Native spirituality. It has nothing to do with salvation. It's a different worldview altogether.

"Along with a gift as powerful as that goes a great responsibility," he continued. "In this age of the seventh fire, we turn and we look back, and we retrace our footsteps. Our footsteps take us back to ancient times and ancient knowledge. We begin to pick up those sacred bundles that have fallen by the wayside because of persecution from the US government and missionaries that tried to erase our identity. Our responsibility is to educate the new people as to how to live in harmony and balance with the natural world." He returned to the idea that humanity is at a perilous crossroads. "These corporate *windigos* have no respect for the natural world," he said. "Their motivation is based on greed and excess. When they acquire more materialistic possessions and money than what they can spend in generations, then they get into power and control, which is even worse." Rose laughed darkly. "That's where your democracy is threatened," he said. "That's what's happening right now."

7

WHICH SHALL RULE, WEALTH OR MAN?

The cost of the conservative war on Wisconsin's political legacy has mostly been borne by the state's citizens. Since 2011, Wisconsin has experienced a dramatic increase in child poverty rates, nonexistent wage growth, steep cuts to K–12 public schools and the state university system, and a significant decline in water quality. Minnesota, by contrast, has invested in its citizens and public institutions. In 2010, the state elected Mark Dayton, of the Democratic-Farmer-Labor Party, who pushed through a tax hike on Minnesota's wealthiest residents—one of the largest in the state's history—and used its revenue to fund all-day kindergarten, expand early childhood education programs, increase funding for the University of Minnesota (which began poaching professors from Wisconsin), and improve water quality.

While the two states' economies differ in significant ways (Wisconsin's is more dependent on manufacturing jobs, which are declining nationally), Minnesota has experienced higher wage growth, higher labor force participation, a lower unemployment rate, and better job growth in higher-wage occupations. Wisconsin, which has passed more than $8 billion in tax cuts since Walker took office, has a budget deficit of nearly $2 billion. The vast majority of those cuts have benefited corporations and the state's wealthiest citizens, at a time when Walker has been forced to issue bonds to fix Wisconsin's dilapidated roads.

Julie Allen, the Scandinavian studies professor, noted how crucial the trade-union movement and the communitarian ethos of Scandinavian Lutheranism had been in fostering the progressivism of the Upper Midwest. In both Wisconsin and Minnesota, that effort translated into strong support for public institutions like state government and their flagship universities. Allen believes that Minnesota's progressive tradition endured partly due to the state's continuous support for the public sector, a tradition that had eroded in Wisconsin before Walker. "Minnesotans have retained more trust in their institutions," she said. "That was lost in Wisconsin—and it wasn't something Scott Walker invented." Though Governor Jim Doyle, a Democrat, didn't carry out his 2002 promise to cut 10,000 state workers fully, his rhetoric helped pave the way for Walker's attack on state workers. "I've made deeper cuts [to state employees] than any governor's ever made," Doyle boasted to a reporter in December 2010, three months before Walker announced Act 10. During Allen's ten years of teaching at the University of Wisconsin, four of which were under Doyle, she got one raise.

Still, Allen loved teaching in Madison—until Walker and his allies made it unbearable. "The rhetoric coming from the governor and state legislature always seemed to be telling us how little our contributions mattered," she said. "We were just mooching off the taxpayer." Allen recently left Madison for Brigham

Young University, and feels valued at her new job. But there was much she missed about Wisconsin. "It was lovely the first five or six years," she said. "Then it got so painful." Like many UW faculty members, Allen believed fervently in the Wisconsin Idea and was heartbroken to see it banished from state government.

In 2015, Walker tried to erase the Wisconsin Idea more literally. Four decades earlier, core tenets of the Wisconsin Idea—service to the state's citizens, a search for truth—had been enshrined in statute. The mission of the university is "to extend knowledge and its application beyond the boundaries of its campuses," the 1974 law reads. "Inherent in this broad mission are methods of instruction, research, extended training and public service designed to educate people and improve the human condition. Basic to every purpose of the system is the search for truth."

Walker's 2015 budget struck these passages. His staff inserted a new clause that the university's mission would be "to meet the state's workforce needs." Walker never announced the change, but it was discovered by the Center for Media and Democracy, buried in the 1,800-page bill. The find prompted a massive and immediate backlash, which included some conservatives. Emails later released between University of Wisconsin administrators and Walker's staff revealed that the university was pressured to accept Walker's revision months earlier, but when Walker rescinded the change, he claimed it was merely a "drafting error."

A RED-WINGED BLACKBIRD darted across the windshield as I parked in front of Robert La Follette's childhood home in Argyle, a village of 850 people twenty miles from the Illinois border. In 2000, a group of civic-minded residents formed Historic Argyle, a local nonprofit, to save La Follette's crumbling home, then on a list of Wisconsin's ten most endangered historic properties. Fifteen years later, with the house largely restored, they marked the 160th anniversary of La Follette's birth with the first "La Follette Days," a chautauqua celebrating the birthday of Wisconsin's Progressive lion. At the third annual event, I joined a small crowd milling about on the front lawn, near a wooden stage straddled by a Wisconsin flag on one end and an American flag on the other. Neighbors caught up with one another, drinking beer in the late-afternoon sun, as they waited for a free talk by Jim Leary, a folklorist at the University of Wisconsin.

Leary has devoted his career to the Wisconsin Idea. Since the 1970s, he has exhumed the forgotten music and folklore of Wisconsin's immigrant and Native communities and brought his findings—the songs of French-Canadian lumberjacks, Finnish miners, Potawatomi ironworkers, and Mexican farmhands—to hundreds of small gatherings like this one. A bearded sixty-five-year-old with a graying ponytail and bushy eyebrows, Leary hopped on stage and began running through a playlist that recounted the state's history through labor songs like the a cappella "Cranberry Song," a lighthearted homage to transnational solidarity among cranberry pickers; "Corrido Pensilvanio," a Mexican-American ballad about steelworkers recruited from Texas who bump into a group of Italian women in Milwaukee on their journey to the Pennsylvania mills; and "Ironworker Blues," a Johnny Cash–tinged rockabilly tune written in the 1960s by an ironworker from northern Wisconsin named Dewain Olby.

After Leary's talk, the High Street Revelers, an old-time string band from Mineral Point, prepared to take the stage. Kristine O'Connor drank a beer in the backyard. O'Connor, a founding member of Historic Argyle, worked on the La Follette renovation, stripping century-old paint off the house with her husband. "If you walk down Main Street, you'll run into people who don't know La Follette even lived here," she said. "That's the main reason why we opened this up again. Because what he stood for was just—he was for the common person." She took a sip of beer. "I think living in Argyle formed a lot of his beliefs." O'Connor equally admired Belle La Follette, Bob's wife and the first woman to graduate from the University of Wisconsin Law School. She particularly liked how, when Bob and Belle married, in 1881, Belle made the Unitarian minister take the word "obey" out of their vows.

"To tell you the truth, I didn't know about Bob La Follette either, until I joined Historic Argyle," O'Connor admitted. She had joined only because she thought a tourist attraction might help her struggling town. "But the more I read about him, the more I thought, Gosh, we need him now." For many years, O'Connor worked at a local bank on Main Street, where she approved personal loans. Lafayette County is one of the poorer counties in Wisconsin, ranking fifty-first out of seventy-two in per capita income. "Divorces and medical bills," she said. "Those are the two things that can just destroy a family." O'Connor watched helplessly as Argyle grew depleted. "The area used to be full of family dairy farms, and most of them have died out," she said. "We've got big corporate farms around here. Some people lost their farms. As farmers got older, the majority of them just sold out, and the younger generation doesn't want a 24/7 day job. When I grew up, a mom and dad could run a farm, and the wife didn't have to work off the farm, you could make a living." Many of O'Connor's friends now commute from Argyle to Madison for work.

"We want people to be aware of Bob La Follette and the importance he has on Wisconsin history," she said. "I hate to say this, but people don't seem to be interested in history. Even local history. You know, they're concerned with putting a meal on the table and meeting their next car payment."

IN JUNE 2017, Randy Bryce officially launched his campaign against Paul Ryan with a two-minute video. It begins with President Trump introducing a smiling Ryan at a press conference focused on repealing Obamacare. "Everybody doesn't get what they want," Ryan says in a cutaway interview. The video moves to green Wisconsin farmland and then to Bryce and his mom, Nancy, sitting in her living room, as Nancy describes the pain from multiple sclerosis and the twenty medicines she needs to function. It's a poignant moment, and Bryce hugs her after she chokes up. Equally memorable is a taunt Bryce delivers at the end of the video. He is at a job site, wearing his hard hat and a blue denim shirt emblazoned with an ironworkers' union logo. "Let's trade places," Bryce says, staring hard at the camera. "Paul Ryan, you can come work the iron, and I'll go to DC." The video went viral. Within days, Bryce was appearing on multiple MSNBC shows, as well as on CNN and other networks.

Soon after the video was released, I saw Bryce at his official launch event in the gymlike meeting hall of UAW Local 72 in Kenosha. Red, white, and blue balloons decorated the hall, and at the end of his speech, everyone gathered together for a posed picture holding a "Randy Bryce" sign. Outside in the hallway, I saw Nancy Bryce, who arrived late. Her MS is making driving more difficult, and she seemed a bit disoriented. She was happy for Bryce, but she had always been happy for him, whether he was unloading boxes at a warehouse or appearing on national television. She never projected her ambitions onto him.

I saw Bryce again a month later in New York City, at a fundraiser at an East Village wine bar. The room was overstuffed with ironworkers, millennial office workers, and a few prominent supporters like Cynthia Nixon, who cohosted the event. Bryce had met earlier that day with New York's mayor, Bill de Blasio, who offered to help him in any way he could. Just two months earlier, Bryce had been struggling to pay his rent after being laid off from the Northwestern Mutual job. Now waiters in New York and Los Angeles recognized him. They called him "Ironstache," after the Twitter handle he came up with during the Act 10 fight, and begged him to defeat Ryan.

IN 2016, Kathy Cramer, a political scientist at the University of Wisconsin, published *The Politics of Resentment*, which detailed the anger in rural Wisconsin that Walker drew on—and stoked—in his attack on the public-sector unions. It was the product of five years of fieldwork: countless predawn drives to drop in on small-town diners, bait shops, and gas stations. Cramer met with thirty-nine different groups in all, including a few in urban and suburban areas, but she concentrated on rural communities. Sometimes her presence made people uncomfortable. On one visit to a group that met at a gas station along the Wisconsin River, the regulars, who had met with her three times before, got up from their table and stood on the other side of the room until she left. Most people were friendly, though, and grew more so over time. Many were thrilled that someone from the distant state capital, which they viewed with fascination and contempt, would be interested in them. Cramer methodically established trust with people who were deeply distrustful of what she represented: the university, Madison, professors. They opened up to her.

The daughter of two public school teachers, Cramer grew up in Grafton, a manufacturing town of ten thousand people on Lake Michigan. Her small-town upbringing and thick Wisconsin accent made it easy for her to ingratiate herself with people from across the state, but as a child she had also experienced some of the same resentment that propelled Act 10. "I was made aware we were sort of wealthy in town because my parents had decent, stable jobs," she said. People were particularly angry that her parents didn't work in the summer, a complaint echoed decades later by the people she interviewed. "They have so much awareness of how teachers' salaries are much higher than everyone else's in town," she said. "That they have health care. That they have pensions and summers off, and their union is protective. They say things like 'the lazy one will never get fired.'"

A Wisconsin labor leader once told me that Act 10 succeeded because Walker transformed the person who spent the day in a classroom teaching his child from "teacher" to "union member." Cramer's research amplified the point. The fierce pride rural people felt for their schools, she said, did not include the teachers who worked in them. "The schools themselves, especially the sports teams, are a source of identity for the community," she said. "A place for people to get together physically and psychologically. When I would hear griping about school consolidation, they often say things like, 'Once the school goes, we're done. That's the end of this place.'"

Cramer saw resentment intensify during the Act 10 protests. "Who are these people with all this time on their hands that they can protest during the day?" was a common complaint she heard. "They saw the protests as an unruly, violent mob, defacing the capitol," she said, an idea trumpeted incessantly by conservative media. In one notorious example during the occupation of the capitol, Bill O'Reilly's program featured a dispatch that cut immediately to violent clashes between police officers and protesters. The only glitch was the California palm trees one could make out in the distance. (After the segment aired, demonstrators in Madison began bringing inflatable plastic palm trees to the capitol.)

Despite the passage of Act 10, Cramer told me her subjects were unsatisfied. "They are still angry," she said. "Less angry than in the moment it happened. In that moment, the number of people who told me their sisters weren't talking to them was remarkable. A lot of that has quieted down, but it's not like they feel that public employees are now on the same playing field. They still feel the public employees are getting too much, because they think they complain too much." Cramer's fieldwork gels with the findings of a 2005 study published in the *Australian Journal of Psychology* that showed that resentment persisted even after the object of the resentment was cut down. In other words, taking something—higher wages, benefits—away from someone else won't make you feel better about not having those things. An earlier study published by the same authors showed that when people were victorious over someone they thought was undeserving, as Cramer's subjects thought of the public employees, it produced schadenfreude, not empathy.

The morning she spoke with me, Cramer had met with one of her regular groups in southeastern Wisconsin. It was late June, eight months after the election, and she asked the participants if they were happy with Trump. "They feel positive about him," she said. "I shouldn't be surprised by that. We know that when people make a choice, they process information accordingly. They're going to convince themselves they made the right choice." I asked her what they wanted him to do. "One of my favorite questions is, 'So what are you hoping is different?'" she said. "'Not much.' The typical answer is: Nothing is going to change around here. I don't hear them believing that he's going to change their community, or their life."

Cramer's research began in 2007, before the collapse of the investment bank Bear Stearns, and ran through the recession and recovery. When she would ask how the local economy was doing, the answer went beyond the recent business cycle. "Oftentimes, they would say, 'It's fine, it's doing pretty good,'" she told me. "I was surprised, and I'd say: 'Really? Okay, so tell me more. Things are picking up around here?' 'Oh no, no, no. See, we've been in poverty for decades.'"

Her fieldwork exposed the volatile mix of hope and fatalism that pervaded rural Wisconsin and might explain why many of her subjects voted first for Barack Obama and then for

Donald Trump. "They are reluctant to put a partisan label on themselves," she said. "I heard a lot of talk about Bernie Sanders, and people feel a lot of fascination with him. They felt he had a really great message, if a little unrealistic. They'll say he was a loose cannon, sort of the way they talk about Trump. The appeal of Trump is the same: someone who is ready to really shake things up. The sense was Sanders recognized them, without condescending to them."

The people Cramer interviewed for *The Politics of Resentment* made no mention of ALEC, or the billionaire donors and corporations that have been writing many of the policies depressing the living standards of working-class people in rural and urban America alike. In her book, Cramer does not address the origins of rural resentment—whether it came from within the people themselves or was fomented by leaders like Walker and Trump. In her office, though, she suggested it might be a combination. "A lot of the sentiments that Walker tapped into were there the first moment I met these groups in 2007," she said. "And yet, like with any human relationship, when you're with a pal and they give a name to a concern you have, then it catalyzes it, it makes it easier for you to recall it, to think about it when it's labeled and packaged for you. You may have felt that way for a good long time, but now it's more accessible."

Yet some of the things she found people angry about seemed to have no clear precedent. "I went into my fieldwork asking about immigration because I thought it often brings up issues of social class, which is what I was interested in," she said. "But it never came up. I think we see the sanctioning much more clearly after the election. Some of those things that are now sanctioned were so forbidden. Now they're on the surface." She mentioned a recent incident at a girls' high school soccer match in Elkhorn, a small town in southeastern Wisconsin. The Elkhorn and Beloit Memorial varsity teams were in the middle of a match when a small group of Elkhorn fans began shouting racist chants. "Donald Trump, build that wall," they yelled at Beloit's Latina and African American players, along with racial epithets. The Beloit girls, too distraught to continue, walked off the field. "One of the girls was cradled in the arms of one of our assistant coaches for a good fifteen to twenty minutes," the Beloit soccer coach told a reporter after the game. He believed the girls on his team would be scarred by the experience. He knew he had been. "Seeing the impact on those kids is something I will never forget," he said.

I asked Cramer what she thought the legacy of divide-and-conquer politics would be. "It's profound," she said, shaking her head. "How do you turn that around? The kinds of people who care about what has happened have already taken sides—for life. They know who the enemies are. How do you turn that around, short of a world war or a Great Depression? What I'm parsing through these days is the enormous sense of loss. Is it that my state has actually changed? Or is it that my sense of the state has changed? It was always understood that Wisconsin was a great place to live and people were decent to one another. I went away to graduate school, and I was always proud to be from this place where people were so nice to one another. As I matured, and as I wrote this book, I wondered: Are we so nice to one another? And have we always been?"

Cramer rattled off some of the uglier moments in the state's recent past—the fight over treaty rights, an outburst of anti-

Semitism in her hometown of Grafton when she was growing up. "What I don't know is the legacy that Walker has left:
What is it? Is it *maybe* a very productive thing? Where we are
realizing we have a whole lot of gunk we need to deal with as
a population? That it's not something that was plopped down
here and given to us; it's something that we were shown by
someone's ability to tap into it."

She went on: "Part of my struggle now is the question of
whether we really have democracy. I believe that there's a role
for ordinary people to do something about what's happening. I'm
hoping so. I think so. If that's the case: What do we do? How do
we ensure that we have leaders who stand on flatbeds and say,
'Hold on, do not go at each other's throats because there's a better
part of us here?' As opposed to, 'You're right.'" She pointed in
the air toward an imaginary enemy. "*They're* the ones.'"

IN SEPTEMBER 2017, Mike Wiggins took me out on his boat
into the Kakagon Sloughs, a vast area of wetlands along the
Lake Superior coast. Known as the "Everglades of the North,"
the sloughs are home to largemouth bass, northern pike, walleye, and most important to the Bad River, the tribe's wild rice
beds. We sped along for nearly thirty minutes until Wiggins
suddenly cut the motor. "This is a good place to talk," he said.
It was dusk, and the mosquitoes swarmed ferociously, but the
otherworldly landscape inspired us to tough it out for a bit.

Wiggins told me he planned to run for tribal chairman
again, after losing the last election in 2015. His heart wasn't
in that race. His battle with GTac had burned him out. The
loss was easier to accept at the time, because GTac had pulled

out. But just a few months later, David Adams, the president of one of the mining companies that owns the mineral rights at the site, said he expected a new company to replace GTac. The mining law GTac helped write and pass would make the process for the next company exponentially easier. Adams told the *Milwaukee Journal-Sentinel* that mining in the Penokee Hills was inevitable.

What drove Wiggins to run again were other, related concerns. In 2017, Republican state senator Tom Tiffany introduced a bill revoking the mining moratorium, the law requiring a company to prove that a sulfide mine can operate for ten years and be closed for another ten without polluting groundwater or surface waters with acid rock drainage. It was passed almost unanimously and signed into law by Governor Tommy Thompson. GTac's bill had tried to get around that by carving out an exception for nonsulfide mining. Wiggins, like many other mining opponents, believed that the ultimate goal of GTac's bill was to weaken Wisconsin environmental protection and wear down the opposition of the state's environmentalists until mining interests could revoke the moratorium, allowing companies an almost unfettered ability to mine precious metals across all of northern Wisconsin. (The moratorium was repealed in December 2017.)

Wiggins was also motivated by alarm at the industry-friendly people, such as Cathy Stepp, whom Trump had appointed to the EPA. Just as concerning was Trump's order to clear the protesters at the Standing Rock reservation in the Dakotas and hang a portrait of Andrew Jackson in the Oval Office. Many Native Americans consider Jackson to be the "American Hitler," because he signed the Indian Removal Act. The law uprooted thousands of people from their ancestral homes, often at gunpoint. One of the removals was the "Trail of Tears," the name the Cherokee gave to their forced journey from the Southeast to reservations in Oklahoma. As many as four thousand Cherokee are estimated to have died along the route.

The mosquitoes picked up, and we decided to head back to shore. Before we did, Wiggins told me about a dream he had a couple of years earlier. He was looking down a wormhole and saw a series of evenly spaced gunnels, like those in a birchbark canoe. "A voice of a spirit in the dream told me that the gunnels represent the many times the world has been redone," he said. "It was pretty infinite. The voice said, 'Look,' and it showed me what's happening right now." The last gunnel in the distance was not evenly spaced; it was terrifyingly close to the previous one, signaling an end coming very soon. To Wiggins, the spirit's message was clear: "This is how fast we're killing the planet right now," he said. "The world is half dead already."

Over coffee at the tribal casino, Wiggins seemed at peace. He knew that humanity was at a crossroads, but he wasn't sure which path humanity would ultimately choose. He would do all that he could to prevent a mine from ever being built in the Penokee Hills.

Two months later, he won his election as tribal chairman.

IN 2017, I met Lori Compas again at Cafe Carpe in Fort Atkinson. Since challenging Scott Fitzgerald in the recall election of 2012, she had taken a full-time job in the marketing department for Spacesaver, a local company that makes office storage equipment, to pay for her son's college tuition at UW-Madison. We sat on the restaurant's back porch, nursing a couple of beers in mild fall weather. When I asked who had run against Fitzgerald when he ran for reelection in 2014, two years after her defeat, she couldn't remember at first and had to Google it. "That's right, Michelle Zahn," she said. Zahn won 37 percent of the vote, worse than Compas. "But that goes back to the gerrymandering," Compas said. "Who are you going to find every four years? You get a sacrificial lamb that puts their name on the ballot, because they think there should be a name on the ballot."

Compas told me that on the day before her recall petitions against Fitzgerald were due at the Government Accountability Board, she had called the state Democratic Party as a courtesy, to tell them she would be dropping them off. "I noticed you're not recalling this guy who really ought to be recalled," she told a party official on the phone. "They asked what time I would be coming." The Democrats had planned an afternoon event announcing the successful recall drive against Walker and the three targeted senators. "They didn't want me to steal their thunder," Compas said, so she agreed to drop her petitions off in the morning.

Despite the lack of support from the Democratic Party, Compas harbored no resentment. "I feel like we didn't need their help," she said. "I also understood their strategy. This is an unwinnable district. They needed to focus their efforts and their limited resources." After looking at the partisan breakdown and their budget, they targeted the districts they thought they could win in a recall election, she said. "I saw it as: We should do this because it needs to be done."

Compas had sparked a democratic revival in her rural district through sheer force of will. As much as anyone I had met, she embodied La Follette's ideal of active citizenship. Whether Compas could have beaten Fitzgerald in a fifty-fifty district remains unknowable, but it was clear that that democratic spirit had withered under the insurmountable onslaught of dark money and gerrymandering. She was focused now on smaller-scale efforts. At her new job, where she estimates 90 percent of her colleagues voted for Trump, she has struck up an unlikely friendship with one of them, an evangelical Christian. "I take my Trump supporter guy out to lunch, or he treats me," she said. "We take turns. I feel like that's how things change. Gradually. As much as I would've liked to wave my magic wand and transform Wisconsin in the recall, it didn't happen. Now we have to get on with the business of living our lives day to day, getting along at work, getting along in these small towns where everyone knows each other and deep down everyone likes each other."

More than anything, Compas is worried about her two children. "It saddens me that my own kids are coming into their own at this time in history," she said. "They have inherited a mess and are going to have to deal with it and the consequences. As will we. I just don't know what to do about it. I feel very content. I feel very happy, but I don't feel fulfilled. During my campaign, I felt fulfilled. I felt like I was doing what I had been born to do. The high school plays I had performed in had taught me how to step into a character, how to speak and be onstage and not be afraid. I felt like I was playing a part. I was being the candidate that I wanted, that I wished *would* exist. I created it, and I was it. And then I lost. Like I said: I'm happy at my job. I love my work. I love my company. I love my coworkers, but I have not felt fulfilled since June of 2012."

IN AUGUST 2017, I flew to Chicago for a CNN-hosted town hall for Paul Ryan in Racine. Randy Bryce was trying to get in, but the event was staged at the Racine Theatre Guild, which seats fewer than four hundred people. Even though Ryan had played a leading role in passing the House's repeal of the Affordable Care Act, a bill that would strip twenty-three million people of their health insurance, there wasn't much opportunity for his constituents to engage him. It had been nearly two years since Ryan's previous town hall, and Ryan's avoidance of them had turned into a local meme. CNN selected the participants, and ultimately Bryce was refused. He saw the CNN town hall as nothing but free publicity for Ryan, and on Twitter called out the event's moderator, Jake Tapper, over it. Bryce promoted a hashtag—#faketownhall— that became a clearinghouse for angry constituents to vent about being shut out.

Like many Wisconsin Republicans, Ryan's distance from the people he represents had grown since the passage of Act 10. He began holding "telephone" town halls; a limited number of constituents were given a call-in number to listen while a few were selected to ask a question. He held "employee" town halls where he dropped by to friendly businesses in his district to take questions from workers. Sometimes they were prescreened by a company manager, like the workers at a town hall at WPC Technologies in Oak Creek, the previous month. The first question of that town hall was: "If you had to make a decision between attending an October regular-season Packers game or a Brewers World Series game: Which one?" It was easy to see why Ryan wanted to avoid an unfiltered public. He and his wife, Janna, had been pushing a stroller in Janesville's first Labor Day parade after Act 10 when they were confronted by protesting teachers. Ryan and his wife looked visibly shaken, and he had to tell them: "This is not the place." The last real town hall he had held in Racine, the district's second most populous city, was in 2013. It had grown contentious when a high school student named Valeria Ruiz asked Ryan about his support for children like her, who had DACA status and arrived as a child in the United States with undocumented parents.

On my drive from Chicago to the Racine town hall, I stopped in Kenosha to see a seventy-six-year-old retired plumber named Tom Nielsen, whose experience with Ryan had contributed to Bryce's decision to run. Six years earlier, Nielsen had become a brief internet sensation when a video showed police officers pinning him to the ground during a Ryan lunch event at the Whitnall Park Rotary Club in Greenfield, a Milwaukee suburb. Tickets cost fifteen dollars, and the venue was filled mainly with Rotary Club members who were given first dibs. To avoid the event being labeled a closed session, a small number of tickets were made available to the public. Wisconsin Jobs Now, a nonprofit advocacy group pushing for higher wages, purchased eight of them and gave one to Nielsen.

When Ryan told the crowd, "Most of our debt, in the future, comes from our entitlement programs," Nielsen erupted. "An entitlement is something I'm entitled to!" Nielsen shouted, as he stood up. "I *paid* into those for fifty years! My unemployment and my Social Security and my Medicare, and now you're gonna—" he was cut off as two police officers grabbed him. The officers dragged him out into the hallway, wrestled him down, and handcuffed him tightly. He was not resisting at all and in fact had a broken collarbone from a car accident a few weeks earlier. The officers pulled his arm back, and the pain was excruciating. As Nielsen was writhing on the floor just outside the ballroom, he could hear Ryan mock him. "I hope he's taking his blood-pressure medication," he said. The crowd laughed.

As I pulled up to Nielsen's house in Kenosha, I saw a "Randy Bryce" sign in the small front yard. Nielsen lives in a duplex on a busy street in a manufacturing-heavy town that's been struggling economically for decades. A white-haired gentle giant, Nielsen led me to his backyard, where he keeps an expansive garden, which was in full bloom. He told me he immigrated to the United States from the Danish island of Falster in 1959, as an eighteen-year-old. "I came with wooden shoes," he recalled. "I was a real tenderfoot, never real masculine. Just a gentle kid from the country." The economy in Denmark was still suffering from the war, and a friend of Nielsen's grandparents sponsored the family to come to Racine.

He hurt his back at his first job, at a farm, so he took work at a factory, then joined the Navy, where he learned plumbing. After getting out in 1964, he got a job as an apprentice and worked as a union plumber for forty years. "Plumbing was a godsend," he said. Nielsen had started paying into his Social Security in 1959, when he worked at the farm. "It was a mockery approach to a serious issue for the working man," he said of Ryan's attacks on the safety net. "He's saying we're going to take Social Security away, then Medicare so they don't rob the national treasury. Well, I don't think *we're* the ones who did that. I signed up for Social Security when I came over to this country, and I worked on the farm making one hundred twenty dollars a month!"

Nielsen said he yelled only because he had no microphone and was worried that people wouldn't understand his accent. When he was arrested, the handcuffs cut off his circulation, so he asked if they could be loosened. "You don't need to secure me," he told one of the officers. "I'm not going anywhere." He told me: "My shoulder hurt like hell because they threw me down. This one young police officer jumped on me. He was trying to bend my wrist to restrain me. I asked him, 'What are you trying to do?' He's breathing heavily. 'You want to bend my wrist?' He couldn't do it because I've been doing plumbing for all these years. I said, 'I'll bend it for you.'" Nielsen was charged with resisting arrest and trespassing even though he had a ticket and did not resist. He was put in a police van and charged with a $1,000 fine that eventually was reduced to a $15 filing fee. He's embarrassed that the video is still on YouTube.

When I got up to leave, Nielsen walked me to my car. "This used to be a busy place," he said, gesturing to Kenosha's rundown streets. "American Motors was here, Chrysler, Jockey underwear, American Brass. They all went by the wayside, all by the wayside." He told me he had another envelope for Bryce, his second donation. The greatest appeal for him seemed to be that Bryce was simply a regular citizen, a worker like himself.

"We don't need a lot of people with classroom knowledge," he said. "We need people who have experience in the field and know people who have suffered, been discriminated against, and got thrown under the rug and mistreated. These people deserve better." As I pulled out heading for Racine, I saw Nielsen pick up his "Randy Bryce" yard sign and move it closer to the street.

As I drove north, the sun finally broke through the thick clouds, but Racine resembled Nielsen's vision of Kenosha: There were nearly as many vacant storefronts as open businesses, and the industrial jobs that had sustained the economy for decades were mostly gone. Republican attacks on the wages of public workers had only furthered the city's hollowing out. Several hours before the town hall was scheduled to begin, dozens of protesters had gathered on a barricaded patch of grass in front of the venue. Many held signs that were merely sheets of paper with their ZIP codes written in black marker, an affirmation of their residency in Ryan's district and a kind of semaphore that they had been shut out of a forum with their representative. Valeria Ruiz, the undocumented immigrant who posed a troubling question to Ryan at his town hall four years earlier, was there.

When Bryce showed up with his campaign staff, he was greeted almost like a rock star. "The ball just keeps getting bigger and bigger," Bill Hyers, Bryce's top campaign strategist, told me, when I asked how it was going. "We'll probably bring in $1.2 million this quarter." Hyers could take or leave the protest, but for Bryce, it seemed like a communion. More than any other group, this crowd, a mixture of older white union workers and Latino immigrants, was his constituency. For them, there was also a special bond. They had never had a candidate like this to bring them together—an ordinary citizen who had been with them in every lost fight since the passage of Act 10.

Ryan's staff had started attacking Bryce; his runaway campaign, and his success at nationalizing this race, seemed to be rattling them. Since Ryan mustered the Obamacare repeal bill through the House, his poll numbers had cratered. Even before that, as he became more identified with Washington, support had softened in his district, which Obama had narrowly won in 2008. His 2012 reelection, when he was Mitt Romney's vice-presidential candidate, was his narrowest win ever. Ryan's attempt to have it both ways with Trump, sometimes mildly criticizing his racism and sexism while aligning himself with the president in attacks on the welfare state, had only weakened his support further.

Bryce did a local TV interview, took selfies with a few young supporters, and then decamped for a nearby bar to talk to a reporter from *Rolling Stone*. Eventually Bryce and his campaign crew decided to watch the town hall from a bar in downtown Milwaukee. "You're like a real-life superhero, Randy," a woman sitting next to him at the bar said. Bryce smiled politely, almost embarrassed. He was focused on tweeting responses to Ryan's town hall.

A Dominican nun, Sister Erica Jordan, had just asked Ryan about how he was holding up the Catholic Church's social teaching that "God is always on the side of the poor to help the poor and dispossessed." Ryan responded by telling her, erroneously, that the United States was in its thirty-second year of a failed war on poverty. He said only "economic opportunity" could lift the poor out of poverty. Bryce retweeted an assessment that Ryan had just mansplained poverty to a nun. "I think he is really naïve," Jordan later told *Commonweal* magazine about the exchange. "Trickle-down economics has never worked."

Afterward, Bryce went to the PBS studio nearby for a remote appearance on Don Lemon's CNN show. His slot kept getting pushed back, and by the time he was on, he seemed a little exhausted. Later he told me that Terry McGowan, the president of Local 139, the operating engineers union, who had been burned by Walker's abandoned promise to stop the right-to-work law, had decided to support Ryan, and not Bryce, in the hope that Ryan would preserve federal prevailing-wage laws. "Divide and conquer," Bryce said. "And after all that."

HAS WISCONSIN'S PROGRESSIVISM been permanently subdued by resentment, fating the state to be a conservative bastion for the foreseeable future? An answer might lie in looking at Richland County, a swath of rich farmland in southwestern Wisconsin. The county was settled by German, Irish, and Norwegian immigrants in the mid-nineteenth century, and since the time of the Civil War, it has voted Republican (with a few exceptions: Bob La Follette's insurgent third-party bid in 1924, FDR's landslide in 1932, and LBJ's in 1964). More recently, however, it has shown itself to be persuadable; it went for Bill Clinton, George W. Bush, and then Barack Obama in each of their respective elections. (In 2008, it delivered 60 percent of the vote to Obama.) In 2016, however, the county went for Donald Trump.

"I'll tell you what I read in that," Dale Schultz, the former Republican state senator who represented the county for more than three decades, told me. "People are mad. They're so mad that they want to throw everybody out, it doesn't matter which side they vote for, they get the same load of crap. Nothing happens, nothing changes, and their life gets more miserable."

Schultz, who voted against Act 10 before retiring in 2015, notes that the rural resentment that helped drive the measure has now come back to bite many of the rural schools used by its supporters. "One of the biggest crises we have right now is that hardly anybody wants to be a teacher," he said. He noted that the University of Wisconsin's education department has seen applications drop by two-thirds. Experienced teachers are increasingly becoming free agents, moving to wealthier suburban districts that can offer better pay and benefits, leaving rural schools even further behind. In 2017, Scott Walker announced his support for a bill allocating $10 million in "sparsity aid" for rural schools with few students, a pittance compared to the hundreds of millions of dollars he has cut from K–12 public education.

Schultz predicts that the downward cycle of bitterness and living standards set in motion by Act 10 could get worse. "I think that the anger now is there and will increase for a different reason," he said. "We have a real problem with income distribution. I'm not an Occupy Wall Street guy, but people can't make it: You can't survive on nine or ten dollars an hour and raise a family. Even if they're working every waking hour, there's not enough money. When you strip away their benefits and people see their standard of living shrinking, well, there's anger there. It may not bubble up today or tomorrow, but if the situation gets bad enough, it will boil over, and the next time around I predict the people on top of the economic heap are going to pay a terrible price for it."

Schultz acknowledged the state's low unemployment rate, but he noted it can be deceptive. "Look at Richland County, we have one of the highest outmigrations of any county in the state," he said. "Because there isn't any opportunity there for young people. More than 20 percent of the county is now older than sixty-five: the only people who move in are old people. Younger people who can't make it drop out, and they work for a cash economy. They find some way of getting by, or they double up on jobs, but the anger is there. When these people find out that they've been badly duped by Trump, I predict they will be *spectacularly* angry."

Despite his votes against Act 10 and the GTac mine, Schultz still considers himself a loyal Republican. "I'm a member of the party of Abraham Lincoln, Teddy Roosevelt, Ike Eisenhower, and Ronald Reagan," he said. "What Trump and these other guys claim to be is not clear to me." He thought the GOP's recent turn evoked aspects of the John Birch Society, the nineteenth century's Know-Nothing party, and the paleoconservative American Party of the 1970s. "One thing I know for certain is what they say is conservative is not conservative at all," he said.

IN THE FALL OF 2017, as a chill set in and the sugar-maple leaves turned to yellow and orange, I returned to La Follette's boyhood home in Argyle. As I crossed the road to the front entrance, Kristine O'Connor's husband, Donald "Doc" O'Connor, clambered out of a red pickup truck. Wearing a UW Badgers sweatshirt, O'Connor, a retired veterinarian, introduced himself with a handshake and a smile that revealed teeth stained yellow-black from years of chewing tobacco. He walked me to a small cottage a hundred feet in front of La Follette's old home, where Kristine was waiting for us. The little house had been donated, and had the only functional bathroom on the property. Kristine handed me a cup of coffee she had brought from the local gas station, one of the few businesses still open in the area.

"Argyle used to have four or five grocery stores, two car dealerships, a dry cleaners, and a hardware store," she said. All of those are gone now, except for one grocery store. Many people in Argyle buy their groceries in Madison. "They can get them cheaper," Kristine explained. "A local grocery store can't match the big stores, which buy in bulk." South Wayne, eleven miles south, where Doc grew up, was more destitute. "It's almost a ghost town," Kristine said, as the three of us settled into beat-up wooden chairs. Doc had recently watched an 8-mm film his mother shot of Main Street in South Wayne in the late 1950s. "My dad was coming out of the restaurant in town with his cup of coffee," Doc said. "The film is only a minute long, and I must have counted fifteen cars going up and down. There were twenty-seven businesses then. There are now two taverns, one gas station, and one small restaurant—that's it."

As a boy, Doc dreamed of becoming a veterinarian, like his father. One of four students to go to college from a graduating class of forty-five, he earned a degree in veterinary medicine at Iowa State and then moved back to South Wayne to open his farm-animal practice. Kristine managed the office, relaying the day's calls to Doc by CB radio. For the next twelve years, he was covering an area of nearly 400 square miles. He worked at least fifteen hours every day except Sunday. "I would get Sunday afternoons from about one to five off," he said. "When people called, I couldn't say no because they were counting on me. There was always an emergency or something."

Doc eventually burned out, and closed his practice after twelve years. Before long, the family farms he used to service began vanishing at an alarming rate. "When I sold out, I had two hundred dairy farms that I worked for, plus four swine farms and one beef farm," he said. "Now there are maybe fifteen to twenty of those left in business." He recalled one particularly devoted farmer. "I would have bet my life that he would die on that dairy farm," Doc said. But three years after Doc quit, the farmer sold his cows. "He went into partnership with another young guy in the carpentry business and found out he could make as much money in two months of carpentry as he could all year on that farm. And he had holidays off, Sundays off. That's what they all found out. The farm input costs were incredibly high, and the profits from sales so low. They were working twelve-to-fifteen-hour days for maybe a dollar, a dollar and a half an hour."

Doc took a job as an animal epidemiologist for the State of Wisconsin, commuting to an office in Madison, an hour and fifteen minutes away. He developed statewide programs to treat avian flu and *Salmonella* poisoning. Under his guidance, Wisconsin became one of the first states to eradicate pseudorabies, an often-fatal viral disease found in pigs, and Doc helped craft national standards for treating the disease. He was also responsible for tracing the origins of foodborne-illness outbreaks, like a rash of *Salmonella* poisoning cases that started with the eggs Benedict served at an Oshkosh restaurant. With the spread of Big Agriculture, the need for this kind of work was greater than it had been when he was growing up.

"When I was a kid, you'd have fifty cows on a farm, and then in the summertime they'd turn 'em out to pasture, then bring them back in to milk 'em and then run 'em back out again," he said. "A cow would cough, and it would just blow out across the hillside. Now you have confinement. You have three hundred head beneath one roof, so if one cow gets a viral pneumonia." He whistled. "It goes right through the whole herd."

Like many state workers, shortly after the passage of Act 10, Doc decided to retire early. "I got to look and figured it out with the gas and an increase in my medical and retirement, I would be making $1,700 more a month sitting at home than if I was still working," he said. Though he made 70 percent of what he would have made in the private sector, he often heard complaints about the state paying for health care for public employees.

Today, the few dairy farms remaining in the area produce more milk than the hundreds of family farms once did, but they offer few decent-paying jobs. "A local dairy about ten minutes from Argyle, with a thousand cows, hires a lot of immigrants," Kristine said. "There's another one out here that milks four hundred cows," Doc added. "He tried to hire high school kids. They milk two or three days, find they don't like it, they leave." Another farmer, right outside Argyle, with five hundred cows, uses robotic milking. "He could go to town while the cows are being milked," Doc said. "He's got a thing on his cellphone, an app, sort of. If something's going on with the milking, he gets a message."

I asked Kristine and Doc to show me South Wayne. On the way, Kristine pointed to the enormous six-bedroom Victorian house where she grew up. "My parents and my grandmother went in together," she said. "They bought it in 1960 for nine thousand dollars. My mother would later tell me there's no house big enough for three generations." She laughed. Her first memory of politics was her parents discussing the 1960 presidential campaign in that house. She was in seventh grade, and John F. Kennedy had made a campaign stop that year in Argyle. "Nobody in my family voted for Kennedy because he was Catholic," she said, shaking her head in disbelief. We passed Argyle's Main Street, which had nearly everything Kristine's family needed when she was growing up. "Going to Monroe was even a big deal," she said. "It was half an hour away. We went there twice a year for our dentist appointment, and that was it."

We passed a country graveyard at the edge of Argyle and continued along winding back roads for several miles until we reached South Wayne. I pulled into a parking stall next to Doc's truck. The street was completely desolate. Not a single car drove by. There was a meat processor still in business up the street and a deserted bar and restaurant on the corner. Doc pointed to his dad's old office, remembering the film his mom had shot. "Every one of these parking stalls here was full," he said, shaking his head. He stared at an empty lot up the street. "That used to be a drugstore," he said.

"That's where his dad would go to buy Christmas presents," Kristine said.

I said goodbye to Doc and Kristine and walked up Main Street. On the corner was a shuttered junk store with a "For Sale" sign next to a notice for an upcoming auction of the store's goods.

Inside the dust-covered window, a carousel pony lay beneath a series of photographs showing various handguns and shotguns that would be auctioned. The shop reminded me of the resentment coursing through Wisconsin, and also something Doc had said back at La Follette's house. "Everybody I talked to that voted for Trump now has nothing good to say about him at all," he told me. "They think he's a nut case. But they think Walker walks on water, because he got rid of all those public-employee unions who were getting all that free money, all that big retirement money."

Staring at that "For Sale" sign on that forlorn street, I knew it was hubris to try and pinpoint the exact source of that resentment, which had propelled Act 10 and Donald Trump's Wisconsin victory. Just as I knew those events could never be isolated from the desolation of places like South Wayne.

EPILOGUE

In March 1864, a decade after Alvan Bovay founded the Republican Party in Ripon, a delegation from the New York Workingmen's Democratic Republican Association came to the White House to offer the country's first Republican president an honorary membership in their labor organization. "None are so deeply interested to resist the present rebellion as the working people," Abraham Lincoln told them, after accepting the honor. "Let them beware of prejudice, working division, and hostility among themselves. The most notable feature of a disturbance in your city last summer was the hanging of some working people by other working people. It should never be so. The strongest bond of human sympathy, outside of the family relation, should be one uniting all working people, of all nations, and tongues, and kindreds."

Scott Walker didn't share Lincoln's view. A century and a half later, he fulfilled a promise to one of his wealthiest donors that he would "use divide and conquer" against Wisconsin's working class to break the power of their unions. His devastating success has allowed for the transformation of Wisconsin into a laboratory for corporate interests and conservative activists, a process that continues unabated. Since Donald Trump's victory, Walker has signed an NRA-supported law removing the age limits for hunting licenses, and more than fifty children under the age of five, and ten under the age of one, are now licensed to hunt in the state. Foxconn has filed an application with the Wisconsin Department of Natural Resources to pump seven million gallons of water a day from Lake Michigan for its proposed plant near Racine, whose subsidy has grown from $3 billion to $4.5 billion in taxpayer money. And a state senate committee has approved a bill, supported by the American Petroleum Institute, to remove all of the state's air-pollution regulations.

Wisconsin's Republicans, enabled by a combination of dark money, gerrymandering, a weak Democratic opposition, and a potent conservative infrastructure, drive a relentless and cohesive party. Dale Schultz, the former Republican state senator, described a Republican caucus meeting he attended a few years back with a prominent conservative lobbyist, which in his view illuminated the Republicans' determination to undo Wisconsin's progressive legacy. "All we need is fifty percent of the vote plus one," the lobbyist told Schultz and his colleagues. "If we get any more than that one vote, then we didn't push the state far enough in the direction we want to push it, because we had votes to spare. And if we lose an election, we'll win it back, and then we'll start up where we left off." Any Republican who defies the party's orthodoxy is shunned, as Schultz was.

Since Walker signed Act 10, Republicans in many other states have passed measures restricting collective bargaining, a focus that has intensified since Trump's victory, as Republicans more fully understand how atomizing labor can help swing elections. An extreme version of Act 10 was passed in Iowa in early 2017, after Republicans seized the governorship and both houses of the state legislature for the first time since 1998. The bill, supported by a "grassroots campaign" run by Americans for Prosperity–Iowa, eviscerated collective bargaining rights for Iowa's 180,000 public workers, and it went further than Act 10 by including police- and fire-department unions in some of the restrictions. Then there was the impending Supreme Court decision in *Janus v. AFSCME*, a closely watched case argued in February 2017. It threatened to nationalize right-to-work for public employees, starving the unions, and in turn, the Democratic Party.

Entrenching conservative control of the states promises a continued assault on public institutions, a process that has already significantly damaged Wisconsin's once widely admired K–12 public school system and its flagship university. Recent research suggests Act 10, which led to an exodus of experienced teachers or their transfer to wealthier school districts, has already reduced test scores in math and science in lower-performing schools. And since the legislature weakened the terms of university tenure in 2016, the University of Wisconsin has been forced to spend money it might otherwise devote to research to prevent poaching of its disenchanted faculty by other top universities. "Republicans are in the process of engineering permanence," Dave Poklinkoski, the president of IBEW Local 2304, told me. "They're destroying the educational institutions. If a population can't think critically or know its history, then it's easy to manipulate and get the desired result, which is staying power." Poklinkoski fears such a population would be swept up in "a permanent resentment," allowing divide-and-conquer politics to dominate indefinitely.

There is one force that can untangle the Gordian knot of divide-and-conquer politics: solidarity. Whether it can flourish without the infrastructure of the labor movement is unclear, but the spirit of it endures in Wisconsin, even with diminished unions. Few things capture that spirit more than Randy Bryce's quixotic campaign against Speaker of the House Paul Ryan. Two days before the Supreme Court heard arguments in *Janus v. AFSCME*, Bryce held a rally in Racine headlined by Senator Bernie Sanders. An exuberant, standing-room-only crowd filled Memorial Hall. "It is no secret to anybody in this room that Randy is not running against any Republican," Sanders said. "That's why, brothers and sisters, the whole country is looking at this particular election, because it's not just another election. It is an election about the future of America. It is—to quote an old union song—it is about which side are you on."

The support for Bryce was a sign of a broader awakening: After seven years of nearly unbroken Republican control of state government, Wisconsin's beleaguered Democrats had begun showing signs of life. There is little doubt that Bryce's success, and the larger shift it embodied, contributed to Paul Ryan's shocking decision to announce his retirement in April 2018. Perhaps Ryan had noticed other warning signs. Just a few months earlier, in a special election for an open state senate seat, a Democrat named Patty Schachtner had trounced her Republican opponent in a rural western district that Trump had carried by eighteen points.

A genial medical examiner and political novice, Schachtner

seemed to be a throwback to the Wisconsin politics of old, even as she embodied a pushback against Trump. "My message has always been: be kind, be considerate, and we need to help people when they're down," she told the Associated Press. The day of the vote, Governor Walker had tweeted his alarm: "Liberal groups and the media have made [the 10th Senate District] a target." After Schachtner's win, Walker wrote another tweet—"WAKE UP CALL"—and painted a stark picture to his donors. "Everything we have done is at risk if we don't win in November," he warned in a fundraising email. "The big government union bosses are back," he told his followers in a video.

Whatever happens in Wisconsin's elections in the coming years, it will likely prove more difficult to rebuild the state's progressive traditions than it was to destroy them. Even during a more sympathetic era, it took three decades for the state government to recognize collective bargaining rights for public workers, and no state has yet repealed a right-to-work law. But watching the crowd at Bryce's rally in Racine, I saw that Walker had never extinguished the movement that rose up to oppose Act 10. The packed auditorium couldn't have been a starker contrast to the deflated workers who lost the right-to-work battle. It reminded me of a remark Bryce had made during that fight, as he drove to another forlorn job site with his hand-copied flyers. It was already clear the effort was doomed; Republicans had the votes lined up. "There's no chance of winning," he told me. "But we're not going to give up." He saw the loss as a chance to build solidarity.

The momentum of Bryce's campaign reminded me of something else, too, something I had seen when I met with him two months after he announced his challenge to Ryan. We were at his apartment in Racine. Clothes, his son's toys, reams of papers were strewn everywhere. In the hallway, I searched for the picture his grandfather had taken of Bryce working on Miller Park. Next to it, I noticed another that I had not remembered. It was a sepia-toned image of Bryce standing on a podium, speaking to a small crowd on behalf of Palermo's Pizza's striking immigrant workers.

Everyone knew that the Palermo's strike, too, was a losing battle; Bryce had even been told to stay away from it by a powerful local union leader. He kept showing up anyway. The picture illustrated the bonds of solidarity Lincoln had spoken of, but it also showed something else, something that had always struck me about Bryce: his commitment remained the same whether anyone was watching or not. It remained the same whether he won or lost. Bryce shared that quality with many other Wisconsinites, whose endless defeats I had followed for the past seven years—Lori Compas, Chris Taylor, Dale Schultz, Mike Wiggins. Despite their losses, none of them would let go of the democratic ideals that Fighting Bob etched into Wisconsin. Their victory has always been to hang on to the memory of that place; to persist, despite what has been destroyed. As long as they did so, as long as they remembered what had been, they might reclaim the state they knew and loved.

ACKNOWLEDGMENTS

Even long after growing up in Wisconsin, I am still awed by the warmth and generosity of the state's citizens. This book's greatest debt is to them, especially the Wisconsinites who shared their lives and struggles with me over the past several years. Their openness, candor, and kindness kept me returning, again and again, to try and understand what had transpired in my home state and why. This book is their book as much as it is mine, and I am forever grateful to them.

My editor at Norton, Matt Weiland, was my guiding spirit. I wish every author had an editor of Matt's patience, good humor, and unshowy brilliance. (A native Minnesotan, Matt bolstered my faith in the "special relationship" between our home states.) Remy Cawley, Matt's assistant, offered her own wise suggestions and helped shepherd the manuscript to its finished form. Managing editor Rebecca Homiski and project editor Susan Sanfrey, along with many other people at Norton, worked tirelessly to bring this book into being. I deeply appreciate all of their efforts behind the scenes.

Sometimes meeting a person feels fated, as was the case

with David McCormick, my deft, tenacious agent, whose enthusiasm and commitment to this book never wavered.

Portions of this story appeared in articles published in the *New York Times Magazine*, the *New York Times* opinion section, and the website of *The New Yorker*. I am grateful to Jake Silverstein, Hugo Lindgren, Andrew Rosenthal, and Amy Davidson Sorkin for publishing those pieces and for their unflagging dedication to the importance of this story. Amy, my former colleague at *The New Yorker* and a farseeing editor and writer there, published my first brief report on the "Cheddar Revolution," unknowingly launching a seven-year odyssey that culminated in this book. And at the *Times*, I have been fortunate to have a remarkable run of editors in Joel Lovell, Luke Mitchell, Aaron Retica, Jessica Lustig, and Bill Wasik. Each has improved my work immeasurably. Philip Montgomery, a master photographer, was a welcome reporting companion who captured the battle over Wisconsin's right-to-work law in breathtaking images, one of which graces the cover of this book.

Sameen Gauhar, a meticulous, thoughtful fact-checker, not only caught my mistakes but also deepened my reporting with her discoveries. Her help assembling the endnotes was just as crucial. The portions of these pages first published by the *New York Times* were fact-checked by a stellar cohort of checkers: Cynthia Cotts, David Ferguson, Rob Liguori, Mark Van de Walle, Gita Daneshjoo, and Kevin McCarthy. Evan Vorpahl, a resourceful and dogged researcher, assisted me in the later stages of writing. Peter Coutu helped in earlier ones.

No thanks would be sufficient to the countless people who shared their knowledge and expertise into Wisconsin's past and present with me. To list every person would be impossible, but I would like to highlight some whose help was invaluable.

I am grateful to Lisa Graves and Nick Surgey, codirectors of Documented, and to Graves's former colleagues at the Center for Media and Democracy for launching ALEC Exposed while Graves was executive director. Mary Bottari, a senior reporter at Center for Media and Democracy, and Brendan Fischer, a top-notch former researcher at CMD, provided immeasurable assistance by illuminating the national and local conservative infrastructure. John Gurda, Milwaukee's unofficial historian laureate, Aims McGuinness, and Anita Zeidler all generously shared their knowledge of Milwaukee's past. Exhuming the state's labor battles, both historic and contemporary, would not have been possible without the insight of David Boucher, David Newby, Sheila Cochran, Paul Secunda, Frank Emspak, Ken Germanson, Jody Spencer, Don Moynihan, and John Matthews.

To understand the legacy of Bob La Follette, the Wisconsin Idea, and the state's progressive roots, I was aided by talks with Nancy Unger, J. David Hoeveler, W. Lee Hansen, and John Witte. To grasp the richness of Ojibwe culture and the tribe's complex history, I leaned on the expertise of Patty Loew, Paul DeMain, and Mel Gaspar.

Wisconsin's environmental tradition and its current battles were detailed by Kerry Schumann, the dearly missed Glenn Stoddard, Dennis Grzezinski, Sandy Lyon, Eric Carson, and Eric Compas.

Many people's help defied categorization. Norm Stockwell, publisher of the *Progressive* magazine, was unfailingly helpful in finding experts in every imaginable Wisconsin subject, no matter how obscure. Rebecca Kemble, Marshall Steinbaum, Kim Phillips-Fein, Jason Stahl, Keri Leigh Merritt, Rob Hansen, Christina Neumann-Ortiz, Steve Born, Katherine Acosta, Chuck Chvala, and Bob Wirch also generously shared their knowledge.

Laura Dresser, a labor economist at the Center on Wisconsin Strategy, provided indispensable statistics research into Wisconsin's economy, as did Matthew Kures at the University of Wisconsin–Extension Center for Community and Economic Development and Jake Rosenfeld of Washington University.

The Economic Policy Institute is a national treasure for reporters covering labor issues and economic inequality. I am particularly thankful for the patient research and expertise of Elise Gould, David Cooper, Robert Scott, and Josh Bivens. The Wisconsin Democracy Campaign, which documents the influence of money on Wisconsin's politics, was equally important. I relied on talks with Matt Rothschild, the current executive director, and Mike McCabe, the previous one, and the work of Michael Buelow, the Democracy Campaign's research director.

I also benefited from the wisdom of several friends who read my countless drafts. Daniel Fromson and Alex Carp were indispensable and kept me from getting lost in the forest. I am also grateful to my soul-mate aunt, Elyse Zukerman, and to Peter Canby, Mary Norris, Rebecca Mead, Michael Azerrad, Harvey Dickson, and Matt Dellinger for their insights and suggestions.

Many family members and friends offered needed encouragement that kept me going, especially my in-laws, Jim and Pat Mapp; my sister, Ariel Kaufman; my neighbors James and Jennie Sheehan; my bandmates of Barbez; and my former teachers Michael Brockmeyer and Steve Stuckert.

A residency at the MacDowell Colony was a heaven-sent, deadline-saving experience. Bob and Mary Buckley provided another refuge, graciously letting me use their beautiful home on the Jersey Shore. Jeff Spitzer-Resnick did the same with his cabin in central Wisconsin.

My deepest gratitude is to my parents, Jerry Kaufman and Judy Zukerman Kaufman, who both died in the past five years. My interest in this story began dramatically one February morning in 2011, when I awoke to find a long email from my mother, then in her seventies, describing arriving home from the Wisconsin State Capitol at one in the morning, having waited with hundreds of others to testify against Governor Walker's attack on collective bargaining rights. Soon afterward, my father participated in one of the early marches at the state capitol, joined by tens of thousands of other engaged citizens like himself. He was then a seventy-seven-year-old retired professor of urban planning, and he told me he sang "God Bless America" at the capitol with thousands of other protestors. This book is a testament to their quiet dignity, their deep faith in democracy, their sense of fairness, and how those values were so intertwined, at least until recently, with those of their beloved state.

At the end of the road, awaiting me always, were my twin stars: my wife, Juliette Mapp, and my son, Luca. No reward was greater than returning home to them.

NOTES

PROLOGUE

5 **banning corporate donations to political candidates**: Lynn Adelman, "How Big Money Ruined Public Life in Wisconsin," *Cleveland State Law Review*, 2017, 1–30.

5 **"Democracy is a life"**: Robert M. La Follette, *La Follette's Autobiography: A Personal Narrative of Political Experiences* (Madison: University of Wisconsin Press, 1968), ix.

5 **In 1911, the state legislature**: For a comprehensive account of the 1911 Wisconsin State Legislature, see *State of Wisconsin: Blue Book, 2011–2012* (Madison: Joint Committee on Legislative Organization, 2011), 100–170.

5 **"laboratory for wise, experimental legislation"**: Theodore Roosevelt's introduction to *The Wisconsin Idea* by Charles McCarthy (New York: Macmillan, 1912), vii.

6 **"laboratories of democracy"**: *New State Ice Co. v. Liebmann*, 285 U.S. 262 (1932). The phrase is derived from Associate Justice Louis Brandeis's dissenting opinion. "It is one of the happy incidents of the federal system that a state may, if its citizens choose, serve as a laboratory; and try novel social and economic experiments without risk to the rest of the country."

6 **has seen one of the largest**: Tim Henderson, "The Shrinking Middle Class, Mapped State by State," Pew Research Center, Mar. 19, 2015.

6 **its poverty rate has climbed to a thirty-year high**: *Significant Changes in Wisconsin Poverty* (Applied Population Lab, University of Wisconsin–Madison, 2015).

6 **University of Wisconsin–Madison has fallen**: Lauren Sorensen, "UW-Madison Shut Out of Top Five Research Institutions for Second Consecutive Year," *Daily Cardinal*, Nov. 30, 2017.

6 **a recent study estimated that 11 percent**: Kenneth R. Mayer, "Estimating the Effect of Voter ID on Nonvoters in Wisconsin in the 2016 Presidential Election," University of Wisconsin–Madison, Department of Political Science, 2017.

6 **the state's roads**: "Best States Rankings," *U.S. News & World Report*, Feb. 28, 2017.

7 **"do it anywhere"**: Scott Walker with Marc Thiessen, *Unintimidated* (New York: Sentinel, 2013), 8.

1. THE PEOPLE'S HOME

9 **"People looked at us with wonder"**: Rasmus B. Anderson and Ole Knudsen Nattestad, "Description of a Journey to North America," *Wisconsin Magazine of History*, Dec. 1917, 149–186. All of the subsequent details of Nattestad's journey are derived from this article.

9 **only 3 percent of the land is arable**: Richard J. Fapso, *Norwegians in Wisconsin* (Madison: Wisconsin Historical Society Press, 2001), 5.

13 **"We have no expectation"**: "An Open Letter from the Pioneers at Muskego to the People of Norway, An Account of Conditions in North America," *Morgenbladet*, April 1, 1845.

13 **Ultimately, 800,000 Norwegians**: "Immigration to the United States, 1789–1930: Scandinavian Immigration," Harvard University Library Open Collections Program, http://ocp.hul.harvard.edu/immigration/scandinavian.html.

13 **On the evening of March 20, 1854**: Frank Abial Flower, *History of the Republican Party: Embracing Its Origin, Growth and Mission* (Springfield, IL: Union Publishing, 1884), 149.

14 **The revised law imposed harsh penalties**: Elizabeth Dale, *Criminal*

Justice in the United States, 1789–1939 (Cambridge, MA: Cambridge University Press, 2011), 13.

15 **Founded in 1849 by David Mapes**: Samuel M. Pedrick, "Sketch of the Wisconsin Phalanx," Proceedings of the State Historical Society of Wisconsin at its 50th annual meeting held Dec. 11, 1902 (Madison, 1903), 190–226.

15 **The community was named for Ceres**: Federal Writers' Project, *The WPA Guide to Wisconsin* (St. Paul: Minnesota Historical Society Press, 2006), 363.

15 **Fourier abhorred modern civilization and advocated sexual freedom**: Jonathan Beecher, *Charles Fourier: The Visionary and His World* (Berkeley: University of California Press, 1986), 207–208.

15 **Among them was a math professor**: "The Cast of Primary Characters Involved in the Birth of the Republican Party," The Little White Schoolhouse, National Historic Site, Ripon, Wisconsin.

16 **Bovay wanted to call his new party "Republican"**: Flower, *History of the Republican Party*, 152.

16 **"advocate calling together in every church"**: Ibid., 160.

17 **abolitionist mob liberated a runaway slave**: Ruby West Jackson and Walter T. McDonald, *Finding Freedom: The Untold Story of Joshua Glover, Runaway Slave* (Madison: Wisconsin Historical Society Press, 2007), 46.

17 **Glover had escaped from slavery**: Ibid., 25–42.

17 **"Free citizens who do not wish to be made slaves"**: Ibid., 46.

17 **The protesters demanded Glover be given a fair trial**: Ibid., 47–70.

18 **"We went into the little meeting"**: Amanda Gesiorski, Naomi Jahn, and Christian Krueger, *Ripon* (Charleston, SC: Arcadia Publishing, 2014), 35.

18 **the idea of "conspicuous consumption"**: Thorstein Veblen, *The Theory of the Leisure Class* (New York: Macmillan, 1912), 68–101.

18 **born to immigrant parents in Cato**: Ronald Fernandez, *Mappers of Society: The Lives, Times, and Legacies of Great Sociologists* (Westport, CT: Praeger, 2003), 176.

19 **"You're not to think you are anything special"**: Aksel Sandemose, *A Fugitive Crosses His Tracks* (New York: Knopf, 1936).

19 **"We should not much care"**: Francis Curtis, *The Republican Party:*

A History of Its Fifty Years' Existence and a Record of Its Measures and Leaders, 1854–1904 (New York: Putnam, 1904), 214.

20 **ruled the Fugitive Slave Act unconstitutional**: Paul Finkelman, ed., *Encyclopedia of African-American History, 1619–1895: From the Colonial Period to the Age of Frederick Douglass* (Oxford: Oxford University Press, 2006), 1.

20 **only non-English-speaking regiment**: Julie Allen, "The Scandinavian Invasion of the Midwest," public lecture at the Wisconsin Historical Museum in Madison, WI, Sept. 15, 2015.

20 **whose first name was Ole**: Ronald Paul Larson, *Wisconsin and the Civil War* (Charleston, SC: History Press, 2017), 98.

21 **Taylor mustered through a bill called the Potter Law**: "Potter Law (1874)." Wisconsin Historical Society.

21 **"These wild terms"**: Gilbert Ernstein Roe, ed., *Selected Opinions of Luther S. Dickson and Edward G. Ryan* (Chicago: Callaghan, 1907), 349.

22 **"As a boy on the farm in Primrose Township,"** *La Follette's Autobiography*, 19.

22 **"There is looming up a new and dark power"**: Robert C. Nesbit, *Wisconsin: A History* (Madison: University of Wisconsin Press, 1989), 384.

22 **Eli Pederson delivered a passionate speech**: Nancy C. Unger, *Fighting Bob La Follette: The Righteous Reformer* (Chapel Hill: University of North Carolina Press, 2008), 74.

23 **"The basic principle of this government"**: Robert M. La Follette, "The Danger Threatening Representative Government," July 4, 1897. Wisconsin Historical Society.

24 **"an experiment station in politics"**: Frederic C. Howe, *Wisconsin: An Experiment in Democracy* (New York: Charles Scribner's Sons, 1912), vii.

24 **condolences to his family**: Unger, *Fighting Bob La Follette*, 305.

25 **at a news conference in 1936**: Franklin D. Roosevelt, "Excerpts from the Press Conference, June 23, 1936," American Presidency Project, University of California, Santa Barbara.

25 **Wisconsinites began migrating into Washington**: For further reading on Wisconsin's contribution to the creation of Social Security, see Theron F. Schlabach, *Edwin E. Witte: Cautious Reformer* (Madison: State Historical Society of Wisconsin, 1969).

25 **"against several of the great disturbing factors"**: "The Committee on Economic Security," Social Security Administration website, accessed Apr. 11, 2018.

26 **Witte's committee studied Scandinavian**: Frances Perkins, "The Roots of Social Security," delivered at Social Security Administration headquarters, Baltimore, Oct. 23, 1962.

26 **When Norwegian women won a series**: Anna Peterson, "Making Women's Suffrage Support an Ethnic Duty: Norwegian American Identity Constructions and the Women's Suffrage Movement, 1880–1925," *Journal of American Ethnic History*, Summer 2011, 5–23.

27 **started a "Jesus USA" club**: Jason Stein, "Scott Walker Learned Early Lessons at Father's Iowa Church," *Milwaukee Journal Sentinel*, Jan. 31, 2015.

27 **empty mayonnaise jar**: Bill Lueders, "Man on a Mission," Wisconsin Center for Investigative Journalism, Jan. 10, 2012.

28 **told Glen Barry, a fellow student**: Alec MacGillis, "The Unelectable Whiteness of Scott Walker," *New Republic*, June 15, 2014.

28 **"Did you know where these flowers"**: Ibid.

28 **he never released his transcript**: Patrick Marley, "Is Finishing College an Issue in Governor's Race?" *Milwaukee Journal Sentinel*, July 31, 2010.

28 **The couple celebrate their anniversary**: Walker, *Unintimidated*, 58.

29 **tens of millions of dollars in pension bonuses**: Bruce Murphy, "How the County's Pension Fund Grew and Benefitted a Few," Urban milwaukee.com, Oct. 10, 2001.

29 **Despite an equal right to spend**: Gordon Lafer, *The One Percent Solution: How Corporations Are Remaking America One State at a Time* (Ithaca, NY: Cornell University Press, 2017), 8.

30 **a week after Lawton dropped out**: Carol E. Lee and Alexander Burns, "Gaspard, Barrett Meet Amid 2010 Buzz," Politico.com, Nov. 4, 2009.

31 **permanently damaged his hand**: Steve Schultze, "Barrett Says His Hand May Be Permanently Damaged," *Milwaukee Journal Sentinel*, Sept. 18, 2009.

31 **the White House reportedly pushed for Barrett to run**: Daniel Bice, "Obama Team Likes Barrett for Governor," *Milwaukee Journal Sentinel*, Oct. 25, 2009.

31 **also received more than $40,000**: Andy Kroll, "Wisconsin Gov. Scott Walker: Funded by the Koch Bros.," MotherJones.com, Feb. 18, 2011.

33 **In the north wing**: Clay Barbour and Mary Spicuzza, "No Pics of Walker and 'Fighting Bob' at Inauguration," *Wisconsin State Journal*, Dec. 31, 2010.

2. DIVIDE AND CONQUER

37 **training site for chemical, biological, and radiological warfare**: "Potential Exposure at Fort McClellan," US Department of Veterans Affairs website, accessed Apr. 11, 2017.

37 **"America's most toxic town"**: Ellen Crean, "Toxic Secret," *60 Minutes*, CBS News, Aug. 28, 2003.

40 **confirming their residency status**: Steven Greenhouse and Steven Yaccino, "Fight Over Immigrant Firings," *New York Times*, July 27, 2012.

40 **The company claimed the firings were unrelated**: Dominique Paul Noth, "The Story Behind the Strike," urbanmilwaukee.com, May 23, 2013.

42 **six bedrooms and eight baths**: Ryan Lizza, "Fussbudget," *New Yorker*, Aug. 6, 2012.

42 **"when I was flipping burgers"**: Peter Hanby, "Ryan Embraces 'Regular Guy' Routine on the Stump in Colorado," CNNpolitics.com, Aug. 14, 2012.

45 **"turn the safety net into a hammock"**: Paul Ryan, at House Republican Fiscal Year 2013 Budget Plan Press Conference, C-SPAN, Mar. 20, 2012: https://www.c-span.org/video/?304994-1/house-republican-fiscal-year-2013-budget-plan.

45 **"What I've been trying to do"**: "Glenn's Soulmate?" *The Glenn Beck Program*, Apr. 12, 2010.

47 **"You still have to negotiate it"**: Daniel Bice, "Video Shows Walker Saying He Would Negotiate Changes," *Milwaukee Journal Sentinel*, Mar. 2, 2012.

47 **"any chance we'll ever get to be a completely red state"**: *As Goes Janesville*, directed by Brad Lichtenstein, 371 Productions, Kartemquin Films, 2012.

48 **"we dropped the bomb"**: The blogger was named Ian Murphy, and the transcript and audio were published initially on Feb. 22, 2011, on the *Beast* website, which has since been discontinued. It can be found at "Transcript of Prank Koch-Walker Conversation," *Wisconsin State Journal*, Feb. 23, 2011.

53 **"the Tunisia of collective bargaining rights"**: Michael Cooper and Katharine Q. Seelye, "Wisconsin Leads Way as Workers Fight State Cuts," *New York Times*, Feb. 18, 2011.

53 **characterized the Madison protests as "riots"**: Paul Ryan interviewed by Joe Scarborough and Mika Brzezinski, *Morning Joe*, MSNBC, Feb. 17, 2011.

53 **He was seen texting**: Dan Kaufman, "Notes on the Cheddar Revolution," *New Yorker*, Feb. 22, 2011.

56 **the bill was "progressive"**: Scott Bauer, "Wisconsin Governor Scott Walker Officially Cuts Collective Bargaining," Associated Press, Mar. 12, 2011.

57 **title of a book about that legislative session**: McCarthy, *The Wisconsin Idea*.

57 **believed in activist government**: J. David Hoeveler, *John Bascom and the Origins of the Wisconsin Idea* (Madison: University of Wisconsin Press, 2016), 39–41, 143–149, 159–160.

57 **"Protection is admitted by all"**: John Bascom, *Sociology* (New York: G. P. Putnam's Sons, 1887), 210–211.

58 **owed his graduation**: Hoeveler, *John Bascom*, 186–187.

58 **"encourage the spirit"**: La Follette, *La Follette's Autobiography*, 14.

58 **"The guiding spirit of my time"**: Ibid., 12.

58 **"Wealth means power"**: John Bascom, "A Christian State," Baccalaureate Sermon, 1887 (Milwaukee, WI: Cramer, Aikens, & Cramer, 1887), 17.

59 **"The long story of failure"**: Interview with D. O. Kinsman, *Wisconsin Magazine of History*, Sept. 1937, 4.

60 **more than 2,500 railroad workers**: *Wisconsin Blue Book*, 2011–2012, 125.

61 **Ely was put on trial**: Gerald F. Vaughn, "Richard T. Ely: Economic Reformer and Champion of Academic Freedom," *Choices* 9, no. 3 (1994): 28–30.

61 **after his dismissal by administrators at Syracuse University**: Dennis Deslippe, Eric Fure-Slocum, and John W. McKerley, *Civic Labors: Scholar Activism and Working-Class Studies* (Urbana: University of Illinois Press, 2016), 13.

61 **they supported eugenics**: Thomas C. Leonard, *Illiberal Reformers: Race, Eugenics & American Economics in the Progressive Era* (Princeton: Princeton University Press, 2016). For more a nuanced assessment: Marshall I. Steinbaum and Bernard A. Weisberger, "The Intellectual Legacy of Progressive Economics: A Review Essay of Thomas C. Leonard's *Illiberal Reformers*," *Journal of Economic Literature* 55, no. 3 (2017): 1064–1083.

62 **Commons advocated for the workers' compensation law**: Richard A. Gonce, "John R. Commons' Successful Plan for Constitutional, Effective Labor Legislation," *Journal of Economic Issues* 40, no. 4 (2006): 1045–1067.

62 **He was also a proponent of a "living wage"**: Donald R. Stabile, The *Living Wage: Lessons From the History of Economic Thought* (Northampton, MA: Edward Elgar Publishing, 2008), 82–85.

62 **"The only way to beat the Socialists"**: McCarthy, *The Wisconsin Idea*, 300.

64 **"In America for the first time"**: John Gurda, *The Making of Milwaukee* (Milwaukee, WI: Milwaukee County Historical Society, 1999), 206.

65 **investing in "public enterprise"**: Ibid., 218–219.

65 **"Some eastern smarties"**: Emil Seidel, *Thy Kingdom Come: Sketches from My Life* (Manuscript at the Wisconsin Historical Society, 1944), 79–80.

67 **"You know, whenever Pharaoh wanted"**: Martin Luther King Jr., "I Have Been to the Mountaintop," Memphis, TN, Apr. 3, 1968.

68 **"The coalition that can have the greatest impact"**: Martin Luther King Jr. letter to Mr. Louis Simon, Amalgamated Laundry Workers, Jan. 16, 1962.

68 **"the strength of labor will fail"**: Martin Luther King Jr., address to AFL-CIO New York City District 65, Sept. 16, 1965.

69 **if unionization rates had remained at 1970s levels**: Jake Rosenfeld and Meredith Kleykamp, "Organized Labor and Racial Wage

Inequality in the United States," *American Journal of Sociology*, Mar. 2012, 1460–1502.

3. THE LAST DEER ON EARTH

75 **eight dollars an acre**: Curt Meine, *Aldo Leopold: His Life and Work* (Madison: University of Wisconsin Press, 1988), 340–342.

76 **delinquent owner**: Aldo Leopold, *A Sand County Almanac and Sketches Here and There* (New York: Oxford University Press, 1949), 9.

76 **love hunting and the outdoors**: Meine, *Aldo Leopold*, 16–19.

77 **"Great gashing gullies are torn"**: Aldo Leopold, "Coon Valley: An Adventure in Cooperative Conservation (1935)," in Curt Meine and Keefe Keeley, eds., *The Driftless Reader* (Madison: University of Wisconsin Press, 2017), 231–237.

77 **A slim majority of the valley's eight hundred farmers**: Douglas Helms, "A Conservation Success Story," *Readings in the History of the Soil Conservation Service* (Washington, DC: Soil Conservation Service, 1992), 51–53.

78 **"In those days we had never heard of passing up"**: Leopold, *A Sand County Almanac*, 130.

79 **"generating new insecurities"**: Curt Meine and Richard L. Wright, eds., *The Essential Aldo Leopold: Quotations and Commentaries* (Madison: University of Wisconsin Press, 1999), 97.

80 **"Chicken of Tomorrow" contest**: Alexis Coe, "Today We're Eating the Winners of the 1948 Chicken of Tomorrow Contest," *Modern Farmer*, May 12, 2014.

80 **today there are fewer than 9,000**: "Wisconsin Milk Cow Herds," Jan. 1, 2018, United States Department of Agriculture, National Agricultural Statistics Services.

83 **In the 1980s, Bresette led**: For a detailed account, see Rick Whaley and Walter Bresette, *Walleye Warriors: The Chippewa Treaty Rights Story* (Center Ossipee, NH: Beech River Books, 2009).

83 **document some of the racism**: "Protests," Great Lakes Indian Fish & Wildlife Commission website, accessed Apr. 11, 2018.

84 **12,000 jobs, more than any other state in the nation**: "Employees on Nonfarm Payrolls by State and Selected Industry Sector, Seasonally Adjusted," Bureau of Labor Statistics, Economic News Release, Mar. 13, 2012.

84 **nearly five thousand jobs**: Larry Sandler and Jason Stein, "State Temporarily Halts Work on Train Project," *Milwaukee Journal Sentinel*, Nov. 4, 2010.

88 **President John F. Kennedy flew in a Marine helicopter**: Bill Christofferson, *The Man from Clear Lake: Earth Day Founder Senator Gaylord Nelson* (Madison: University of Wisconsin Press, 2004), 181.

89 **"This section of Wisconsin"**: President John F. Kennedy, "Remarks Upon Arrival at the Airport, Ashland, Wisconsin," Sept. 24, 1963.

89 **they stood rapt**: Christofferson, *The Man from Clear Lake*, 14.

89 **"the philosophy and the purpose of the Wisconsin Idea"**: Ibid., 81.

89 **As governor, he launched a program to buy private land**: Ibid., 142–147.

91 **he decided to stage a national teach-in**: The teach-in movement was born in 1965, in the living room of my uncle Arnold S. Kaufman, a professor of political philosophy at the University of Michigan.

91 **"Earth Day can—and it must—lend a new urgency"**: Gaylord Nelson, "Earth Day Speech," in *The Environmental Moment: 1968–1972*, ed. David Stradling (Seattle: University of Washington Press, 2012), 85–86.

93 **"A land ethic changes the role"**: Leopold, *A Sand County Almanac*, 204.

94 **More than five hundred years ago**: For a captivating account of Ojibwe culture and history, see Patty Loew, *Indian Nations of Wisconsin: Histories of Endurance and Renewal* (Madison: Wisconsin Historical Society Press, 2013), 59–98.

96 **agency had been burned down**: Interview with Joe Rose, tribal elder, Bad River Band of Lake Superior Chippewa.

96 **"We wish to . . . be permitted to remain here"**: Loew, *Indian Nations of Wisconsin*, 67.

96 **They set out for Washington**: Chief Buffalo's journey is documented in *Early Life Among the Indians: Reminiscences from the Life of Benj. G. Armstrong* (Ashland, WI: A. W. Bowron, 1892), 9–54.

96 **"To give up this trip"**: Ibid., 18.

99　**"The woodcock is a living refutation"**: Leopold, *A Sand County Almanac*, 34.

101　**warned of the dangers of global warming**: Barbara Reynolds, "Alaska Oil Spill: A Disaster Like This Affects Whole World," *USA Today*, Mar. 29, 1989.

101　**When Norwegian and German farmers**: Christofferson, *The Man from Clear Lake*, 10–11.

103　**help them fight a utility company**: Ibid., 246–249.

103　**He could barely walk**: Interview with Sandy Lyon, organizer of the protest.

105　**One of the primary targets was Jessica King**: For more on GTac's role in King's campaign, see Theodoric Meyer's "In Wisconsin, Dark Money Got a Mining Company What It Wanted," *ProPublica*, Oct. 14, 2014.

106　**several hundred people gathered on the grass**: Dan Kaufman, "The Fight for Wisconsin's Soul," *New York Times*, Mar. 29, 2014.

106　**"Lake Superior, the Apostle Islands"**: Kennedy, "Remarks Upon Arrival at the Airport, Ashland, Wisconsin."

108　**"We have a lot to learn from your nations"**: President Barack Obama, "President Obama Delivers Remarks at White House–Tribal Nations Conference," *Washington Post*, Nov. 5, 2009.

109　**Wiggins mentioned an earlier mining fight**: Loew, *Indian Nations of Wisconsin*, 40–41.

109　**"Even as the Chippewa spearers and white anglers"**: Michael O'Brien, *Exxon and the Crandon Mine Controversy* (Middletown, WI: Badger Books, 2008), 74.

4. THE MODEL FOR THE COUNTRY

114　**"What Scott Walker is doing with the public unions"**: Stacey Singer, "David Koch Intends to Cure Cancer in His Lifetime and Remake American Politics," *Palm Beach Post*, Feb. 20, 2012.

114　**Nearly $140 million**: "Recall Race for Governor Cost $81 Million," Wisconsin Democracy Campaign, July 25, 2012.

115　**"This is a gubernatorial race"**: Geneva Sands, "Obama Campaign

Downplays Importance of Wisconsin Recall in November," *The Hill*, May 30, 2012.

115 **"He knew a significant number of his supporters"**: Walker, *Unintimidated*, 172.

116 **"run by private corporations"**: President William J. Clinton, State of the Union address, Jan. 25, 1994.

116 **"You've done some things we agree with"**: Joy Resmovits, "Arne Duncan Meetings with Rahm Emanuel, Scott Walker Don't Address Teachers Union Controversy," *Huffington Post*, Sept. 9, 2011.

117 **Mayer has called "weaponized philanthropy"**: Jane Mayer, *Dark Money: The Hidden History of the Billionaires Behind the Rise of the Radical Right* (New York: Random House, 2016), 30.

119 **According to Allen-Bradley's official corporate history**: John Gurda, *The Bradley Legacy: Lynde and Harry Bradley, Their Company, and Their Foundation* (Lynde and Harry Bradley Foundation, 1992), 90. Most of the details about the company and its founders are derived from Gurda's history.

119 **But the foundation's politics would soon become clear**: Ibid. 124–126.

120 **At the Olin Foundation, Joyce had helped fund**: Mayer, *Dark Money*, 107–109.

120 **"Perhaps more than any other person"**: Barbara Miner, "Voucher's Money Man," *Rethinking Schools*, Fall 2001.

120 **$1 million in grants to Charles Murray to coauthor *The Bell Curve***: Ronald Samuda, *Psychological Testing of American Minorities: Issues and Consequences* (Thousand Oaks, CA: Sage, 1998), 198.

121 **Grebe had known Walker since the 1980s**: Patrick Healy and Monica Davey, "Behind Scott Walker, a Longstanding Conservative Alliance Against Unions," *New York Times*, June 8, 2015.

122 **boasted of passing two hundred bills**: Laura Sullivan, "Shaping State Laws with Little Scrutiny," *NPR Morning Edition*, Oct. 29, 2010.

123 **ALEC's model right-to-work bill**: ALEC's model bill can be accessed on its website: https://www.alec.org/model-policy/right-to-work-act/.

123 **The Wisconsin version**: Wisconsin's SB 44, the right-to-work law, can be read here: https://docs.legis.wisconsin.gov/2015/related/proposals /sb44.

125 **cut funding for public schools**: Matthew DeFour, "Budget Cuts Hundreds of Millions of Dollars from Schools," *Wisconsin State Journal*, Mar. 2, 2011.

127 **In 1984, ALEC released its first model bill**: Brendan Fischer and Zachary Peters, "ALEC Continued to Cash In on Kids in 2015 and Beyond," Center for Media and Democracy, Mar. 8, 2016.

128 **"I always loved going"**: "The United States of ALEC," *Moyers & Company*, Sept. 28, 2012.

128 **"freedom granted by the Constitution"**: Kim Phillips-Fein, *Invisible Hands: The Businessmen's Crusade Against the New Deal* (New York: W. W. Norton, 2009), 3.

128 **"We had to struggle with the old enemies"**: President Franklin D. Roosevelt, Address Announcing the Second New Deal, Oct. 31, 1936.

129 **"Should any political party"**: Michael Kazin, Rebecca Edwards, and Adam Rothman, eds., *The Concise Princeton Encyclopedia of American Political History* (Princeton, NJ: Princeton University Press, 2011), 223.

129 **gave every GE plant supervisor**: Phillips-Fein, *Invisible Hands*, 101.

129 **Grede had railed against the New Deal**: Tula A. Connell, *Conservative Counterrevolution: Challenging Liberalism in 1950s Milwaukee* (Urbana: University of Illinois Press, 2016), 1.

129 **"out of consideration for the men"**: William J. Grede, "Observations of a Free Market Operator," *Rampart Journal of Individualist Thought*, Summer 1966, 35–45.

130 **Loock also wrote a memo to company staff**: Gurda, *The Bradley Legacy*, 115.

130 **One episode attacked**: Phillips-Fein, *Invisible Hands*, 83.

131 **Powell mailed Sydnor a manifesto**: "Powell Memorandum: Attack on American Free Enterprise System," Powell Archives, Washington and Lee University School of Law.

132 **confidential memo was never mentioned in Powell's confirmation hearings**: Ibid.

132 **to a few of his friends**: Phillips-Fein, *Invisible Hands*, 161.

132 **details the evolution of William J. Baroody**: Jason Stahl, *Right Moves*:

The Conservative Think Tank in American Political Culture Since 1945 (Chapel Hill: University of North Carolina Press, 2016).

133 **His father, Ignatius, immigrated from Germany**: Bruce Weber, "Paul Weyrich, 66, a Conservative Strategist, Dies," *New York Times*, Dec. 18, 2008.

133 **"All of a sudden lobbyists were telling me"**: David Grann, "Robespierre of the Right," *New Republic*, Oct. 27, 1997.

133 **"All I did was sit there"**: Weber, "Paul Weyrich, 66, a Conservative Strategist, Dies."

134 **persuaded Joseph Coors**: Mayer, *Dark Money*, 77–78.

134 **at the direction of the Illinois state representative Donald Totten**: Alan Crawford, *Thunder on the Right: The 'New Right' and the Politics of Resentment* (New York: Pantheon Books, 1980), 12–14.

134 **sued for sex discrimination**: Interview with Nick Surgey.

134 **"So many of our Christians"**: Michael Waldman, *The Fight to Vote* (New York: Simon & Schuster, 2017), 185.

135 **"that the federal government did not create the states"**: President Ronald Reagan, Inaugural Address, Jan. 20, 1981.

135 **"I want to congratulate you"**: President Ronald Reagan, "Remarks at a White House Briefing for the American Legislative Exchange Council," Dec. 12, 1986.

136 **"The evil empire can be dissolved"**: Lee Edwards, *The Power of Ideas: Heritage Foundation at 25 Years* (Ottawa, IL: Jameson Books, 1997), 91.

137 **a fund-raising consultant named Kate Doner**: Ed Pilkington, "Scott Walker, the John Doe Files and How Corporate Cash Influences American Politics," *Guardian*, Sept. 14, 2016.

137 **"The governor is encouraging all to invest"**: Ibid.

138 **"I would give the greatest sunset"**: Ayn Rand, *The Fountainhead* (New York: New American Library, 1943), 463.

139 **O'Keefe's Wisconsin Club for Growth**: Interview with Eric O'Keefe.

140 **"beautiful beyond expectation"**: "New Glarus: The Emigration," New Glarus Historical Society, 2009.

142 **Cronon's entry included a brief history of ALEC**: William Cronon, "Who's Really Behind Recent Republican Legislation in Wisconsin

and Elsewhere? (Hint: It Didn't Start Here)," *Scholar as Citizen*, Mar. 15, 2011.

142 **Stephan Thompson, sent a letter to the university's legal office**: William Cronon, "Abusing Open Records to Attack Academic Freedom," *Scholar as Citizen*, Mar. 24, 2011.

142 **A national outcry over academic freedom**: Dee J. Hall and Clay Barbour, "UW Releases Some of Professor's Emails to GOP; Withholds Others," *Wisconsin State Journal*, Apr. 1, 2011.

142 **Wisconsin has enacted 162 of these laws**: Molly Beck, "Memo: GOP Lawmakers Passed 128 Measures Limiting Local Control," *Wisconsin State Journal*, May 20, 2016. Updated figures provided by the Legislative Reference Bureau.

144 **With no assistance from the state Democratic Party**: Dan Kaufman, "How Did Wisconsin Become the Most Politically Divisive Place in America?" *New York Times Magazine*, May 24, 2012.

146 **The gerrymandering plans were drawn up**: Emily Bazelon, "The New Front in the Gerrymandering Wars: Democracy vs. Math," *New York Times Magazine*, Aug. 29, 2017.

146 **$400,000 in taxpayer money**: Patrick Marley, Daniel Bice, and Jason Stein, "Lawmakers Were Made to Pledge Secrecy Over Redistricting," *Milwaukee Journal Sentinel*, Feb. 6, 2012.

146 **"Republicans have been keeping our promises"**: Jason Stein and Patrick Marley, "GOP Redistricting Maps Make Dramatic Changes," *Milwaukee Journal Sentinel*, July 8, 2011.

150 **An NRA lobbyist**: "ALEC Castle Doctrine," *ALEC Exposed*, Center for Media and Democracy, accessed Apr. 10, 2018.

150 **The bill soon began appearing**: John Nichols, "How ALEC Took Florida's 'License to Kill' Law National," *The Nation*, Mar. 22, 2012.

150 **A pressure campaign persuaded dozens**: Eric Lichtblau, "Martin Death Spurs Group to Readjust Policy Focus," *New York Times*, Apr. 17, 2012; Ed Pilkington, "ALEC Facing Funding Crisis from Donor Exodus in Wake of Trayvon Martin Row," *Guardian*, Dec. 3, 2013.

151 **"We need to stomp out local control"**: Chris Taylor, "ALEC Otherworld," *Progressive*, May 13, 2014.

158 **"The federal government has taken too much tax money"**: President

Ronald Reagan, "Address Before a Joint Session of the Indiana State Legislature in Indianapolis," Feb. 9, 1982.

158 **an out-of-state group linked to the Koch brothers**: Brendan Fischer, "Ads Telling Voters 'Recall Is Not the Wisconsin Way' Funded by Out-of-State Koch Network," Center for Media and Democracy, Jan. 8, 2014.

159 **"The rest of the country is watching you"**: Andy Kroll, "Scott Walker's Divide-and-Conquer Strategy Is 'The New Model for the Country,' *Mother Jones*, June 2, 2012.

159 **Walker raised $30 million to Barrett's $4 million**: Patrick Marley and Jason Stein, "Walker Wins Recall Race over Barrett," *Milwaukee Journal Sentinel*, June 6, 2012.

5. WORKER AGAINST WORKER

162 **seventy-five molders walked off their jobs**: Darryl Holter, ed., *Workers and Unions in Wisconsin: A Labor History Anthology* (Madison: State Historical Society of Wisconsin, 1999), 42.

162 **Kohler had gathered his handpicked officials**: Ibid, 103.

162 **Kohler refused to meet with the independent union**: Walter H. Uphoff, *Kohler on Strike: Thirty Years of Conflict* (Boston: Beacon Press, 1966), 35–102.

163 **It was one of the most rancorous, and longest**: Ibid.

164 **6.5 percent**: "Union Members Summary," Bureau of Labor Statistics, Jan. 19, 2018.

164 **By 1964, twenty states were right-to-work**: For a complete list of right-to-work states, see National Right to Work Legal Defense Foundation, www.nrtw.org.

165 **"I just attended"**: Brendan Fischer, "Wisconsin Introduces Word-for-Word ALEC Right-to-Work Bill," Center for Media and Democracy, Feb. 20, 2015.

165 **In 1941**: Dan Kaufman, "Scott Walker and the Fate of the Union," *New York Times Magazine*, June 12, 2015.

165 **coined the slogan "right to work"**: William Ruggles, "Magna Carta," *Dallas Morning News*, Sept. 1, 1941.

166 **"White women and white men"**: Stetson Kennedy, *Southern Exposure: Making the South Safe for Democracy* (Tuscaloosa: University of Alabama Press, 1991), 84.

167 **enthusiastic support of the oil magnate Fred Koch**: Daniel Schulman, *Sons of Wichita: How the Koch Brothers Became America's Most Powerful and Private Dynasty* (New York: Grand Central, 2014), 49.

167 **"I have no interest in a right-to-work law"**: Patrick Marley, "Walker Says He Will Do 'Everything in My Power' to Prevent Right-to-Work Bill," *Milwaukee Journal Sentinel*, Mar. 11, 2012.

168 **Ironwork, for example, is a dangerous job**: Christopher Cannon, Alex McIntyre, and Adam Pearce, "The Deadliest Jobs in America," *Bloomberg News*, May 13, 2015.

168 **the fatality rate in construction trades**: Roland Zullo, "Right-to-Work Laws and Fatalities in Construction," *Journal of Labor and Society* 14, no. 4 (2011): 225–234.

171 **"It means turning worker against worker"**: Jason Stein and Patrick Marley, "In Film, Walker Talks of 'Divide and Conquer' Union Strategy," *Milwaukee Journal Sentinel*, Mar. 10, 2012.

172 **they did drive down wages**: Lafer referenced Elise Gould and Heidi Shierholz's "The Compensation Penalty of 'Right-to-Work' Laws," Economic Policy Institute Briefing Paper, Feb. 17, 2011.

173 **A labor organizer, it turned out, had told**: Jason Stein, "Protest Planned for the End of Committee Hearing," *Milwaukee Journal Sentinel*, Feb. 24, 2015.

175 **"If I can take on 100,000 protesters"**: Erik Lorenzsonn and Shawn Johnson, "Walker: 'If I Can Take on 100k Protesters, I Can Do the Same' with Islamic Terrorists," Wisconsin Public Radio, Feb. 26, 2015.

176 **"You can't parachute in here from Manhattan"**: Eli Stokols, "Why Wisconsin's 'Never Trump' Movement Is Different," *Politico*, Mar. 30, 2016.

178 **had paid for billboards across the South**: Gurda, *The Making of Milwaukee*, 363.

178 **The smears contributed**: Matthew J. Prigge, "Dixie North: George

Wallace and the 1964 Wisconsin Presidential Primary," *Shepherd Express*, Dec. 22, 2015.

178 **"they beat up old ladies"**: Rick Perlstein, *Before the Storm: Barry Goldwater and the Unmaking of the American Consensus* (New York: Nation Books, 2009), 321.

178 **"Send them back to Africa"**: Patrick D. Jones, *The Selma of the North: Civil Rights Insurgency in Milwaukee* (Cambridge, MA: Harvard University Press, 2009), 66.

178 **"would destroy the union seniority system"**: Joshua Zeitz, *Building the Great Society: Inside Lyndon Johnson's White House* (New York: Viking, 2018), 95.

178 **"If I ever had to leave Alabama"**: Jones, *The Selma of the North*, 67.

179 **AFL-CIO poll**: Philip A. Klinkner with Rogers M. Smith, *The Unsteady March: The Rise and Decline of Racial Equality in America* (Chicago: University of Chicago Press, 1999), 291.

179 **A post-vote analysis comparing**: Barbara J. Miner, *Lessons from the Heartland: A Turbulent Half-Century of Public Education in an Iconic American City* (New York: New Press, 2013), 43.

183 **"labor unions are nothing but blood-sucking parasites"**: Nelson Lichtenstein, *The Retail Revolution: How Wal-Mart Created a Brave New World of Business* (New York: Picador, 2010), 196.

183 **a former Walmart board member**: Brian Ross, Maddy Sauer, and Rhonda Schwartz, "Clinton Remained Silent as Walmart Fought Unions," ABC News, Jan. 31, 2008.

183 **"She was not a dissenter"**: Stephen Braun, "At Walmart, Clinton Didn't Upset Any Carts," *Los Angeles Times*, May 19, 2008.

186 **net loss of roughly 40,000 jobs in Wisconsin**: Robert E. Scott and Elizabeth Glass, "Trade Deficits with TPP Countries Cost More Than 2 Million U.S. Jobs in 2015," Economic Policy Institute Briefing Paper, Mar. 3, 2016.

191 **Wisconsin's union density has declined**: Molly Beck, "Union Membership Down Nearly 40 Percent Since Act 10," *Wisconsin State Journal*, Jan. 27, 2017.

191 **with the exponential rise in income inequality**: Evan Butcher, "Union

Membership and Income Inequality," Center for Economic and Policy Research, Sept. 9, 2015.

191 **suggests that right-to-work laws decrease the Democratic presidential vote share**: James Feigenbaum, Alexander Hertel-Fernandez, and Vanessa Williamson, "Bargaining Table to the Ballot Box: Political Effects of Right to Work Laws," National Bureau of Economic Research, Jan. 2018.

192 **the first step the Nazi Party took**: William L. Shirer, *The Rise and Fall of the Third Reich: A History of Nazi Germany* (New York: Simon & Schuster, 1960), 213.

192 **"Donald Trump's unexpected victory in 2016"**: Grover Norquist, "Why Republicans (and Trump) May Still Win Big in 2020—Despite 'Everything,'" *Ozy*, May 28, 2017.

193 **scarring them and eventually impairing their lung capacity**: Uphoff, *Kohler on Strike*, 13–14.

196 **He described a letter he received**: President Ronald Reagan, "Remarks at the National Conference of the Building and Construction Trades Department, AFL-CIO," Mar. 30, 1981.

199 **Trump had used undocumented Polish workers**: Charles V. Bagli, "Trump Paid over $1 Million in Labor Settlement, Documents Reveal," *New York Times*, Nov. 27, 2017.

6. THE SEVENTH FIRE

201 **twenty-seven members of its scientific staff**: Lee Bergquist, "Fifty-Seven DNR Staff Receive Layoff Notices Amid Talk of Budget Cuts," *Milwaukee Journal Sentinel*, Apr. 22, 2015.

203 **"A great general has said that the only good Indian is a dead one"**: "'Kill the Indian, and Save the Man': Capt. Richard H. Pratt on the Education of Native Americans," Carlisle Indian School Digital Resource Center, accessed Apr. 11, 2018.

209 **Over the opposition of a group of Wisconsin environmentalists**: Dan Kaufman, "The Other Pipeline You Should Worry About," *New York Times*, Jan. 16, 2015.

210 **likened the company's employees to "Keystone Kops"**: "Pipeline Rupture and Oil Spill Accident Caused by Organizational Failures and Weak Regulations," National Transportation Safety Board, Office of Public Affairs, July 10, 2012.

211 **"Chamber of Commerce mentality"**: Ron Seely, "Cathy Stepp, Outspoken Critic of DNR, Picked to Head Agency," *Wisconsin State Journal*, Dec. 30, 2010.

211 **"they don't pay taxes and they don't sign our paychecks"**: Pat Nash, "DNR Skipping the Natural Resources Part of Its Duties," *Baraboo News Republic*, Apr. 15, 2016.

212 **Drafting documents obtained through an open-records request**: Danielle Kaeding, "Documents Show Energy Firm Helped Craft Changes to States Eminent Domain Law," Wisconsin Public Radio, July 9, 2015.

213 **adjacent pipeline**: Dan Egan, "Greasing Oil's Path," *Milwaukee Journal Sentinel*, Nov. 9, 2017.

213 **Albaugh described a closed-door Republican caucus meeting**: Patrick Marley, "Ex-GOP Staffer Says Senators Were 'Giddy' Over Voter ID Law," *Milwaukee Journal Sentinel*, May 16, 2016.

216 **Kessler came across an article**: Nicholas Stephanopoulos and Eric McGhee, "Partisan Gerrymandering and the Efficiency Gap," University of Chicago Public Law and Legal Theory Working Paper, 2014.

218 **contents of a hard drive**: Bazelon, "The New Front in the Gerrymandering Wars."

221 **"Adamczyk said he felt 'passionately that the name Tia Nelson should not be listed'"**: Board Meeting Minutes, Board of Commissioners of Public Lands, State of Wisconsin, Jan. 6, 2015.

221 **alleged that Nelson had engaged in active "time theft"**: Ibid., Mar. 3, 2015.

221 **victim of Republican vindictiveness**: Bill Lueders, "In the 'Cubby Hole' with Doug La Follette," *Isthmus*, Aug. 22, 2015.

222 **"by the water cooler"**: Julie Bosman, "Wisconsin Agency Bans Activism on Climate," *New York Times*, Apr. 9, 2015.

223 **"Earth's climate is changing"**: Steven Verburg, "DNR Wipes Cause of Climate Change from Website," *Wisconsin State Journal*, Dec. 30, 2016.

225 **hackers from a group called Anonymous Poland**: Daniel Bice, "Hacked Records Show Bradley Foundation Taking Its Conservative Wisconsin Model National," *Milwaukee Journal Sentinel*, May 5, 2017.

7. WHICH SHALL RULE, WEALTH OR MAN?

233 **fund all-day kindergarten**: Lawrence R. Jacobs, "Right vs. Left in the Midwest," *New York Times*, Nov. 23, 2013.

233 **declining nationally**: Drew. D. Silver, "Most Americans Unaware That as U.S. Manufacturing Jobs Have Disappeared Output Has Grown," Pew Research Center, July 25, 2017.

234 **"I've made deeper cuts"**: "Doyle 'Surprised' State Contracts Not Approved," *Upfront with Mike Gousha*, WISN-TV, Dec. 19, 2010.

235 **struck these passages**: Mary Bottari, "Walker Strikes Truth and Wisconsin Idea from UW Mission in Budget," Center for Media and Democracy, Feb. 4, 2015.

239 **detailed the anger in rural Wisconsin**: Katherine J. Cramer, *The Politics of Resentment: Rural Consciousness in Wisconsin and the Rise of Scott Walker* (Chicago: University of Chicago Press, 2016).

241 **resentment persisted**: Norman T. Feather and Katherine Nairn, "Resentment, Envy, Schadenfreude, and Sympathy: Effects of Own and Other's Deserved or Undeserved Status," *Australian Journal of Psychology* 57, no. 2 (2005): 87–102.

242 **victorious over someone they thought was undeserving**: Norman T. Feather and Rebecca Sherman, "Envy, Resentment, Schadenfreude, and Sympathy: Reactions to Deserved and Undeserved Achievement and Subsequent Failure," *Personality and Social Psychology Bulletin* 28, no. 7 (2002): 953–961.

244 **"Donald Trump, build that wall"**: Chris Gothner, "District Investigating Racist Chants Directed at Beloit Soccer Players," Channel 3000 .com, Apr. 10, 2016.

246 **mining in the Penokee Hills**: Lee Bergquist, "Mining Inevitable at Vast Wisconsin Iron Ore Site, Owner Says," *Milwaukee Journal Sentinel*, Aug. 10, 2015.

250 **would strip twenty-three million people of their health insurance**:

Congressional Budget Office Cost Estimate, American Health Care
Act of 2017, May 24, 2017.

255 **"I think he is really naïve"**: John Gehrig, "The Catholic Sister Who
Challenged Paul Ryan on CNN: An Interview with Sister Jordan,"
Commonweal Magazine, Aug. 24, 2017.

EPILOGUE

265 **"None are so deeply interested to resist"**: *The Martyr's Monument,
Being the Patriotism and Political Wisdom of Abraham Lincoln* (New
York: American News, 1865), 257.

267 **Recent research suggests Act 10, which led to an exodus of experi-
enced teachers**: E. Jason Baron, "The Effect of Teachers' Unions on
Student Achievement: Evidence from Wisconsin's Act 10," Florida
State University, Working Paper, Aug. 18, 2017.

INDEX